Matrices, Vectors, and 3D Math

A Game Programming Approach with MATLAB®

Scott Stevens

Matrices, Vectors, and 3D Math
A Game Programming Approach with MATLAB®
©2012, Worldwide Center of Mathematics, LLC
www.centerofmath.org
ISBN-10: 0-9842071-8-X
ISBN-13: 978-0-9842071-8-3

Contents

Preface

This textbook originates from the class notes used in a math course developed at Champlain College for Software Engineer and Game Programming majors. I wrote this book because I could not find a suitable text which satisfied the following criteria.

- The course covers basic topics from Linear Algebra and Calculus III.

- The course can be completed in one semester.

- The course has a single semester of college-level calculus as a prerequisite.

- The course is suited for Software Engineer and Game Programming majors as well as a variety of other students interested in mathematics.

Creating such a course/text was not an easy task. I am, after all, a mathematician and was accustomed to teaching the standard sequence of 4-credit Calculus courses and then Linear Algebra where everything fits nicely where it belongs with minimal gaps in the underlying knowledge structure. However, the students taking this course did not have that kind of credit allowance in their curriculum. So I tried to create a course which was founded on a solid mathematical structure but allowed students to start doing interesting and moderately sophisticated mathematics in a short period of time.

As it turned out, the field of game-programming provided the perfect back-drop for such a course. What started out as a math course for game-programmers quickly, and quite naturally, became a sequence of game programming objectives that motivated the very topics I wanted to cover in mathematics. After having taught this course many times I am now of the belief that more math courses and topics should be motivated by such objectives. The reason is simple. It does not take long to describe the objective in a programmable game. There are many examples. You want the ball (or object or figure) to move around in a realistic manner. You want to know if it has hit anything else in its world. You want to determine an appropriate response to such a collision. You want to graphically represent these objects and reactions in a visually realistic way. These relatively simple objectives lead, quite naturally, to the development of many of the topics in mathematics often motivated by less visible and more abstract applications. In this course the bigger objectives are less like *determine where the projectile hits the ground* and more like *animate the entire trajectory of the projectile for the first 10 seconds of flight including bounces*. Obviously the second objective entails the first but covers so much more and, in the end, produces an answer that the students can not only visualize but actually watch on the computer screen.

Obviously, programmable software is required for a course such as this. There are many options and we considered quite a few before choosing MATLAB® . There are *game engines*, *physics engines*, and game development software. These options (while quite appealing to many of the students) were dropped as these software packages generally do most, if not all, of the math for you. This is a math course and that would defeat the purpose. There are a few suitable mathematical software packages that were considered. We eventually chose MATLAB® because, in my opinion, programming in MATLAB® is very simple, the graphics are superb, animations are easily created, and the software is reasonably priced. However, there are plenty of people who would prefer other packages. Unfortunately, we could only pick one, so we chose MATLAB® . Perhaps future versions of this text will be written for other packages.

As with any motivating applications in a math course, some time must be dedicated to teaching/learning the background information. In this case, that background comes in the form of programming, graphing, and making animations in MATLAB® . There is a brief but fairly thorough introduction to MATLAB® in the appendix. This appendix is complete with an assignment that, once completed, should have the students fairly comfortable with the software and how to use it for the purposes of this course. This is usually completed in less than two class meetings. In order to expedite this part of the learning curve, all of the code used for demonstration purposes, and some problem set *starter code* can be downloaded from the textbook companion website found at

http://cosmos.champlain.edu/people/stevens/MV3D/index.html

Many of the problems and projects within the text can be completed by downloading the appropriate demonstration or *starter* code and making minimal yet significant alterations. I.e., Students should not have to write much code from scratch.

While the students who use this book should have completed a college-level calculus course, that does not always ensure they have a good grasp of trigonometry. For this reason, there is also an appendix on trigonometry, complete with a summary problem set. Additionally, the Differentiation Appendix provides a few tables of standard differentiation rules.

The course has been a pleasure to develop and teach. This book has been a necessary part of that process. I now appreciate Game Programming for its bountiful supply of applied math problems and suspect that it will play a larger role in motivating math students in the future. I hope you enjoy teaching or learning mathematics with the aid of this book. It was fun to write. As I tell my students quite often - *I wish I had taken this course when I was in college.* I really do.

Scott Stevens
May 2012

Chapter 1

Introduction to Linear Algebra

Linear Algebra is a branch of mathematics concerned with the study of linear systems, vectors, vector spaces, matrices, transformations, and much more. It can be presented in a very abstract manner which includes the algebraic properties of vector spaces and subspaces. It has extensive applications in the natural and social sciences. However, we will restrict our study of linear algebra to include only the most basic applications which we will need in studying systems of equations and the geometry of two- and three-dimensional space.

1.1 Systems of Linear Equations - Row Reduction

Often in mathematics we are concerned with solving equations. Specifically, if we want to solve an equation for a particular variable we are guaranteed to be able to do it provided the equation is linear in that variable. For example, consider the equation

$$x^5 + \sin x - 72y = 105 - 12y. \tag{1.1}$$

This equation is linear in y and it would be easy to solve this equation for y. However, the equation is not linear in x and hence solving this equation for x would be far more difficult and, in this case, impossible to solve algebraically. In order to solve this equation for x we would have to use a *numerical* method. In this chapter, we will focus on solving equations for variables that appear linearly.

Before you get too excited about this simple task, the situation is more complicated than you might first think. For example, consider solving the simple equation $ax = b$ for x. If $a \neq 0$, then $x = b/a$, if $a = 0$ there are two options. What are they? This same situation occurs with systems of linear equations but it is harder tell whether we have one, infinitely many, or no solutions. For example, use whatever method you can to find the solutions to the following systems of equations.

$$(1) \quad \begin{matrix} x & + & y & = & 4 \\ 3x & + & y & = & 4 \end{matrix} \qquad (2) \quad \begin{matrix} x & + & y & = & 4 \\ 3x & + & 3y & = & 12 \end{matrix} \qquad (3) \quad \begin{matrix} x & + & y & = & 4 \\ 3x & + & 3y & = & 10 \end{matrix}$$

Answers: (1) $x = 0$, $y = 4$, (2) infinitely many solutions, (3) no solutions. Think about determining where two lines intersect. They can intersect at a point, infinitely many points (same line), or not at all (parallel).

There are many ways you could have solved the previous systems of equations. Some ways are better than others depending on the equations involved. In this chapter we formalize our approach to this type of problem by using a standard method which will produce a solution every time one exists. This method is called **Gaussian elimination**. The previous systems of equations were *two-by-two* systems. This means there were two equations and two unknowns (x and y). Gaussian elimination can be used on these and larger systems as well. Since we don't want to run out of letters, we will just order our variables with subindexes. First, create the **augmented matrix** representing the system of equations. This consists of the **coefficient matrix**, a vertical line, and the column of constants.

System of Equations   **Augmented Matrix**

$$
\begin{aligned}
2x_1 + 4x_2 + 6x_3 &= 18 \\
4x_1 + 5x_2 + 6x_3 &= 24 \\
3x_1 + x_2 - 2x_3 &= 4
\end{aligned}
\qquad
\left[\begin{array}{ccc|c}
2 & 4 & 6 & 18 \\
4 & 5 & 6 & 24 \\
3 & 1 & -2 & 4
\end{array}\right]
$$

We will perform Gaussian elimination on the augmented matrix. The goal is to perform various row operations which result in equivalent systems until the coefficient matrix has one's on the diagonal and zeros below the diagonal.

The Idea Behind Gaussian Elimination

1. Work from the top left to the bottom right of the coefficient matrix.

2. At each column get a 1 on the diagonal and all zeros below it.

3. Continue this and try to get 1's along the diagonal and zeros below it.

4. This is called **row-echelon form.**

$$
\left[\begin{array}{cccc|c}
1 & * & * & * & * \\
0 & 1 & * & * & * \\
0 & 0 & 1 & * & * \\
0 & 0 & 0 & 1 & *
\end{array}\right]
$$

Once the augmented matrix is in row echelon form, we can use **back substitution** to solve for the variables. We'll get to this later. There are only three types of row operations required to get the augmented matrix into row echelon form.

ROW OPERATIONS [notation]:

1. Multiply a row by a number. $[R_i \rightarrow a\, R_i]$

2. Add/subtract a multiple of one row to/from another and replace it. $[R_i \rightarrow R_i \pm aR_j]$

3. Switch any two rows. $[R_i \leftrightarrow R_j]$

Example 1

System of Equations	Augmented Matrix	Row Operation(s)

$$\begin{aligned} 2x_1 + 4x_2 + 6x_3 &= 18 \\ 4x_1 + 5x_2 + 6x_3 &= 24 \\ 3x_1 + x_2 - 2x_3 &= 4 \end{aligned} \qquad \left[\begin{array}{ccc|c} 2 & 4 & 6 & 18 \\ 4 & 5 & 6 & 24 \\ 3 & 1 & -2 & 4 \end{array}\right] \qquad R_1 \to 1/2\, R_1$$

$$\begin{aligned} x_1 + 2x_2 + 3x_3 &= 9 \\ 4x_1 + 5x_2 + 6x_3 &= 24 \\ 3x_1 + x_2 - 2x_3 &= 4 \end{aligned} \qquad \left[\begin{array}{ccc|c} 1 & 2 & 3 & 9 \\ 4 & 5 & 6 & 24 \\ 3 & 1 & -2 & 4 \end{array}\right] \qquad \begin{aligned} R_2 &\to R_2 - 4R_1 \\ R_3 &\to R_3 - 3R_1 \end{aligned}$$

$$\begin{aligned} x_1 + 2x_2 + 3x_3 &= 9 \\ -3x_2 - 6x_3 &= -12 \\ -5x_2 - 11x_3 &= -23 \end{aligned} \qquad \left[\begin{array}{ccc|c} 1 & 2 & 3 & 9 \\ 0 & -3 & -6 & -12 \\ 0 & -5 & -11 & -23 \end{array}\right] \qquad R_2 \to -1/3\, R_2$$

$$\begin{aligned} x_1 + 2x_2 + 3x_3 &= 9 \\ x_2 + 2x_3 &= 4 \\ -5x_2 - 11x_3 &= -23 \end{aligned} \qquad \left[\begin{array}{ccc|c} 1 & 2 & 3 & 9 \\ 0 & 1 & 2 & 4 \\ 0 & -5 & -11 & -23 \end{array}\right] \qquad R_3 \to R_3 - (-5)\, R_2$$

$$\begin{aligned} x_1 + 2x_2 + 3x_3 &= 9 \\ x_2 + 2x_3 &= 4 \\ - 1x_3 &= -3 \end{aligned} \qquad \left[\begin{array}{ccc|c} 1 & 2 & 3 & 9 \\ 0 & 1 & 2 & 4 \\ 0 & 0 & -1 & -3 \end{array}\right] \qquad R_3 \to -1\, R_3$$

$$\begin{aligned} x_1 + 2x_2 + 3x_3 &= 9 \\ x_2 + 2x_3 &= 4 \\ x_3 &= 3 \end{aligned} \qquad \left[\begin{array}{ccc|c} 1 & 2 & 3 & 9 \\ 0 & 1 & 2 & 4 \\ 0 & 0 & 1 & 3 \end{array}\right] \qquad \begin{aligned} &\text{This is} \\ &\textbf{Row Echelon Form} \end{aligned}$$

Gaussian Elimination Stops Here.

You solve for the variables using **back substitution**. This means you start at the last equation and solve for the last variable and work your way to the first equation substituting the values you find along the way.

- The third equation is $x_3 = 3$ or $\mathbf{x_3 = 3}$.

- The second equation is $x_2 + 2x_3 = 4$ or $x_2 + 6 = 4$ or $\mathbf{x_2 = -2}$.

- The first equation is $x_1 + 2x_2 + 3x_3 = 9$ or $x_1 - 4 + 9 = 9$ or $\mathbf{x_1 = 4}$.

- The solution is $x_1 = 4$, $x_2 = -2$, $x_3 = 3$.

You can continue with **Gauss-Jordan Elimination**:

System of Equations	Augmented Matrix	Row Operation(s)
$\begin{aligned} x_1 + 2x_2 + 3x_3 &= 9 \\ x_2 + 2x_3 &= 4 \\ x_3 &= 3 \end{aligned}$	$\left[\begin{array}{ccc|c} 1 & 2 & 3 & 9 \\ 0 & 1 & 2 & 4 \\ 0 & 0 & 1 & 3 \end{array}\right]$	$\begin{aligned} R_2 &\to R_2 - 2\,R_3 \\ R_1 &\to R_1 - 3\,R_3 \end{aligned}$
$\begin{aligned} x_1 + 2x_2 &= 0 \\ x_2 &= -2 \\ x_3 &= 3 \end{aligned}$	$\left[\begin{array}{ccc|c} 1 & 2 & 0 & 0 \\ 0 & 1 & 0 & -2 \\ 0 & 0 & 1 & 3 \end{array}\right]$	$R_1 \to R_1 - 2\,R_2$
$\begin{aligned} x_1 &= 4 \\ x_2 &= -2 \\ x_3 &= 3 \end{aligned}$	$\left[\begin{array}{ccc|c} 1 & 0 & 0 & 4 \\ 0 & 1 & 0 & -2 \\ 0 & 0 & 1 & 3 \end{array}\right]$	This is **Reduced Row Echelon Form**

Gauss-Jordan Elimination Complete: $x_1 = 4$, $x_2 = -2$, $x_3 = 3$
While this is nice, Gaussian elimination with back-substitution is more efficient so we will stick with that.

Example 2

System of Equations	Augmented Matrix	Row Operation(s)
$\begin{aligned} -3x_1 - 8x_2 - 8x_3 &= -7 \\ 2x_1 + 6x_2 + 10x_3 &= 9 \\ 1x_1 + 3x_2 + 4x_3 &= 3 \end{aligned}$	$\left[\begin{array}{ccc|c} -3 & -8 & -8 & -7 \\ 2 & 6 & 10 & 9 \\ 1 & 3 & 4 & 3 \end{array}\right]$	$R_1 \leftrightarrow R_3$
$\begin{aligned} 1x_1 + 3x_2 + 4x_3 &= 3 \\ 2x_1 + 6x_2 + 10x_3 &= 9 \\ -3x_1 - 8x_2 - 8x_3 &= -7 \end{aligned}$	$\left[\begin{array}{ccc|c} 1 & 3 & 4 & 3 \\ 2 & 6 & 10 & 9 \\ -3 & -8 & -8 & -7 \end{array}\right]$	$\begin{aligned} R_2 &\to R_2 - 2R_1 \\ R_3 &\to R_3 + 3R_1 \end{aligned}$
$\begin{aligned} 1x_1 + 3x_2 + 4x_3 &= 3 \\ 2x_3 &= 3 \\ x_2 + 4x_3 &= 2 \end{aligned}$	$\left[\begin{array}{ccc|c} 1 & 3 & 4 & 3 \\ 0 & 0 & 2 & 3 \\ 0 & 1 & 4 & 2 \end{array}\right]$	$R_2 \leftrightarrow R_3$
$\begin{aligned} 1x_1 + 3x_2 + 4x_3 &= 3 \\ x_2 + 4x_3 &= 2 \\ 2x_3 &= 3 \end{aligned}$	$\left[\begin{array}{ccc|c} 1 & 3 & 4 & 3 \\ 0 & 1 & 4 & 2 \\ 0 & 0 & 2 & 3 \end{array}\right]$	$R_3 \to 1/2\,R_3$

$$
\begin{array}{rcrcrcr}
1x_1 & + & 3x_2 & + & 4x_3 & = & 3 \\
 & & x_2 & + & 4x_3 & = & 2 \\
 & & & & x_3 & = & 3/2
\end{array}
\qquad
\left[\begin{array}{ccc|c}
1 & 3 & 4 & 3 \\
0 & 1 & 4 & 2 \\
0 & 0 & 1 & 3/2
\end{array}\right]
$$

This is
Row Echelon Form

Gaussian Elimination Stops Here. You solve for the variables using **back substitution**.

- The third equation is $1x_3 = 3/2$ or $\mathbf{x_3 = 3/2}$.

- The second equation is $x_2 + 4x_3 = 2$ or $x_2 + 6 = 2$ or $\mathbf{x_2 = -4}$.

- The first equation is $x_1 + 3x_2 + 4x_3 = 3$ or $x_1 - 12 + 6 = 3$ or $\mathbf{x_1 = 9}$.

- The solution is $x_1 = 9$, $x_2 = -4$, $x_3 = 3/2$.

From now on, the preceding sequence of row operations will be denoted simply by

$$
\left[\begin{array}{ccc|c}
-3 & -8 & -8 & -7 \\
2 & 6 & 10 & 9 \\
1 & 3 & 4 & 3
\end{array}\right]
\sim
\left[\begin{array}{ccc|c}
1 & 3 & 4 & 3 \\
2 & 6 & 10 & 9 \\
-3 & -8 & -8 & -7
\end{array}\right]
\sim
\left[\begin{array}{ccc|c}
1 & 3 & 4 & 3 \\
0 & 0 & 2 & 3 \\
0 & 1 & 4 & 2
\end{array}\right]
\sim
\left[\begin{array}{ccc|c}
1 & 3 & 4 & 3 \\
0 & 1 & 4 & 2 \\
0 & 0 & 2 & 3
\end{array}\right]
\sim
\left[\begin{array}{ccc|c}
1 & 3 & 4 & 3 \\
0 & 1 & 4 & 2 \\
0 & 0 & 1 & 3/2
\end{array}\right]
$$

and it is up to you to properly infer the associated row operations. If you can get one matrix from another by performing any number of sequential row operations, the matrices are called **row equivalent**. We use the symbol $\sim$ to represent row equivalence.

In both of the previous examples we were **lucky**. Why?

1. We didn't have to deal with fractions. In most problems there will inevitably be more complicated calculations. In the future, we will be using a computer to perform Gaussian elimination. For now, the problems won't get too *messy*.

2. We were dealing with a **square system of equations**. This means the number of equations is the same as the number of variables resulting in a square coefficient matrix. It is the most common type of system of equations. This represents our best shot at getting a unique solution. We'll deal with non-square systems later.

3. We were able to get all ones down the diagonal of the coefficient matrix with all zeros below it. As such, we were able to obtain a unique solution. This doesn't always happen. When it doesn't we can get different solution options. This is especially frequent when dealing with non-square systems but it can happen with square systems as well.

There are two types of systems of equations and three types of solutions.

1. A **consistent system** has at least one solution:

   (a) A unique solution like in the previous examples, or

   (b) infinitely many solutions which occur from a **dependent** system.

2. An **inconsistent** system has no solutions.

Example 3: Infinite Number of Solutions $\rightarrow$ Consistent and Dependent System

$$
\begin{array}{rcrcrcl}
2x_1 & + & 4x_2 & + & 6x_3 & = & 18 \\
4x_1 & + & 5x_2 & + & 6x_3 & = & 24 \\
2x_1 & + & 7x_2 & & 12x_3 & = & 30
\end{array}
$$

$$
\left[\begin{array}{ccc|c}
2 & 4 & 6 & 18 \\
4 & 5 & 6 & 24 \\
2 & 7 & 12 & 30
\end{array}\right]
\sim
\left[\begin{array}{ccc|c}
1 & 2 & 3 & 9 \\
4 & 5 & 6 & 24 \\
2 & 7 & 12 & 30
\end{array}\right]
\sim
\left[\begin{array}{ccc|c}
1 & 2 & 3 & 9 \\
0 & -3 & -6 & -12 \\
0 & 3 & 6 & 12
\end{array}\right]
\sim
\left[\begin{array}{ccc|c}
1 & 2 & 3 & 9 \\
0 & 1 & 2 & 4 \\
0 & 3 & 6 & 12
\end{array}\right]
\sim
\left[\begin{array}{ccc|c}
1 & 2 & 3 & 9 \\
0 & 1 & 2 & 4 \\
0 & 0 & 0 & 0
\end{array}\right]
$$

Here, the third equation has essentially disappeared - it is meaningless: $0x_1 + 0x_2 + 0x_3 = 0$. This has infinitely many solutions. So, we turn to the second equation: $x_2 + 2x_3 = 4$ and let x_3 be a **free variable**. This is done by setting $x_3 = t$ where t represents any real number.

Let $x_3 = t$

From the second equation:

$x_2 + 2x_3 = 4$

$x_2 = 4 - 2x_3$

$x_2 = 4 - 2t$

From the first equation:

$x_1 + 2x_2 + 3x_3 = 9$

$x_1 = 9 - 2x_2 - 3x_3$

$x_1 = 9 - 2(4 - 2t) - 3t$

$x_1 = 9 - 8 + 4t - 3t$

$x_1 = 1 + t$

The **general solution** is given in the form

$$
\left[\begin{array}{c}
x_1 \\
x_2 \\
x_3
\end{array}\right]
=
\left[\begin{array}{c}
1 + t \\
4 - 2t \\
t
\end{array}\right]
\quad \text{for} \quad -\infty < t < \infty.
$$

This actually represents a line in 3 space. A **particular solution** is found by assigning any number to the parameter t. For example, it we set $t = 0$, a particular solution is $x_1 = 1$, $x_2 = 4$, and $x_3 = 0$.

Example 4: No Solutions $\rightarrow$ An inconsistent system

$$
\begin{array}{rcrcrcl}
 & & 2x_2 & + & 3x_3 & = & 4 \\
2x_1 & - & 6x_2 & + & 7x_3 & = & 15 \\
x_1 & - & 2x_2 & + & 5x_3 & = & 10
\end{array}
$$

$$
\left[\begin{array}{ccc|c}
0 & 2 & 3 & 4 \\
2 & -6 & 7 & 15 \\
1 & -2 & 5 & 10
\end{array}\right]
\sim
\left[\begin{array}{ccc|c}
1 & -2 & 5 & 10 \\
2 & -6 & 7 & 15 \\
0 & 2 & 3 & 4
\end{array}\right]
\sim
\left[\begin{array}{ccc|c}
1 & -2 & 5 & 10 \\
0 & -2 & -3 & -5 \\
0 & 2 & 3 & 4
\end{array}\right]
\sim
\left[\begin{array}{ccc|c}
1 & -2 & 5 & 10 \\
0 & -2 & -3 & -5 \\
0 & 0 & 0 & -1
\end{array}\right].
$$

The third equation says $0x_1 + 0x_2 + 0x_3 = -1$. This equation has no solutions and so the system of equations has no solution and we call the system **inconsistent**.

Chapter 1.1 Worksheet

Use Gaussian elimination with back-substitution to determine if the system of equations is consistent (has at least one solution). If it is consistent, solve for the variables. If you get infinitely many solutions, give the **general solution** in terms of a parameter (t) and give one **particular solution**.

1.

$$\begin{aligned} x_1 - 3x_3 &= 8 \\ 2x_1 + 2x_2 + 9x_3 &= 7 \\ x_2 + 5x_3 &= -2 \end{aligned}$$

$$\begin{bmatrix} 1, & 0, & -3 & | & 8 \\ 2, & 2, & 9 & | & 7 \\ 0, & 1, & 5 & | & -2 \end{bmatrix} \sim \begin{bmatrix} 1, & 0, & -3 & | & 8 \\ 0, & 1, & 5 & | & -2 \\ 2, & 2, & 9 & | & 7 \end{bmatrix} \sim$$

$$\begin{bmatrix} 1, & 0, & -3 & | & 8 \\ 0, & 1, & 5 & | & -2 \\ 0, & 2, & 15 & | & -9 \end{bmatrix} \sim \begin{bmatrix} 1, & 0, & -3 & | & 8 \\ 0, & 1, & 5 & | & -2 \\ 0, & 0, & 5 & | & -5 \end{bmatrix} \sim \begin{bmatrix} 1, & 0, & -3 & | & 8 \\ 0, & 1, & 5 & | & -2 \\ 0, & 0, & 1 & | & -1 \end{bmatrix}$$

$X_3 = -1$

$x_2 + 5x_3 = -2$

$x_2 - 5 = -2$

$\boxed{x_2 = 3}$

$x_1 - 3x_3 = 8$

$x_1 + 3 = 8$

$\boxed{x_1 = 5}$

2.

$$\begin{aligned} x_2 - 4x_3 &= 8 \\ 2x_1 - 3x_2 + 2x_3 &= 1 \\ 5x_1 - 8x_2 + 7x_3 &= 1 \end{aligned}$$

$$\begin{bmatrix} 0, & 1, & -4 & | & 8 \\ 2, & -3, & 2 & | & 1 \\ 5, & -8, & 7 & | & 1 \end{bmatrix} \sim \begin{bmatrix} 0, & 1, & -4 & | & 8 \\ 2, & 1, & 14 & | & -21 \\ 5, & -8, & 7 & | & 1 \end{bmatrix} \sim \begin{bmatrix} 0, & 1, & -4 & | & 8 \\ 2, & 1, & 14 & | & -21 \\ 1, & -10, & -21 & | & 63 \end{bmatrix} \sim \begin{bmatrix} 1, & -10, & -21 & | & 63 \\ 2, & 1, & 14 & | & -21 \\ 0, & 1, & -4 & | & 8 \end{bmatrix} \sim$$

$$\begin{bmatrix} \\ \\ \end{bmatrix}$$

No Solutions

3.

$$\begin{aligned} x_1 + 2x_2 + 6x_3 &= 10 \\ x_1 + 5x_3 &= 6 \\ 2x_2 + x_3 &= 4 \end{aligned}$$

Chapter 1.1 Problem Set

Numbers with an asterisk[*] have solutions in the back of the book.

1. At the very beginning of this section we noticed that solving 2 equations in 2 unknowns was like determining if and how two lines can intersect in a plane. Now suppose we have 3 planes (geometric plane, not a flying machine) in three dimensional space. When and how can they intersect?

[handwritten: Vector space. R^3]

[handwritten: When they have the same x, y, and z values.]

2.[*] Use Gaussian elimination with back-substitution to determine if the system of equations is consistent (has at least one solution). If it is consistent, solve for the variables. If you get infinitely many solutions, give the **general solution** in terms of a parameter (t) and give one **particular solution**.

[handwritten matrices:]
$$\begin{bmatrix} 1 & 3 & -1 & | & 1 \\ 0 & 1 & -1 & | & 1 \\ 2 & -1 & 5 & | & 2 \end{bmatrix}$$
$$\begin{bmatrix} -2 & -6 & 2 & | & -2 \\ 0 & 1 & -1 & | & 1 \\ 0 & -7 & 7 & | & 0 \end{bmatrix}$$
[handwritten: No solution]

(a)
$$\begin{aligned} x + 3y - z &= 1 \\ y - z &= 1 \\ 2x - y + 5z &= 2 \end{aligned}$$

(b)
$$\begin{aligned} x + 3y - z &= 1 \\ y - z &= 1 \\ 2x - y + 5z &= -5 \end{aligned}$$

[handwritten work, partly crossed out: y = 1 + t]

(c)
$$\begin{aligned} x - 3z &= -5 \\ 2x + y + 2z &= 7 \\ 3x + 2y + z &= 7 \end{aligned}$$

3. Use Gaussian elimination with back-substitution to determine if the system of equations is consistent (has at least one solution). If it is consistent, solve for the variables. If you get infinitely many solutions, give the **general solution** in terms of a parameter (t) and give one **particular solution**.

(a)
$$\begin{aligned} x_1 + x_2 + 2x_3 &= 8 \\ -x_1 - 2x_2 + 3x_3 &= 1 \\ 3x_1 - 7x_2 + 4x_3 &= 10 \end{aligned}$$

(b)
$$\begin{aligned} x_1 + 2x_2 &= 0 \\ 2x_1 + x_2 + 3x_3 &= 0 \\ -2x_2 + 2x_3 &= 0 \end{aligned}$$

(c)
$$\begin{aligned} x_1 + 2x_2 &= 1 \\ 2x_1 + x_2 + 3x_3 &= 2 \\ -2x_2 + 2x_3 &= 3 \end{aligned}$$

4.[*] Use Gaussian elimination with back-substitution to determine if the system of equations is consistent (has at least one solution). If it is consistent, solve for the variables. If you get infinitely many solutions, give the **general solution** in terms of a parameter (t) and give one **particular solution**.

(a)
$$\begin{aligned} x + 2y + 3z &= 6 \\ 2y - z &= 1 \\ x + 4y + 2z &= 7 \end{aligned}$$

(b)
$$\begin{aligned} x + 2y + 3z &= 2 \\ 2y - z &= -3 \\ x + 4y + 2z &= -5 \end{aligned}$$

(c)
$$\begin{aligned} x + 2y + 3z &= -8 \\ 2y - z &= 10 \\ x + 4y + z &= 6 \end{aligned}$$

1.2 Matrices and Vectors - Basic Properties

1. **Some Definitions about Matrices**

   (a) An m **x** n **matrix** is a rectangular array of numbers with $\underline{m \text{ rows}}$ and $\underline{n \text{ columns}}$.

   $$A = \begin{bmatrix} a_{11} & a_{12} & a_{13} & \cdots & a_{1n} \\ a_{21} & a_{22} & a_{23} & \cdots & a_{2n} \\ \vdots & \vdots & \vdots & \vdots & \vdots \\ a_{m1} & a_{m2} & a_{m3} & \cdots & a_{mn} \end{bmatrix} = [a_{ij}]$$

   (b) The **dimension** of A is m by n or m **x** n.

   (c) Two matrices are **equivalent** if they have the same dimension and corresponding entries are equal.

   (d) The matrix of all zeros is called the **zero matrix** denoted **0**.
   For example

   $$\mathbf{0} = \begin{bmatrix} 0 & 0 \\ 0 & 0 \end{bmatrix} \qquad \mathbf{0} = \begin{bmatrix} 0 & 0 & 0 \\ 0 & 0 & 0 \\ 0 & 0 & 0 \end{bmatrix} \qquad \mathbf{0} = \begin{bmatrix} 0 & 0 & 0 & 0 \\ 0 & 0 & 0 & 0 \end{bmatrix}$$

   (e) The n **x** n matrix with ones along the diagonal and zeros elsewhere is called the **identity matrix** and is denoted I_n. For example,

   $$I_2 = \begin{bmatrix} 1 & 0 \\ 0 & 1 \end{bmatrix} \qquad I_3 = \begin{bmatrix} 1 & 0 & 0 \\ 0 & 1 & 0 \\ 0 & 0 & 1 \end{bmatrix} \qquad I_4 = \begin{bmatrix} 1 & 0 & 0 & 0 \\ 0 & 1 & 0 & 0 \\ 0 & 0 & 1 & 0 \\ 0 & 0 & 0 & 1 \end{bmatrix}$$

   (f) If $A = [a_{ij}]$, the **transpose** of A, denoted A^T, is defined by $a_{ij}^T = a_{ji}$. (switch rows and columns). For example,

   $$\text{if} \quad A = \begin{bmatrix} 1 & 2 & 3 \\ 4 & 5 & 6 \\ 7 & 8 & 9 \end{bmatrix} \quad \text{then} \quad A^T = \begin{bmatrix} 1 & 4 & 7 \\ 2 & 5 & 8 \\ 3 & 6 & 9 \end{bmatrix}$$

   (g) If $A^T = A$, then A is called **symmetric.** For example,

   $$A = \begin{bmatrix} 1 & 2 & 3 \\ 2 & 5 & 6 \\ 3 & 6 & 9 \end{bmatrix} \quad \text{is symmetric}$$

2. **Some Operations on Matrices**

   (a) **Scalar Multiplication:** When a matrix is multiplied by a number (scalar) this is called scalar multiplication. Each term in the matrix is multiplied by the scalar.

$$\text{if} \quad A = \begin{bmatrix} 1 & -1 & 1 \\ 0 & 1 & 6 \end{bmatrix} \quad \text{then} \quad 3A = \begin{bmatrix} 3 & -3 & 3 \\ 0 & 3 & 18 \end{bmatrix}$$

   (b) **Matrix Addition:** Matrices of the same dimensions are added term by term.

$$\text{if} \quad A = \begin{bmatrix} 1 & -1 & 1 \\ 0 & 1 & 6 \end{bmatrix} \quad \text{and} \quad B = \begin{bmatrix} 2 & 1 & 0 \\ 1 & 0 & -1 \end{bmatrix} \quad \text{then} \quad A + B = \begin{bmatrix} 3 & 0 & 1 \\ 1 & 1 & 5 \end{bmatrix}$$

3. **Properties of Matrix Addition and Scalar Multiplication:**

   Assume A and B are matrices of the same dimension and r is a scalar (number).

   (a) Commutative Property of Addition: $A + B = B + A$

   (b) Associative Property of Addition: $(A + B) + C = A + (B + C)$

   (c) Identity property of Addition: $A + \mathbf{0} = A$

   (d) Distributive property of scalar multiplication: $r(A + B) = rA + rB$

4. **Row and Column Vectors**

   A **row vector** is a 1 by n matrix: A **column vector** is an m by 1 matrix:

$$x = [x_1, x_2, \ldots, x_n]$$

$$y = \begin{bmatrix} y_1 \\ y_2 \\ y_3 \\ \vdots \\ y_m \end{bmatrix}$$

   You can get a column vector from a row vector by taking the transpose. For example,

$$[1, 2, 3]^T = \begin{bmatrix} 1 \\ 2 \\ 3 \end{bmatrix}.$$

   This notation is regularly used to save space.

5. **Some More Operations on Vectors and Matrices**

   (a) The **Dot Product**

   Two vectors of the same length may be multiplied by the dot product:

   $$x \cdot y = [x_1, x_2, \ldots, x_n] \cdot [y_1, y_2, \ldots, y_n] = x_1 y_1 + x_2 y_2 + \ldots x_n y_n$$

   Example: Find $x \cdot y$ for $x = [2, 3, 4]$ and $y = [-1, 7, -3]$ Answer: $x \cdot y = -2 + 21 - 12 = 7$

   (b) **Matrix Multiplication**

   Two matrices can be multiplied as follows.

   If A is m x n given by $A = [a_{ij}]$ and B is n by p given by $[b_{ij}]$ then $AB = C$ is m by p where

   $$C_{ij} = \text{i'th row of A dotted with the j'th column of B}$$

   Example: Find AB when $A = \begin{bmatrix} 1 & -1 & 1 \\ 0 & 1 & 6 \end{bmatrix}$ and $B = \begin{bmatrix} 1 & -1 \\ 0 & 1 \\ 2 & 3 \end{bmatrix}$

   Answer: $AB = \begin{bmatrix} 1+0+2 & -1-1+3 \\ 0+0+12 & 0+1+18 \end{bmatrix} = \begin{bmatrix} 3 & 1 \\ 12 & 19 \end{bmatrix}$

6. **Properties of Matrix Multiplication**

   (a) If A is an m x n matrix and B is an n x p matrix, then AB is an m x p matrix.

   (b) Associative: $A(BC) = (AB)C$

   (c) Distributive: $A(B + C) = AB + AC$ and $(A + B)C = AC + BC$

   (d) Identity: If A is n x n then $AI_n = I_n A = A$.

   (e) Zero: $A\,\mathbf{0} = \mathbf{0}$ and $\mathbf{0}A = \mathbf{0}$ where $\mathbf{0}$ is the zero matrix of appropriate dimension.

   (f) $(AB)^T = B^T A^T$

7. **Warning: Order Matters!**

   (a) No Commutative Law! $AB \neq BA$ unless you get real lucky.

   (b) By definition, the dot product of two vectors always yields a scalar ($x \cdot y = y \cdot x$). However, on most software, the dot product is just a form of matrix multiplication. It depends on how you define your vectors but quite often $x \cdot y \neq y \cdot x$.

8. **Linear Systems $\iff$ Matrix Equations**

Any linear system can be expressed as a matrix equation.

(a) **Example:** The system of equations defined by

$$
\begin{array}{rcrcrcrcr}
x_1 & - & x_2 & + & x_3 & + & 2x_4 & = & 1 \\
    &   & x_2 & + & 6x_3 & + & 2x_4 & = & 0 \\
x_1 &   &   & + & 7x_3 & + & 5x_4 & = & 3
\end{array}
$$

can be expressed as $Ax = b$ where

$$
\begin{array}{ccc}
\begin{bmatrix} 1 & -1 & 1 & 2 \\ 0 & 1 & 6 & 2 \\ 1 & 0 & 7 & 5 \end{bmatrix} & \begin{bmatrix} x_1 \\ x_2 \\ x_3 \\ x_4 \end{bmatrix} = & \begin{bmatrix} 1 \\ 0 \\ 3 \end{bmatrix} \\
A & x \qquad = & b.
\end{array}
$$

(b) **Example:** Going the other way, the matrix equation $Ax = b$:

$$
\begin{array}{ccc}
\begin{bmatrix} 1 & 0 & -3 \\ 2 & 2 & 9 \\ 0 & 1 & 5 \end{bmatrix} & \begin{bmatrix} x_1 \\ x_2 \\ x_3 \end{bmatrix} = & \begin{bmatrix} 8 \\ 7 \\ -2 \end{bmatrix} \\
A & x \qquad = & b.
\end{array}
$$

represents the linear system

$$
\begin{array}{rcr}
x_1 - 3x_3 & = & 8 \\
2x_1 + 2x_2 + 9x_3 & = & 7 \\
x_2 + 5x_3 & = & -2
\end{array}
$$

9. **Solving Linear Systems:** In MATLAB® you can solve the system of equations defined by $Ax = b$ with:[1]

$$
\text{x = A\textbackslash b}
$$

If there is a unique solution, this works perfectly. If there are infinitely many solutions or no solutions, it gets a little tricky. We'll investigate all three situations in the worksheet.

---

[1]Note, the backslash command in A\b is **not** the division symbol.

- **MATLAB**® : Vectors and Vector Operations (Vectors.m)

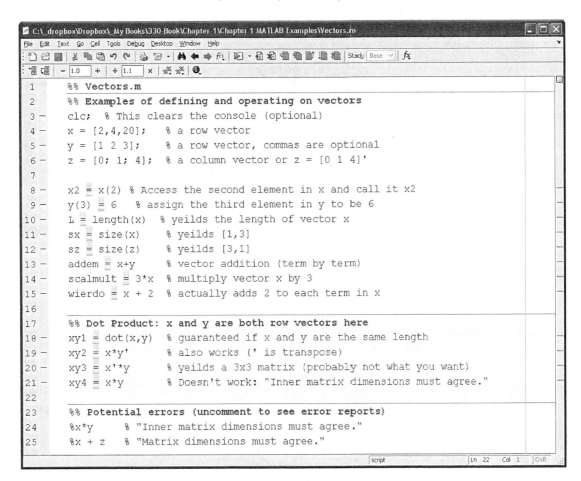

```matlab
%% Vectors.m
%% Examples of defining and operating on vectors
clc;   % This clears the console (optional)
x = [2,4,20];   % a row vector
y = [1 2 3];    % a row vector, commas are optional
z = [0; 1; 4];  % a column vector or z = [0 1 4]'

x2 = x(2) % Access the second element in x and call it x2
y(3) = 6   % assign the third element in y to be 6
L = length(x)  % yeilds the length of vector x
sx = size(x)     % yeilds [1,3]
sz = size(z)     % yeilds [3,1]
addem = x+y      % vector addition (term by term)
scalmult = 3*x   % multiply vector x by 3
wierdo = x + 2   % actually adds 2 to each term in x

%% Dot Product:  x and y are both row vectors here
xy1 = dot(x,y)  % guaranteed if x and y are the same length
xy2 = x*y'      % also works (' is transpose)
xy3 = x'*y      % yeilds a 3x3 matrix (probably not what you want)
xy4 = x*y       % Doesn't work: "Inner matrix dimensions must agree."

%% Potential errors (uncomment to see error reports)
%x*y     % "Inner matrix dimensions must agree."
%x + z   % "Matrix dimensions must agree."
```

- **MATLAB®** : Matrices, Vectors as Matrices, Solving Linear Systems (Matrices.m)

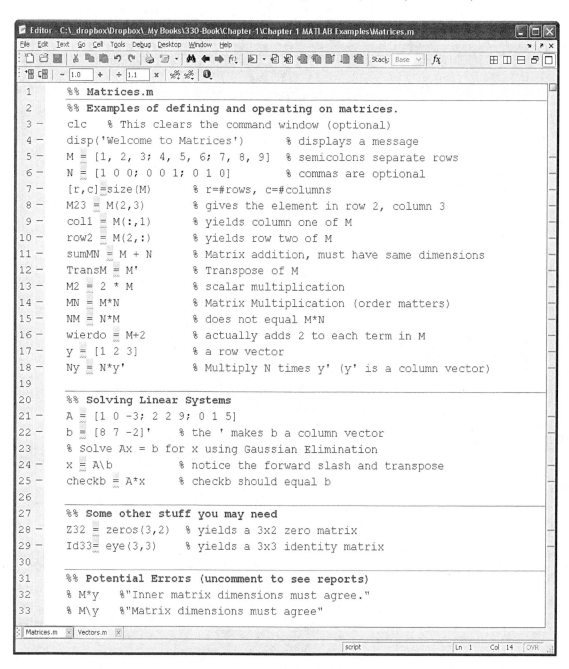

```matlab
%% Matrices.m
%% Examples of defining and operating on matrices.
clc      % This clears the command window (optional)
disp('Welcome to Matrices')       % displays a message
M = [1, 2, 3; 4, 5, 6; 7, 8, 9]  % semicolons separate rows
N = [1 0 0; 0 0 1; 0 1 0]          % commas are optional
[r,c]=size(M)        % r=#rows, c=#columns
M23 = M(2,3)         % gives the element in row 2, column 3
col1 = M(:,1)        % yields column one of M
row2 = M(2,:)        % yields row two of M
sumMN = M + N        % Matrix addition, must have same dimensions
TransM = M'          % Transpose of M
M2 = 2 * M           % scalar multiplication
MN = M*N             % Matrix Multiplication (order matters)
NM = N*M             % does not equal M*N
wierdo = M+2         % actually adds 2 to each term in M
y = [1 2 3]          % a row vector
Ny = N*y'            % Multiply N times y' (y' is a column vector)

%% Solving Linear Systems
A = [1 0 -3; 2 2 9; 0 1 5]
b = [8 7 -2]'        % the ' makes b a column vector
% Solve Ax = b for x using Gaussian Elimination
x = A\b              % notice the forward slash and transpose
checkb = A*x         % checkb should equal b

%% Some other stuff you may need
Z32 = zeros(3,2)     % yields a 3x2 zero matrix
Id33= eye(3,3)       % yields a 3x3 identity matrix

%% Potential Errors (uncomment to see reports)
% M*y    %"Inner matrix dimensions must agree."
% M\y    %"Matrix dimensions must agree"
```

Some MATLAB® commands for vectors and matrices:

- Vectors

    - v = [2 4 6] or v = [2, 4, 6] yields a row vector.
    - v = [2;4;6] or v = [2 4 6]' yields a column vector.
    - v(2) yields the second element in v.
    - v(2:3) = yields elements 2 through 3 of v.
    - v(1) = 0 replaces the 2 with a zero
    - v(4) = 0 appends a zero to v now: v = [2 4 6 0]
    - [m,n] = size(v) yields (m = 1 and n = 3) or (m = 3 and n = 1)
    - v = 0:0.5:2 yields v = [0 0.5 1 1.5 2]

- Matrices

    - A = [1 2 3; 4 5 6; 7 8 9] or [1,2,3;4,5,6;7,8,9] (semicolon seperates rows)
    - [m,n] = size(A) yields m = number of rows in A and n = the number of columns in A.
    - A(1,2) yields the element in row 1 and column 2 of A.
    - A(:,2) yields the second column of A.
    - A(2,:) yields teh second row of A.
    - A(1:2,3:4) = yields rows 1 to 2 and columns 3 to 4 of A.
    - A([1 3 2],[1 3]) = yields rows 1 3 2 and columns 1 3 of A.
    - A + B yields term by term addition (appropriate dimensions reguired)
    - A * B yields normal matrix multiplication (appropriate dimensions required)
    - A∧2 = A * A
    - A.∧2 squares each entry in A.
    - A./2 divides each entry in A by 2.
    - cos(A) takes the cosine of each term in A.
    - eye(n) yields the n x n identity matrix
    - zeros(n,m) yields an n x m zero matrix
    - ones(n,m) yields an n x m matrix of all ones.
    - transpose(A) yields the transpose of A.
    - A' = conjugate transpose (or just transpose if real)
    - inv(A) yields the inverse of A if one exists.
    - det(A) yields the determinent of A.
    - x = A\b produces a solution to Ax = b. (forward slash).

Chapter 1.2 Worksheet

1. (**MATLAB**®) Recall the following systems that you solved by hand in Section 1.1.

   (a)   (b)   (c)

$$\begin{aligned} x_1 - 3x_3 &= 8 \\ 2x_1 + 2x_2 + 9x_3 &= 7 \\ x_2 + 5x_3 &= -2 \end{aligned} \qquad \begin{aligned} x_2 - 4x_3 &= 8 \\ 2x_1 - 3x_2 + 2x_3 &= 1 \\ 5x_1 - 8x_2 + 7x_3 &= 1 \end{aligned} \qquad \begin{aligned} x_1 + 2x_2 + 6x_3 &= 10 \\ x_1 + 5x_3 &= 6 \\ 2x_2 + x_3 &= 4 \end{aligned}$$

You should have found that (a) had a unique solution $[x_1, x_2, x_3] = [5, 3, -1]$, (b) (inconsistent) had no solutions, and (c) (dependent) had infinitely many solutions of the form $[x_1, x_2, x_3] = [6 - 5t, 2 - \frac{t}{2}, t]$.

Assignment: Use MATLAB® to solve these three systems of equations. You should run into problems. You will get warnings for parts (b) and (c). In part (b) MATLAB® actually gives you a solution that is not a solution and in part (c) MATLAB® does not return a solution.

Chapter 1.2 Problem Set

Numbers with an asterisk[*] have solutions in the back of the book.

1.[*] (**Written**) Perform the requested operations on the given vectors by hand and confirm with **MATLAB**® .

$$x = [1, 2, 3] \qquad y = \begin{bmatrix} 4 \\ 5 \\ 6 \end{bmatrix}$$

(a) Find $x \cdot y$ (the dot product of x and y).

(b) Find xy (matrix multiplication).

(c) Find yx (matrix multiplication).

(d) **Notice** that the dot product is just a type of matrix multiplication if you line it up correctly.

2. (**Written**) Perform the following operations by hand and confirm with **MATLAB**® .

$$A = \begin{bmatrix} 2 & -5 \\ 0 & 4 \end{bmatrix}, \quad B = \begin{bmatrix} 3 & 2 \\ -1 & 1 \end{bmatrix}, \quad \text{and} \quad x = \begin{bmatrix} 2 \\ -3 \end{bmatrix}$$

(a) Find A^T and B^T

(b) Find $\frac{1}{2}A$ (scalar multiplication)

(c) Find $A + B$

(d) Find $2(A + B)$ and $2A + 2B$.

(e) Find AB and BA.

(f) Find Ax and Bx.

3.[*] (**Written**) Perform the following operations by hand and confirm with **MATLAB**® .

$$M = \begin{bmatrix} 1 & 0 & 0 \\ 0 & 2 & 0 \\ 0 & 0 & 5 \end{bmatrix} \quad N = \begin{bmatrix} -1 & 3 & -2 \\ 10 & 1 & 1 \\ 0 & 2 & 3 \end{bmatrix} \quad x = \begin{bmatrix} 1 \\ 0 \\ -1 \end{bmatrix} \quad y = \begin{bmatrix} -6 \\ 10 \\ 1 \end{bmatrix}$$

(a) Find M^T and N^T

(b) Find MN and NM.

(c) Find Mx,

(d) Find the dot product $x \cdot y$.

(e) Find $3x - 2y$

4.[*] (**Written**) Perform the following operations by hand and confirm with **MATLAB**® .

$$A = \begin{bmatrix} 1 & 2 & 0 \\ 0 & 4 & -2 \\ 1 & 0 & 3 \end{bmatrix}, \quad B = \begin{bmatrix} 3 & 2 & -1 \\ 0 & 1 & 0 \\ -1 & 2 & 3 \end{bmatrix}, \quad C = \begin{bmatrix} 3 & 0 & 0 \\ 0 & 2 & 0 \\ 0 & 0 & 4 \end{bmatrix} \quad \text{and} \quad x = \begin{bmatrix} 2 \\ -3 \\ 0 \end{bmatrix}$$

(a) Find AB

(b) Find AC and CA. What was the effect on A of these two multiplications.

(c) Find Ax, Bx, and Cx. Comment on what happens to x when multiplied by C.

5. (**MATLAB**®) Write a program that

(a) demonstrates $AB \neq BA$.

(b)[*] displays the error message when you try to multiply matrices of inappropriate sizes.

(c) demonstrates $(AB)^T = B^T A^T$.

(d) creates a symmetric matrix S and shows that $S^T = S$.

(e) creates a 3 x 3 matrix by multiplying a 3 x 1 and 1 x 3 vector.

(f) demonstrates the dot product.

(g) demonstrates the distributive properties.

6.[*] (**MATLAB**®) Solve the following systems using MATLAB® .

(a)
$$\begin{aligned} x - 3z &= -5 \\ 2x + y + 2z &= 7 \\ 3x + 2y + z &= 7 \end{aligned}$$

(b)
$$\begin{aligned} x_1 + x_2 + 2x_3 &= 8 \\ -x_1 - 2x_2 + 3x_3 &= 1 \\ 3x_1 - 7x_2 + 4x_3 &= 10 \end{aligned}$$

7. (**MATLAB**®) Solve the following systems using MATLAB® .

(a)
$$\begin{aligned} x + 2y + 3z &= -8 \\ 2y - z &= 10 \\ x + 4y + z &= 6 \end{aligned}$$

(b)
$$\begin{aligned} x_1 + x_2 &= -0.25 \\ -x_1 + 3x_3 &= 5.50 \\ -7x_2 + 4x_3 &= 13.25 \end{aligned}$$

8. (**MATLAB**®) Find the inverse of a matrix by solving systems for the e_i vectors.

In the vector space $\mathbb{R}^3$ (defined later) the standard basis consists of these three vectors.

$$e_1 = \begin{bmatrix} 1 \\ 0 \\ 0 \end{bmatrix} \quad e_2 = \begin{bmatrix} 0 \\ 1 \\ 0 \end{bmatrix} \quad e_3 = \begin{bmatrix} 0 \\ 0 \\ 1 \end{bmatrix}$$

Consider the 3 by 3 matrix A

$$A = \begin{bmatrix} 0 & 1 & 2 \\ 1 & 0 & 3 \\ 4 & -3 & 8 \end{bmatrix}$$

Assignment:

(a) Write a program that solves the three systems $Ax_i = e_i$ for x_i.

(b) Use these three solutions, x_1, x_2, x_3, as the first three columns in a new matrix called B.

(c) Now check $A B$ and $B A$.

(d) You should get the identity matrix I_3 in both cases.

(e) Describe the relationship between A and B.

MATLAB® Help: Once you have found x1, x2, and x3, you can make the matrix B by

`B(:,1) = x1; B(:,2) = x2; B(:,3) = x3`   or   `B = [x1 x2 x3]`

1.3   Inverses and Determinants

If you came across the scalar equation $ax = b$ and you want to solve for x, you would just divide both sides of the equation by a and get $x = b/a$. This is all well and good if $a \neq 0$. If $a \neq 0$ then a has a multiplicative inverse which we denote by $1/a$ or $^{-1}$. If $a = 0$ then we have problems. Specifically, zero has no multiplicative inverse. This is summed up by the rule: *You can't divide by zero.*

It would be nice if there was a simple rule like this for matrix equations in the form $Ax = b$. It turns out, there is. It goes like this: *If the determinant of a matrix is zero, it has no inverse.* This section describes the process of determining whether or not a matrix has an inverse and, if there is one, how to get it.

1. **Matrix Inverse:** Assume A is a square, n x n, matrix. If there exists an n x n matrix B such that

$$AB = BA = I_n$$

then B is called the **inverse** of A, denoted by A^{-1}, and A is called **invertible**. In this case A is also called **nonsingular**. If A does not have an inverse it is called **singular**.

2. **Inverse of a 2 by 2 matrix**

$$\text{If} \quad A = \begin{bmatrix} a & b \\ c & d \end{bmatrix} \quad \text{then} \quad A^{-1} = \frac{1}{ad - bc} \begin{bmatrix} d & -b \\ -c & a \end{bmatrix}$$

Notice: The number $ad - bc$ determines whether A has an inverse or not. This number is called the **determinant** of a 2 by 2 matrix.

3. **Solution to a Matrix Equation:** If A is an n by n invertible matrix, then the system of equations expressed by $Ax = b$ has a solution defined by $x = A^{-1}b$.

$$Ax = b \quad \rightarrow \quad x = A^{-1}b$$

4. **Example:** Use the method above to solve the system
$$\begin{array}{rcrcl} x_1 & + & 2x_2 & = & 5 \\ 3x_1 & + & 4x_2 & = & 6 \end{array}$$

Here, $A = \begin{bmatrix} 1 & 2 \\ 3 & 4 \end{bmatrix}$ and $b = \begin{bmatrix} 5 \\ 6 \end{bmatrix}$ so $A^{-1} = \dfrac{1}{(1)(4) - (2)(3)} \begin{bmatrix} 4 & -2 \\ -3 & 1 \end{bmatrix} = \dfrac{-1}{2} \begin{bmatrix} 4 & -2 \\ -3 & 1 \end{bmatrix}$

and
$$\begin{bmatrix} x_1 \\ x_2 \end{bmatrix} = A^{-1}b = \frac{-1}{2} \begin{bmatrix} 4 & -2 \\ -3 & 1 \end{bmatrix} \begin{bmatrix} 5 \\ 6 \end{bmatrix} = \frac{-1}{2} \begin{bmatrix} 8 \\ -9 \end{bmatrix} = \begin{bmatrix} -4 \\ 4.5 \end{bmatrix}$$

Check:
$$\begin{array}{rcrclclcl} x_1 & + & 2x_2 & = & -4 + 2(4.5) & = & -4 + 9 & = & 5 \\ 3x_1 & + & 4x_2 & = & 3(-4) + 4(4.5) & = & -12 + 18 & = & 6 \end{array}$$

5. **Inverse Theorems:** Assume A and B are both invertible matrices and k is a scalar.

   (a) $(AB)^{-1} = B^{-1}A^{-1}$

   (b) $(A^{-1})^{-1} = A$

   (c) $(A^T)^{-1} = (A^{-1})^T$

   (d) $(kA)^{-1} = \dfrac{1}{k}A^{-1}$

6. **Getting the inverse of larger matrices by row operations:**

   You want to find the matrix X such that
   $$AX = I_n$$

   Set up the augmented matrix $[A|I_n]$ where I_n is the nxn identity matrix. Perform row operations until A is equivalent to I_n then the right half is the inverse of A. In other words convert $[A|I_n] \sim [I_n|A^{-1}]$ using row operations (if possible).

7. **Example:** Find the inverse of $A = \begin{bmatrix} 1 & 2 & 3 \\ 4 & 9 & 12 \\ 2 & 7 & 5 \end{bmatrix}$.

   Set up the augmented matrix $[A|I_3]$
   and perform row operations to get $[I_3|A^{-1}]$

   $$[A|I_3] = \left[\begin{array}{ccc|ccc} 1 & 2 & 3 & 1 & 0 & 0 \\ 4 & 9 & 12 & 0 & 1 & 0 \\ 2 & 7 & 5 & 0 & 0 & 1 \end{array}\right]$$

   $$\sim \left[\begin{array}{ccc|ccc} 1 & 2 & 3 & 1 & 0 & 0 \\ 0 & 1 & 0 & -4 & 1 & 0 \\ 0 & 3 & -1 & -2 & 0 & 1 \end{array}\right]$$

   $$\sim \left[\begin{array}{ccc|ccc} 1 & 2 & 3 & 1 & 0 & 0 \\ 0 & 1 & 0 & -4 & 1 & 0 \\ 0 & 0 & -1 & 10 & -3 & 1 \end{array}\right]$$

   $$A^{-1} = \begin{bmatrix} 39 & -11 & 3 \\ -4 & 1 & 0 \\ -10 & 3 & -1 \end{bmatrix}.$$

   $$\sim \left[\begin{array}{ccc|ccc} 1 & 2 & 3 & 1 & 0 & 0 \\ 0 & 1 & 0 & -4 & 1 & 0 \\ 0 & 0 & 1 & -10 & 3 & -1 \end{array}\right]$$

   $$\sim \left[\begin{array}{ccc|ccc} 1 & 2 & 0 & 31 & -9 & 3 \\ 0 & 1 & 0 & -4 & 1 & 0 \\ 0 & 0 & 1 & -10 & 3 & -1 \end{array}\right]$$

   $$\sim \left[\begin{array}{ccc|ccc} 1 & 0 & 0 & 39 & -11 & 3 \\ 0 & 1 & 0 & -4 & 1 & 0 \\ 0 & 0 & 1 & -10 & 3 & -1 \end{array}\right] = [I_3|A^{-1}]$$

8. Definition: If $A = \begin{bmatrix} a & b \\ c & d \end{bmatrix}$, then the **determinant** of A, denoted $\det(A)$ or $|A|$, is $ad - bc$.

note: Early it was shown that if $\det(A) = 0$ then A does not have an inverse. This carries over to larger matrices but we must first define and be able to calculate the determinant of larger matrices.

9. **Finding the determinant of larger matrices:** Assume A is a square n by n matrix.

   (a) **Definition:** The ij^{th} **minor of** A is the $(n-1)$ x $(n-1)$ matrix M_{ij} resulting from A when the ith row and jth column are removed.

   (b) **Definition:** The ij^{th} **cofactor of** A is denoted A_{ij} and defined by

$$A_{ij} = (-1)^{i+j}|M_{ij}|$$

The **determinant of** A, denoted $\det(A)$ or $|A|$, is given by

$$\det(A) = a_{11}A_{11} + a_{12}A_{12} + \ldots + a_{1n}A_{1n}.$$

In the above case we have found the cofactor expansion of A along the first row. We can find the determinant of A by expanding along any row i

$$\det(A) = a_{i1}A_{i1} + a_{i2}A_{i2} + \ldots + a_{in}A_{in}.$$

or any column j

$$\det(A) = a_{1j}A_{1j} + a_{2j}A_{2j} + \ldots + a_{nj}A_{nj}.$$

Example: Find the determinant of $A = \begin{bmatrix} 2 & 4 & 6 \\ 0 & 1 & 0 \\ 2 & 3 & -1 \end{bmatrix}$

- by expanding along the first row

$$\det(A) = (-1)^{(1+1)}(2)\begin{vmatrix} 1 & 0 \\ 3 & -1 \end{vmatrix} + (-1)^{(1+2)}(4)\begin{vmatrix} 0 & 0 \\ 2 & -1 \end{vmatrix} + (-1)^{(1+3)}(6)\begin{vmatrix} 0 & 1 \\ 2 & 3 \end{vmatrix}$$
$$\det(A) = (2)(-1-0) - (4)(0-0) + (6)(0-2) = -2 - 0 - 12 = \mathbf{-14}.$$

- by expanding along the second row

$$\det(A) = (-1)^{(2+1)}(\mathbf{0})\begin{vmatrix} 4 & 6 \\ 3 & -1 \end{vmatrix} + (-1)^{(2+2)}(\mathbf{1})\begin{vmatrix} 2 & 6 \\ 2 & -1 \end{vmatrix} + (-1)^{(2+3)}(\mathbf{0})\begin{vmatrix} 2 & 4 \\ 2 & 3 \end{vmatrix}$$
$$\det(A) = -(0)(-4-18) + (1)(-2-12) - (0)(6-8) = 0 - 14 - 0 = \mathbf{-14}.$$

- by expanding along the first column

$$\det(A) = (-1)^{(1+1)}(\mathbf{2})\begin{vmatrix} 1 & 0 \\ 3 & -1 \end{vmatrix} + (-1)^{(1+2)}(\mathbf{0})\begin{vmatrix} 4 & 6 \\ 3 & -1 \end{vmatrix} + (-1)^{(1+3)}(\mathbf{2})\begin{vmatrix} 4 & 6 \\ 1 & 0 \end{vmatrix}$$
$$\det(A) = (2)(-1-0) - (0)(-4-18) + (2)(0-6) = -2 - 0 - 12 = \mathbf{-14}.$$

10. **Warning:** Using cofactors to calculate the determinant of a matrix can be impossibly time consuming even for a computer when the matrix gets too big. There is a way around this. We will not go into the procedure but it reduces to performing Gaussian elimination while keeping track of the row operations. It is also worth noting that problems can arise even when the determinant is not zero.

11. **Determinant Theorems:**

    (a) If A is a triangular matrix (upper or lower) then $\det(A) = a_{11}\, a_{22} \ldots a_{nn}$

    (b) $\det(A^T) = \det(A)$

    (c) $\det(AB) = \det(A)\det(B)$

    (d) If A is invertible then $\det(A^{-1}) = \dfrac{1}{\det(A)}$.

12. **Super Theorem Version-1:** Let A be an $n\,x\,n$ matrix. The following are equivalent (TFAE)

    - $Ax = b$ has a unique solution for any b.

    - A is invertible (nonsingular or has an inverse).

    - $A \sim I_n$. (A is row equivalent to the identity matrix).

    - $\det(A) \neq 0$.

13. **MATLAB®** : Inverses and Determinants (`InversesAndDeterminants.m`)

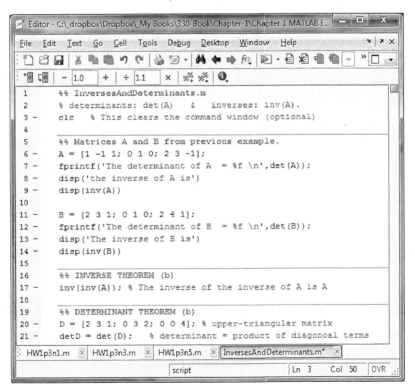

```
1      %% InversesAndDeterminants.m
2      % determinants: det(A)    &    inverses: inv(A).
3 -    clc    % This clears the command window (optional)
4
5      %% Matrices A and B from previous example.
6 -    A = [1 -1 1; 0 1 0; 2 3 -1];
7 -    fprintf('The determinant of A  = %f \n',det(A));
8 -    disp('the inverse of A is')
9 -    disp(inv(A))
10
11 -   B = [2 3 1; 0 1 0; 2 4 1];
12 -   fprintf('The determinant of B  = %f \n',det(B));
13 -   disp('The inverse of B is')
14 -   disp(inv(B))
15
16     %% INVERSE THEOREM (b)
17 -   inv(inv(A)); % The inverse of the inverse of A is A
18
19     %% DETERMINANT THEOREM (b)
20 -   D = [2 3 1; 0 3 2; 0 0 4]; % upper-triangular matrix
21 -   detD = det(D);   % determinant = product of diagonoal terms
```

Chapter 1.3 Worksheet

1. (**MATLAB**®) Recall the systems you solved by hand in Section 1.1 and with MATLAB® in 1.2:

(a)   (b)   (c)

$$
\begin{aligned}
x_1 - 3x_3 &= 8 \\
2x_1 + 2x_2 + 9x_3 &= 7 \\
x_2 + 5x_3 &= -2
\end{aligned}
\qquad
\begin{aligned}
x_2 - 4x_3 &= 8 \\
2x_1 - 3x_2 + 2x_3 &= 1 \\
5x_1 - 8x_2 + 7x_3 &= 1
\end{aligned}
\qquad
\begin{aligned}
x_1 + 2x_2 + 6x_3 &= 10 \\
x_1 + 5x_3 &= 6 \\
2x_2 + x_3 &= 4
\end{aligned}
$$

You should have found that (a) had a unique solution $[x_1, x_2, x_3] = [5, 3, -1]$, (b) (inconsistent) had no solutions, and (c) (dependent) had infinitely many solutions of the form $[x_1, x_2, x_3] = [6 - 5t, 2 - \frac{t}{2}, t]$.

Assignment: Enter the coefficient matrices into MATLAB® , then find the determinants and inverses of these three matrices. You should run into problems.

For part (a), you should get a non-zero determinant and nice inverse matrix. For part (b), you should get something very close to zero for the determinant, and when you try to find its inverse you should get a warning and an inverse with crazy huge numbers. For part (c) you should get zero for the determinant and when you try to get its inverse you get a message that the matrix is singular and it returns a matrix of non-numbers.

Chapter 1.3 Problem Set

Numbers with an asterisk[*] have solutions in the back of the book.

1. (**Written**) Find the determinants by hand. If the determinant is non-zero, find the inverse of the matrix again by hand. Check your answer with software.

   (a) $A = \begin{bmatrix} 1 & 2 \\ 4 & 7 \end{bmatrix}$

   (b)[*] $B = \begin{bmatrix} 1 & 0 & -2 \\ -3 & 1 & 4 \\ 2 & -3 & 4 \end{bmatrix}$

   (c) $C = \begin{bmatrix} 1 & -2 & 1 \\ 4 & -7 & 3 \\ -2 & 6 & -4 \end{bmatrix}$

2. (**Written**) Consider the 2 x 2 matrix: $A = \begin{bmatrix} a & 5 \\ 1 & 3 \end{bmatrix}$.

   For what value of a does this matrix **NOT** have an inverse?

3.[*] (**MATLAB®**) Consider the matrix A and the the three b vectors below.

$$A = \begin{bmatrix} 0 & 1 & 2 \\ 1 & 0 & 3 \\ 4 & -3 & 8 \end{bmatrix} \qquad b_1 = \begin{bmatrix} 3 \\ 1 \\ 0 \end{bmatrix}, b_2 = \begin{bmatrix} 1 \\ 1 \\ 1 \end{bmatrix}, \text{ and } b_3 = \begin{bmatrix} 0 \\ 0 \\ 0 \end{bmatrix}$$

   (a) Use MATLAB® to Find A^{-1} and use this to solve the three equations

$$Ax_1 = b_1 \qquad Ax_2 = b_2 \qquad Ax_3 = b_3$$

   (b) Now use the MATLAB® backslash command (x = A\b) to solve the same equations. Do your answers agree?

4.[*] In the MATLAB® file InversesAndDeterminants.m, Inverse theorem (b) and determinant theorem (a) were demonstrated numerically. Write a MATLAB® program that demonstrates inverse theorems (a), (c), (d), and the determinant theorems (b), (c) and (d).

1.4   Vector Spaces: $\mathbb{R}^2$ and $\mathbb{R}^3$

Motivation:

When modeling three dimensional interactions we want to know where an object is and if it has hit anything else as it moves around. The object might have a complex shape, but we can enclose it in an ellipsoid (example below) and then determine if the ellipsoid has hit anything. This is much easier but not as easy as it gets because even an ellipsoid is not uniform in shape. It is extra difficult when trying to determine a collision response. The **Unit Sphere** is really nice. If the center gets less than one unit from another object - there is a collision. Furthermore, the response is easier to predict. Ask anyone who tries to grab a football after it hits the ground. It would be a lot easier if it was spherical. So, if we can work in a world where all ellipsoids are actually spheres, life just got a lot easier. Making the transformation from the real world with ellipsoids, to a convenient world of spheres, requires a *change of basis* transformation. After this transformation is made, we do all of our calculations in the convenient world of spheres and then transform back to the world of ellipsoids to see what actually happens. That's the goal, but there is a lot to do first.

Ellipsoid
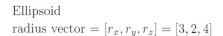

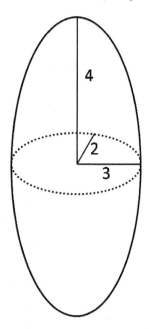

Unit Sphere

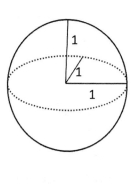

The different *worlds* of ellipses and spheres are actually different mathematical representations of the same space - a vector space. In this chapter, we will not be going into all the different kinds of vector spaces. We will cover the material needed to handle basic tasks in 2 and 3 dimensional space. We will start with the general properties of any vector space and investigate the two most important vector spaces for our purposes. These are $\mathbb{R}^2$ and $\mathbb{R}^3$.

1. **General Vector Spaces:** A vector space is a set V, whose elements are called vectors. If a vector x is in the vector space, we say $x \in V$. A vector space has two operations; addition and scalar multiplication. These operations must satisfy the following properties.

   (a) Addition is a binary operation on V which is both commutative and associative.

       i. If $x \in V$ and $y \in V$ then $x + y \in V$.   **closure under addition**

       ii. For all x, y, and z in V, $(x + y) + z = x + (y + z)$.   **associative property of addition**

       iii. If x and y are in V, then $x + y = y + x$.   **commutative property of addition**

   (b) There is a vector $\mathbf{0} \in V$ such that $x + \mathbf{0} = x$ for all $x \in V$.   **additive identity**

   (c) If $x \in V$ then there is a vector $-x$ such that $x + (-x) = \mathbf{0}$.   **additive inverse**

   (d) If $x \in V$ and α is a scalar (real number), then $\alpha x \in V$.   **closure under scalar multiplication**

   (e) Scalar Multiplication Properties.

       i. If x and y are in V and α is a scalar, then $\alpha(x + y) = \alpha x + \alpha y$.   **distributive property 1**

       ii. If $x \in V$ and α and β are scalars, then $(\alpha + \beta)x = \alpha x + \beta x$.   **distributive property 2**

       iii. If $x \in V$ and α and β are scalars, then $\alpha(\beta x) = (\alpha\beta)x$.   **associative law of scalar mult.**

       iv. For every vector $x \in V$, $1\,x = x$.   **scalar multiplicative identity**

2. **The Vector Space** $\mathbb{R}^3$ **:** This represents the three dimensional space in which we live and may try to recreate on the computer. In this notation, the funny looking $\mathbb{R}$ represents real numbers, and the three represents how many of them we have. A vector in $\mathbb{R}^3$ is essentially a point in 3-space. For example the vector $[2, -3, 4]^T$ is the point obtained by going 2 units in the x-direction, -3 units in the y-direction, and 4 units in the z-direction.

$$\mathbb{R}^3 = \left\{ x = \begin{bmatrix} x_1 \\ x_2 \\ x_3 \end{bmatrix}, \text{ where } x_1, x_2, x_3 \in \mathbb{R} \right\} \qquad \textbf{example: } x = \begin{bmatrix} 2 \\ -3 \\ 4 \end{bmatrix} \in \mathbb{R}^3$$

3. **The Vector Space** $\mathbb{R}^2$ **:** This represents the 2 dimensional space in the plane. It is actually a vector subspace of $\mathbb{R}^3$. A vector in $\mathbb{R}^2$ is essentially a point in 2-space. For example the vector $[2, -2]$ is the point obtained by going 2 units in the x-direction and -2 units in the y-direction.

$$\mathbb{R}^2 = \left\{ x = \begin{bmatrix} x_1 \\ x_2 \end{bmatrix}, \text{ where } x_1, x_2 \in \mathbb{R} \right\} \qquad \textbf{example: } x = \begin{bmatrix} 2 \\ -2 \end{bmatrix} \in \mathbb{R}^2$$

4. While it would takes some time to prove, you should be able to convince yourself that both $\mathbb{R}^2$ and $\mathbb{R}^3$ are vector spaces. In both of these cases, a **scalar** (α) is just a real number.

5. **The Vector Space** $\mathbb{R}^n$ **:** This vector space looks just like $\mathbb{R}^2$ and $\mathbb{R}^3$ except each vector has n terms. For example, $\mathbb{R}^4$ may be considered $\mathbb{R}^3$ with an additional element representing time.

6. **Linear Combinations:** Let v_1, v_2, $\ldots$, v_n be vectors in a vector space V, and $a_1 a_2, \ldots a_n$ be scalars from the same vector space. Any vector x in the form

$$x = a_1 v_1 + a_2 v_2 + \ldots + a_n v_n$$

is called a **liner combination** of v_1, v_2, $\ldots$, v_n. The scalars; $a_1, a_2, \ldots, a_n$, are called the **coefficients** of the linear combination.

(a) **Generating Linear Combinations:**

In practice, linear combinations are generated via matrix multiplication.

First, create a column vector containing the coefficients $a = [a_1, a_2, \ldots a_n]^T$. Then multiply this on the left by the matrix M whose columns are $v_1 \ldots v_n$.

$$x = a_1 v_1 + a_2 v_2 + \ldots + a_n v_n = Ma = \begin{bmatrix} \vdots & \vdots & \vdots & \vdots \\ v_1 & v_2 & \cdots & v_n \\ \vdots & \vdots & \vdots & \vdots \end{bmatrix} \begin{bmatrix} a_1 \\ a_2 \\ \vdots \\ a_n \end{bmatrix}$$

Example in $\mathbb{R}^2$: Let $v_1 = [-1, 0]$ and $v_2 = [3, 4]$ find the linear combination $x = -2v_1 + 5v_2$. First we define our matrix M whose columns are v_1 and v_2 then

$$x = Ma = \begin{bmatrix} -1 & 3 \\ 0 & 4 \end{bmatrix} \begin{bmatrix} -2 \\ 5 \end{bmatrix} = \begin{bmatrix} 17 \\ 20 \end{bmatrix}$$

(b) **Determining Linear Combinations:**

Often we will want to know what linear combination of a given set of vectors produces a specific vector. In this case we are looking for the coefficients of the linear combination. This task is accomplished by solving a linear system.

Example in $\mathbb{R}^3$: Consider the vectors: $v_1 = \begin{bmatrix} 1 \\ -1 \\ 2 \end{bmatrix}$, $v_2 = \begin{bmatrix} 1 \\ 0 \\ 3 \end{bmatrix}$, $v_3 = \begin{bmatrix} 2 \\ -1 \\ 6 \end{bmatrix}$.

Express the vector $x = [4, -1, 14]^T$ as a linear combination of v_1, v_2, v_3. Ie. Find a_1, a_2, a_3 such that $x = a_1 v_1 + a_2 v_2 + a_3 v_3$.

Solution: You must solve the matrix equation $V\mathbf{a} = x$ for $\mathbf{a}$, or

$$\begin{bmatrix} 1 & 1 & 2 \\ -1 & 0 & -1 \\ 2 & 3 & 6 \end{bmatrix} \begin{bmatrix} a_1 \\ a_2 \\ a_3 \end{bmatrix} = \begin{bmatrix} 4 \\ -1 \\ 14 \end{bmatrix}$$

You can solve this by hand or use software to obtain the solutions $[a_1, a_2, a_3] = [-2, 0, 3]$.

7. **The Standard Bases for $\mathbb{R}^2$ and $\mathbb{R}^3$:**

   In a general vector space, all vectors must be identifiable as a unique **linear combination** of the vector space's **basis** vectors. Each vector is then uniquely identified by the coefficients used in this linear combination. The **standard basis** is really nice because the coefficients in this linear combination are just the numbers in the vector. This seems redundant and it is. However, when we start using different bases, it is not.

   (a) The **standard basis** for $\mathbb{R}^2$ consists of the two vectors e_1 and e_2 defined by

   $$e_1 = \begin{bmatrix} 1 \\ 0 \end{bmatrix} \quad e_2 = \begin{bmatrix} 0 \\ 1 \end{bmatrix}.$$

   This basis works wonderfully well because any vector in $\mathbb{R}^2$ can be easily expressed as a **linear combination** of these 2 vectors. For example, the vector $[2, -2]^T$ can be expressed as

   $$\begin{bmatrix} 2 \\ -2 \end{bmatrix} = 2 \begin{bmatrix} 1 \\ 0 \end{bmatrix} - 2 \begin{bmatrix} 0 \\ 1 \end{bmatrix} = 2e_1 - 2e_2$$

   (b) The **standard basis** for $\mathbb{R}^3$ consists of the three vectors e_1, e_2, and e_3 defined by

   $$e_1 = \begin{bmatrix} 1 \\ 0 \\ 0 \end{bmatrix} \quad e_2 = \begin{bmatrix} 0 \\ 1 \\ 0 \end{bmatrix} \quad e_3 = \begin{bmatrix} 0 \\ 0 \\ 1 \end{bmatrix}.$$

   Again, this basis works wonderfully well because any vector in $\mathbb{R}^3$ can be easily expressed as a **linear combination** of these 3 vectors. For example, the vector $[2, -3, 4]^T$ can be expressed as

   $$\begin{bmatrix} 2 \\ -3 \\ 4 \end{bmatrix} = 2 \begin{bmatrix} 1 \\ 0 \\ 0 \end{bmatrix} - 3 \begin{bmatrix} 0 \\ 1 \\ 0 \end{bmatrix} + 4 \begin{bmatrix} 0 \\ 0 \\ 1 \end{bmatrix} = 2e_1 - 3e_2 + 4e_3$$

Chapter 1.4 Problem Set

Numbers with an asterisk[*] have solutions in the back of the book.

1.[*] (**Written**) Verify that the linear combination of vectors on the left side of the $=$ sign can be expressed as the matrix multiplication on the right.

$$a_1 \begin{bmatrix} 1 \\ 0 \\ 2 \end{bmatrix} + a_2 \begin{bmatrix} -2 \\ 1 \\ -3 \end{bmatrix} + a_3 \begin{bmatrix} 2 \\ 5 \\ 0 \end{bmatrix} = \begin{bmatrix} 1 & -2 & 2 \\ 0 & 1 & 5 \\ 2 & -3 & 0 \end{bmatrix} \begin{bmatrix} a_1 \\ a_2 \\ a_3 \end{bmatrix}$$

2. (**Written/MATLAB®**) Consider the vectors $v_1 = [1, 4]$ and $v_2 = [2, 7]$. Express the following vectors as a linear combination of these vectors. Ie. Find a_1 and a_2 such that $x = a_1 v_1 + a_2 v_2$.

   (a)[*] $x = [-2, 3]$

   (b) $x = [0, -4]$

3. (**Written/MATLAB®**) Consider the vectors $v_1 = [1, -3, 2]$, $v_2 = [0, 1, -3]$, and $v_3 = [-2, 4, 4]$. Express the following vectors as a linear combination of these vectors. Ie. Find a_1, a_2, and a_3 such that $x = a_1 v_1 + a_2 v_2 + a_3 v_3$.

   (a)[*] $x = [1, 1, 1]$

   (b) $x = [7, -3, 0]$

4. (**Written/MATLAB®**) Express the vector $[1, 7, 8]^T$ as a linear combination of the vectors $[2, 0, 0]^T$, $[0, \frac{1}{2}, 0]^T$, $[0, 0, 4]^T$.

1.5 Linear Independence, Span, Basis, Dimension

In the previous section we saw the two primary vector spaces that we will use. These were $\mathbb{R}^2$ and $\mathbb{R}^3$. We also saw the convenient standard basis for each of these vector spaces. However, every vector space has infinitely many bases and using an alternative basis will prove to be helpful down the road. Here we will investigate what makes a basis and what a basis tells us about the vector space.

1. A quick refresher of the important material from last section.

   (a) **Linear Combinations:** Let v_1, v_2, ..., v_n be vectors in a vector space V, and $a_1 a_2, \ldots a_n$ be scalars from the same vector space. Any vector x in the form

   $$x = a_1 v_1 + a_2 v_2 + \ldots + a_n v_n$$

   is called a **liner combination** of v_1, v_2, ..., v_n. The scalars; $a_1, a_2, \ldots, a_n$, are called the **coefficients** of the linear combination.

   $$x = a_1 v_1 + a_2 v_2 + \ldots + a_n v_n = Ma = \begin{bmatrix} \vdots & \vdots & \vdots & \vdots \\ v_1 & v_2 & \ldots & v_n \\ \vdots & \vdots & \vdots & \vdots \end{bmatrix} \begin{bmatrix} a_1 \\ a_2 \\ \vdots \\ a_n \end{bmatrix}$$

   (b) The **standard basis** for $\mathbb{R}^2$ consists of the two vectors e_1 and e_2 defined by

   $$e_1 = \begin{bmatrix} 1 \\ 0 \end{bmatrix} \quad e_2 = \begin{bmatrix} 0 \\ 1 \end{bmatrix}.$$

   (c) The **standard basis** for $\mathbb{R}^3$ consists of the three vectors e_1, e_2, and e_3 defined by

   $$e_1 = \begin{bmatrix} 1 \\ 0 \\ 0 \end{bmatrix} \quad e_2 = \begin{bmatrix} 0 \\ 1 \\ 0 \end{bmatrix} \quad e_3 = \begin{bmatrix} 0 \\ 0 \\ 1 \end{bmatrix}.$$

2. **Preliminary Definition of a Basis:** A basis for a given vector space is any smallest collection of vectors from that space that can be linearly combined to obtain any other vector in that space. Or, put in a way containing definitions to follow: A basis is any collection of **linearly independent vectors** from the vector space that **span** the entire vector space.

   It seems complicated. It's not so bad. Here we go.

3. **Span:** The vectors v_1, v_2, ..., v_n in a vector space V, are said to span V, if every vector in V can be written as a linear combination of them. That is, for every $x \in V$, there are scalars, a_1, a_2, ..., a_n, such that $x = a_1v_1 + a_2v_2 + \ldots + a_nv_n$

In Practice for $\mathbb{R}^n$:

Create the matrix M whose columns are $v_1 \ldots v_n$ and determine if the system $Ma = x$ has a solution for any $x \in V$.

$$Ma = \begin{bmatrix} \vdots & \vdots & \vdots & \vdots \\ v_1 & v_2 & \ldots & v_n \\ \vdots & \vdots & \vdots & \vdots \end{bmatrix} \begin{bmatrix} a_1 \\ a_2 \\ \vdots \\ a_n \end{bmatrix} = \begin{bmatrix} x_1 \\ x_2 \\ \vdots \\ x_n \end{bmatrix}$$

Example in $\mathbb{R}^2$: Verify that the vectors $v_1 = [-1, 0]$ and $v_2 = [3, 4]$ span $\mathbb{R}^2$.

Let $x = [x_1, x_2]^T$ be any vector in $\mathbb{R}^2$. Create the matrix M whose columns are v_1 and v_2. Can we solve the equation $Ma = x$ for a?

$$\begin{bmatrix} -1 & 3 \\ 0 & 4 \end{bmatrix} \begin{bmatrix} a_1 \\ a_2 \end{bmatrix} = \begin{bmatrix} x_1 \\ x_2 \end{bmatrix}$$

Yes! Since the $\det(M) = $ -4, we know by the **Super Theorem Version-1** that M has an inverse and we can solve for a by $a = M^{-1}x$. So, we have proven that v_1 and v_2 span $\mathbb{R}^2$.

4. **Linear Independence:** Let v_1, v_2, ..., v_n be vectors in a vector space V. The vectors are said to be linearly dependent if there exists n scalars a_1, a_2, ..., a_n not all zero such that

$$a_1v_1 + a_2v_2 + \ldots + a_nv_n = \mathbf{0}.$$

If the vectors are not linearly dependent they are said to be **linearly independent**.

In Practice for $\mathbb{R}^n$:

Set up the equation: $Ma = 0$ and solve for a

$$Ma = \begin{bmatrix} \vdots & \vdots & \vdots & \vdots \\ v_1 & v_2 & \ldots & v_n \\ \vdots & \vdots & \vdots & \vdots \end{bmatrix} \begin{bmatrix} a_1 \\ a_2 \\ \vdots \\ a_n \end{bmatrix} = \begin{bmatrix} 0 \\ 0 \\ \vdots \\ 0 \end{bmatrix}$$

If the system has a non-zero solution (at least one term in a is not zero) then the vectors are **dependent**. If the only solution is $a_1 = a_2 = \ldots a_n = 0$, then the vectors are linearly **independent**.

Example in $\mathbb{R}^2$: Verify that the vectors $v_1 = [-1, 0]$ and $v_2 = [3, 4]$ are linearly independent.

We must ask ourselves: Is there a non-zero solution to the following equation?

$$\begin{bmatrix} -1 & 3 \\ 0 & 4 \end{bmatrix} \begin{bmatrix} a_1 \\ a_2 \end{bmatrix} = \begin{bmatrix} 0 \\ 0 \end{bmatrix}$$

Since $\det(M) = $ -4, we know by **Super Theorem Version-1** that M has an inverse and $a = M^{-1}0 = [0, 0]^T$. Since the only solution is the zero vector, we have proven that v_1 and v_2 are linearly independent.

5. **Basis:** A finite set of vectors $\{v_1, v_2, \ldots, v_n\}$ is a **basis** for a vector space V if and only if

   (a) $\{v_1, v_2, \ldots, v_n\}$ are linearly independent and
   (b) $\{v_1, v_2, \ldots, v_n\}$ spans V.

   In Practice for $\mathbb{R}^n$: We create the nxn matrix M whose columns are $v_1 \ldots v_n$. If $\det(M) = 0$, the vectors do not form a basis, if $\det(M) \neq 0$, the vectors do form a basis.

   Example in $\mathbb{R}^2$: Verify that the vectors $v_1 = [-1, 0]$ and $v_2 = [3, 4]$ form a basis for $\mathbb{R}^2$.

   Previously we demonstrated that v_1 and v_2 were linearly independent and span $\mathbb{R}^2$ which proves they form a basis. A quick way to both conclusions is noting that the determinant of M was nonzero.

6. **Dimension:** The dimension of a vector space V is the number of vectors in every basis for V. Note: Once you find a basis for V you know that the dimension of V is the number of vectors in that basis and all bases will have the same number of vectors = the dimension of V.

   Example in $\mathbb{R}^2$: Verify that the vector space $\mathbb{R}^2$ has dimension 2.

   Previously we determined that the two vectors $v_1 = [-1, 0]$ and $v_2 = [3, 4]$ form a basis for $\mathbb{R}^2$. As such, all bases for $\mathbb{R}^2$ will have 2 vectors and the dimension of $\mathbb{R}^2$ is 2.

7. **Example from $\mathbb{R}^3$.** Recall, I claimed that $\{e_1, e_2, e_3\}$ form a basis for $\mathbb{R}^3$. Verify the following.

   (a) Show that e_1, e_2, and e_3 are linearly independent.
   (b) Show that e_1, e_2, and e_3 span $\mathbb{R}^3$.
   (c) Show that e_1, e_2, and e_3 form a basis for $\mathbb{R}^3$.
   (d) Verify that the dimension of $\mathbb{R}^3$ is 3.

   Answer: Creating the matrix M whose columns consist of e_1, e_2, and e_3

   $$M = \begin{bmatrix} 1 & 0 & 0 \\ 0 & 1 & 0 \\ 0 & 0 & 1 \end{bmatrix}$$

   Since $\det(M) \neq 0$, we know these vectors are linearly independent, span $\mathbb{R}^3$, and form a basis for $\mathbb{R}^3$. As such, the dimension of $\mathbb{R}^3$ is 3 (as you probably could have guessed).

8. **Another Example:** Prove the vectors $v_1 = [3, 0, 0]$, $v_2 = [0, 2, 0]$, $v_3 = [0, 0, 4]$ form a basis for $\mathbb{R}^3$.

   $$\det(M) = \det\left(\begin{bmatrix} 3 & 0 & 0 \\ 0 & 2 & 0 \\ 0 & 0 & 4 \end{bmatrix}\right) = 24$$

   Easy, since the determinant of this matrix is not zero, we have a basis.
   Note: If we have an ellipsoid with radius vector [3,2,4], this radius vector becomes [1,1,1] with respect to this basis. The ellipsoid becomes a unit sphere!

9. **Super Theorem Version-2:** Let A be an $n \times n$ matrix. The following are equivalent (TFAE)

> (a) $Ax = b$ has a unique solution for any b.
>
> (b) A is invertible (nonsingular or has an inverse).
>
> (c) $A \sim I_n$. (A is row equivalent to the identity matrix).
>
> (d) $\det(A) \neq 0$.
>
> (e) The columns of A are linearly independent.
>
> (f) The columns of A span $\mathbb{R}^n$.
>
> (g) The columns of A form a basis for $\mathbb{R}^n$

10. Some other stuff worth knowing:

   (a) **A nice result for $\mathbb{R}^n$:** If x and y are both non-zero vectors in $\mathbb{R}^n$ and $x \cdot y = 0$ then x and y are linearly independent.

   (b) **Standard Basis for $\mathbb{R}^n$:** The standard basis for $\mathbb{R}^n$ is the set $\{e_1, e_2, \ldots e_n\}$ where e_k has zeros everywhere except in the kth position where it has a one.

   (c) **Linear Independence 2:** A set of vectors are said to be linearly independent if none of them can be obtained as a linear combination of the others.

11. **Examples in $\mathbb{R}^3$**

   Determine if the given vectors form a basis for $\mathbb{R}^3$. Comment on their linear independence and whether or not they span $\mathbb{R}^3$

   (a) $\quad v_1 = \begin{bmatrix} 1 \\ -1 \\ 2 \end{bmatrix}, v_2 = \begin{bmatrix} 2 \\ 0 \\ 1 \end{bmatrix}, v_3 = \begin{bmatrix} 1 \\ -2 \\ 5 \end{bmatrix}$

   Answer: Create the matrix M:

   $$M = \begin{bmatrix} \vdots & \vdots & \vdots \\ v_1 & v_2 & v_3 \\ \vdots & \vdots & \vdots \end{bmatrix} = \begin{bmatrix} 1 & 2 & 1 \\ -1 & 0 & -2 \\ 2 & 1 & 5 \end{bmatrix} \text{ and } \det(M) = 1(0+2) - 2(-5+4) + 1(-1-0) = 3.$$

   Here we use the **Super Theorem** and conclude that since $\det(M) \neq 0$, the vectors **are linearly independent**, they **do span** $\mathbb{R}^3$, and they **do form a basis** for $\mathbb{R}^3$.

(b) $\quad v_1 = \begin{bmatrix} 1 \\ -1 \\ 2 \end{bmatrix}, v_2 = \begin{bmatrix} 2 \\ 0 \\ 1 \end{bmatrix}, v_3 = \begin{bmatrix} 4 \\ -2 \\ 5 \end{bmatrix}$

Answer: Create the matrix M:

$$M = \begin{bmatrix} \vdots & \vdots & \vdots \\ v_1 & v_2 & v_3 \\ \vdots & \vdots & \vdots \end{bmatrix} = \begin{bmatrix} 1 & 2 & 4 \\ -1 & 0 & -2 \\ 2 & 1 & 5 \end{bmatrix} \text{ and } \det(M) = 1(0+2) - 2(-5+4) + 4(-1-0) = 0.$$

Here we use the **Super Theorem** and conclude that since $\det(M) = 0$, the vectors are **not** linearly independent, they do **not** span $\mathbb{R}^3$, and they do **not** form a basis for $\mathbb{R}^3$. You might have noticed that $u_3 = 2u_1 + u_2$ and so these vectors can not be linearly independent.

(c) $\quad v_1 = \begin{bmatrix} 1 \\ -1 \\ 2 \end{bmatrix}, v_2 = \begin{bmatrix} 2 \\ 0 \\ 1 \end{bmatrix}$

Answer: Since the matrix M will not result in a square matrix, we can not use the Super Theorem. However, since any basis for $\mathbb{R}^3$ must have 3 vectors we can conclude that these vectors do **not** form a basis for $\mathbb{R}^3$. Therefore, they must be linearly dependent and/or not span $\mathbb{R}^3$. We can tell that they are linearly independent because one is not a linear combination of the others (one is not a scalar multiple of the other). So, it must be that they do not span $\mathbb{R}^3$. This should make sense: You can not span a 3-dimensional space with only two vectors.

(d) $\quad v_1 = \begin{bmatrix} 1 \\ -1 \\ 2 \end{bmatrix}, v_2 = \begin{bmatrix} 2 \\ 0 \\ 1 \end{bmatrix}, v_3 = \begin{bmatrix} 3 \\ 1 \\ 3 \end{bmatrix}, v_4 = \begin{bmatrix} 2 \\ 4 \\ 6 \end{bmatrix}$

Answer: Since the matrix M will not result in a square matrix, we can not use the Super Theorem. However, since any basis for $\mathbb{R}^3$ must have 3 vectors we can conclude that these vectors do **not** form a basis for $\mathbb{R}^3$. Therefore, they must be linearly dependent and/or not span $\mathbb{R}^3$. Determining which of these is the case is quite tricky and requires Gaussian elimination on a non-square matrix. Exploring this further requires knowing more about linear algebra such as **rank** and **nullity** of a matrix. We will not go into this but there is a good chance that these vectors will span $\mathbb{R}^3$ but are not linearly independent.

Chapter 1.5 Problem Set

Numbers with an asterisk* have solutions in the back of the book.

1. **(Written/MATLAB®)** For each of the sets of vectors below answer the following. 1) Determine whether the vectors are linearly independent or dependent. 2) If they are linearly dependent, find a non-zero linear combination of the vectors which results in the zero vector. 3) Finally, does the set form a basis for $\mathbb{R}^3$?

   (a)* $v_1 = \begin{bmatrix} 1 \\ 2 \\ 3 \end{bmatrix}, \quad v_2 = \begin{bmatrix} 0 \\ 1 \\ 5 \end{bmatrix}, \quad v_3 = \begin{bmatrix} 2 \\ 5 \\ 11 \end{bmatrix}$

   (b) $v_1 = \begin{bmatrix} 1 \\ 2 \\ 3 \end{bmatrix}, \quad v_2 = \begin{bmatrix} 0 \\ 1 \\ 5 \end{bmatrix}, \quad v_3 = \begin{bmatrix} 2 \\ 5 \\ 10 \end{bmatrix}$

   (c)* $v_1 = \begin{bmatrix} 1 \\ 2 \\ 3 \end{bmatrix}, \quad v_2 = \begin{bmatrix} 0 \\ 1 \\ 5 \end{bmatrix}$

2. Determine whether the given vectors form a basis for $\mathbb{R}^3$.

   (a)* $v_1 = \begin{bmatrix} 1 \\ -1 \\ 2 \end{bmatrix}, v_2 = \begin{bmatrix} 1 \\ 0 \\ 3 \end{bmatrix}, v_3 = \begin{bmatrix} 3 \\ -4 \\ 5 \end{bmatrix}$

   (b) $u_1 = \begin{bmatrix} 1 \\ -1 \\ 2 \end{bmatrix}, u_2 = \begin{bmatrix} 1 \\ 1 \\ 3 \end{bmatrix}, u_3 = \begin{bmatrix} 2 \\ 3 \\ 13 \end{bmatrix}$

1.6   Change of Basis

1. **Possible Motivation** (revisited):

   Suppose we have an ellipsoid with a radius vector of $[3, 2, 4]$ and want to convert this ellipsoid to a unit sphere with radius vector $[1, 1, 1]$. The idea is to find a basis for $\mathbb{R}^3$ so that the ellipsoid with respect to this basis has radius vector $[1, 1, 1]$. This is not so hard but converting everything else to this basis is the tricky part. In this sense we need to determine how to perform a **change of basis** transformation.

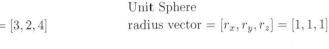

   Ellipsoid
   radius vector $= [r_x, r_y, r_z] = [3, 2, 4]$

   Unit Sphere
   radius vector $= [r_x, r_y, r_z] = [1, 1, 1]$

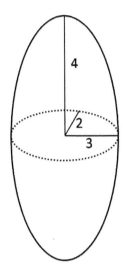
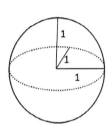

2. Basis Definition (revisited)

   A **basis** is any minimal collection of vectors such that any vector in the vector space can be expressed as a linear combination of these vectors. We have two simple bases for $\mathbb{R}^3$ from the last section. One is the standard basis e_1, e_2, and e_3. The other is $v_1 = [3, 0, 0]^T$, $v_2 = [0, 2, 0]^T$, and $v_3 [0, 0, 4]^T$ which contain the three axis radii from the ellipsoid. For example,

   With respect to the standard basis
   the radius vector is $[3, 2, 4]$ because

   With respect to v_1, v_2, and v_3,
   the radius vector is $[1, 1, 1]$ because

$$\begin{bmatrix} 3 \\ 2 \\ 4 \end{bmatrix} = \mathbf{3} \begin{bmatrix} 1 \\ 0 \\ 0 \end{bmatrix} + \mathbf{2} \begin{bmatrix} 0 \\ 1 \\ 0 \end{bmatrix} + \mathbf{4} \begin{bmatrix} 0 \\ 0 \\ 1 \end{bmatrix}$$

$$\begin{bmatrix} 3 \\ 2 \\ 4 \end{bmatrix} = \mathbf{1} \begin{bmatrix} 3 \\ 0 \\ 0 \end{bmatrix} + \mathbf{1} \begin{bmatrix} 0 \\ 2 \\ 0 \end{bmatrix} + \mathbf{1} \begin{bmatrix} 0 \\ 0 \\ 4 \end{bmatrix}$$

3. **Change of Basis** Let A and B be two different sets of basis vectors for $\mathbb{R}^n$ defined by

$$A = \{u_1, u_2, \ldots u_n\} \quad \text{and} \quad B = \{v_1, v_2, \ldots, v_n\}.$$

Now define the matrices U and V with these basis vectors as columns by

$$U = \begin{bmatrix} \vdots & \vdots & \vdots & \vdots \\ u_1 & u_2 & \ldots & u_n \\ \vdots & \vdots & \vdots & \vdots \end{bmatrix} \quad \text{and} \quad V = \begin{bmatrix} \vdots & \vdots & \vdots & \vdots \\ v_1 & v_2 & \ldots & v_n \\ \vdots & \vdots & \vdots & \vdots \end{bmatrix}$$

If x is a vector in $\mathbb{R}^n$ we can write

$$x = a_1 u_1 + a_2 u_2 + \ldots a_n u_n = Ua \quad \textbf{or} \quad x = b_1 v_1 + b_2 v_2 + \ldots b_n v_n = Vb$$

where a is the column vector $[a_1, a_2, \ldots, a_n]^T$ and $b = [b_1, b_2, \ldots b_n]^T$.

4. **Transformation Matrix** If x is a vector in $\mathbb{R}^n$, then x can be expressed in either form

$$x = Ua \quad \text{or} \quad x = Vb.$$

If we have a and want to find b we must solve the equation

$$Ua = Vb$$

for b. Since the columns of V form a basis for $\mathbb{R}^n$ it has an inverse and

$$b = V^{-1}Ua = Ta \tag{1.2}$$

The matrix $T = V^{-1}U$ is the transformation matrix from basis A to basis B and T^{-1} is the transformation matrix from basis B to basis A.

5. **Important Observation:** If $A = \{e_1, e_2, \ldots, e_n\}$ is the standard basis and you want to express a vector $x = [x_1, x_2, \ldots, x_n]^T$ in terms of a different basis $B = \{v_1, v_2, \ldots, v_n\}$, then equation (1.2) yields

$$b = V^{-1}Ux = V^{-1}x \tag{1.3}$$

because U is just the identity matrix. Now the transition matrix T is just V^{-1}.

Therefore, converting x to a different basis is a matter of finding the inverse of the matrix with columns consisting of the vectors of the different basis. Then multiply by x.

6. **Example in** $\mathbb{R}^2$ **:** Here we start with an ellipse in $\mathbb{R}^2$ with radius vector $[2,3]$. We want to convert this into the same vector space with basis vectors $v_1 = [2,0]$ and $v_2 = [0,3]$. We will call the space using this basis the *ellipse space*. With this basis, our ellipse becomes a unit circle. The transformation matrix is given by T where

$$T = V^{-1} = \left[\begin{array}{cc} 2 & 0 \\ 0 & 3 \end{array} \right]^{-1} = \left[\begin{array}{cc} \frac{1}{2} & 0 \\ 0 & \frac{1}{3} \end{array} \right].$$

So, in order to transform our ellipse into *Ellipse Space* we multiply each point of the ellipse by the transformation matrix $T = V^{-1}$.

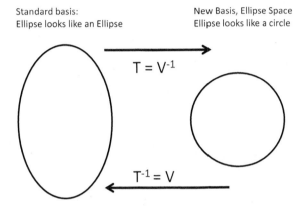

Under this transformation, points inside, on, and outside of the ellipse remain inside, on, and outside of the unit circle respectively. This gives us a way to determine whether or not the ellipse has collided with something else (code on the next page).

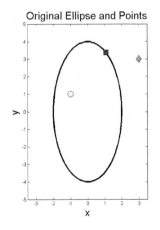

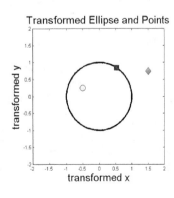

7. MATLAB® code for the Ellipse Transformation

This program transforms an ellipse into a unit circle in *Ellipse Space*. It also hits three points with the same transformation. **Important for Collision Detection:** Interior and exterior points are preserved by the transformation.

```
1    %% EllipseTransform.m:    Transforming an Ellipse into a Circle
2 -  clc; clf;  % Clear the command window and the figure window
3
4    %% THE ELLIPSE AND POINTS WITH STANDARD BASIS
5 -  t = linspace(0,2*pi,100);  % t = a vector of 100 values between 0 and 2 pi.
6 -  x = 2 * cos(t);            % the x-values in the ellipse
7 -  y = 4 * sin(t);            % the y-values in the ellipse
8 -  P1 = [-1 1];    % a point inside the ellipse
9 -  P2 = [3 3];     % a point outside the ellipse
10 - P3 = [2*cos(1) 4*sin(1)]; % a point on the ellipse
11 - subplot(121)  % a 1x2 array of graphs - first plot
12 - plot(x,y,'-k','linewidth',3); hold on;  %Plot the ellipse and hold it.
13 - plot(P1(1), P1(2),'ok','MarkerFaceColor','yellow','MarkerSize',12) % plot P1
14 - plot(P2(1), P2(2),'dk','MarkerFaceColor','green','MarkerSize',12) % plot P2
15 - plot(P3(1), P3(2),'sk','MarkerFaceColor','blue','MarkerSize',12) % plot P3
16 - axis equal  % keeps axis scalings equal (circles look like circles)
17 - axis([-3.5,3.5,-5,5]);  %usage: axis([xmin, xmax, ymin, ymax]);
18 - title('Original Ellipse and Points','fontsize',22)  % graph title
19 - xlabel('x','fontsize',22); ylabel('y','fontsize',22)    % axis labels
20
21   %% THE Transformed ELLIPSE AND POINTS IN ELLIPSE SPACE
22 - V = [2 0; 0 4]; % New Basis Matrix: columns from the basis in ellipse space
23 - T= inv(V);  % The Transition matrix from standard to ellipse space.
24 - xyTran = T*[x;y];  % Transform ellipse points into ellipse space
25 - xTran = xyTran(1,:);  % The x-values in ellipse space
26 - yTran = xyTran(2,:);  % The y-values in ellipse space
27 - P1Tran = T*P1';    % Transform points into ellipse space
28 - P2Tran = T*P2';    % Transform P2 into ellipse space
29 - P3Tran = T*P3';    % Transform P3 into ellipse space
30 - subplot(122) % a 1x2 array of graphs - second plot
31 - plot(xTran,yTran,'-k','linewidth',3); hold on;  %Plot the transformed ellipse
32 - plot(P1Tran(1), P1Tran(2),'ok','MarkerFaceColor','yellow','MarkerSize',12)
33 - plot(P2Tran(1), P2Tran(2),'dk','MarkerFaceColor','green','MarkerSize',12)
34 - plot(P3Tran(1), P3Tran(2),'sk','MarkerFaceColor','blue','MarkerSize',12)
35 - axis equal  % keeps axis scalings equal (circles look like circles)
36 - axis([-2,2,-2,2]);  %usage: axis([xmin, xmax, ymin, ymax]);
37 - xlim([-2,2]); ylim([-2,2]);  % the x and y axis limits [(min,max)]
38 - title('Transformed Ellipse and Points','fontsize',22)  % graph title
39 - xlabel('transformed x','fontsize',22); ylabel('transformed y','fontsize',22)
```

Chapter 1.6 Problem Set

Numbers with an asterisk[*] have solutions in the back of the book.

1. **(Change of Basis)** Express the given point in $\mathbb{R}^3$ with respect to a new basis consisting of the vectors: $v_1 = [1, 2, 1]^T$, $v_2 = [2, 3, 0]^T$, $v_3 = [0, 0, 2]^T$.

    (a)[*] $P = (2, 0, 3)$

    (b) $P = (1, 2, 3)$

2.[*] **(Written/MATLAB®)** Consider a 2D ellipse centered at the origin with radius vector $[r_x, r_y] = [3, 2]$. For each point p, determine whether the point lies inside the ellipse, on the ellipse, or outside of the ellipse. I want you to verify your answer beyond just visual inspection. **Strategy:** Using a change of basis transformation, convert the ellipse to a unit circle via a transition matrix T. Express the point (x, y) in terms of the new basis called (x_{new}, y_{new}). Then if $x_{new}^2 + y_{new}^2 = 1$, the new point lies on the unit circle and the original point lies on the ellipse. Again, I want you to verify this answer beyond visual inspection.

    (a)[*] Where does the point $p = (1.8, 1.8)$ lie with respect to the ellipse?

    (b) Where does the point $p = (-1.8, 1.3)$ lie with respect to the ellipse?

    (c) Where does the point $p = (1.50, 1.73)$ lie with respect to the ellipse?

3. Play the same game as above only consider the ellipsoid in $\mathbb{R}^3$ with radius vector $r = [1, 2, 3]$.

    (a)[*] Where does the point $p = (0.5, 1.5, 2.0)$ lie with respect to the ellipsoid?

    (b) Where does the point $p = (-0.25, 1.25, 1.9)$ lie with respect to the ellipsoid?

4. **(Written/MATLAB®)** Consider a 2D ellipse centered at the origin with radius vector $[r_x, r_y] = [3, 2]$, and the line $y = \frac{5}{7}x + 4$ pictured in the figure. Using a change of basis transformation, convert the ellipse to a circle. What does this transformation do to the line. Ie. Give the equation for this line in the new coordinate system. What is the slope of the new line with respect to the new axes? How does it compare to the slope of the original line? What is the y-intercept with respect to the new bases? How does it compare to the original y-intercept?

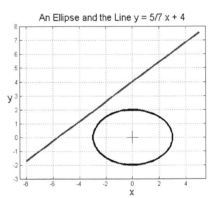

Hint: Take a couple of points from the original line, and transform these to two new points in the new basis. Now create the equation for the line from these two new points.

5. (**MATLAB**®)Collision Detection Assignment: Write a program that determines whether a given point lies inside or outside of an ellipse.

Your program must first graph an ellipse where the user is prompted to determine the x-radius, and the y-radius. Make sure your graph represents the ellipse to scale (it must look like an ellipse using equal scaling in the x and y direction) with a little extra room on all sides. Then prompt the user to click a point on the graph. Your program must determine whether the chosen point lies inside, on, or outside the ellipse. The program (in MATLAB®) is started for you below.

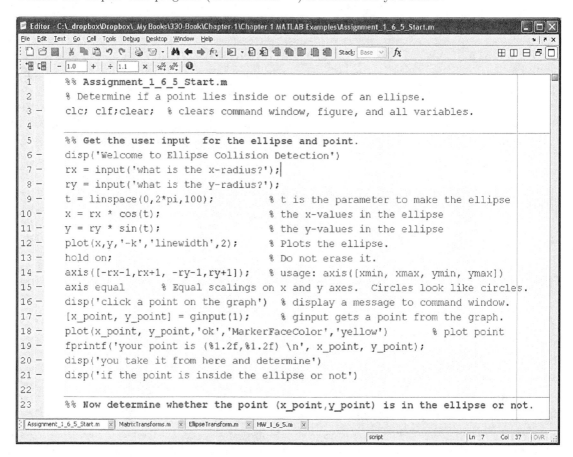

```matlab
1      %% Assignment_1_6_5_Start.m
2      % Determine if a point lies inside or outside of an ellipse.
3  -   clc; clf;clear;  % clears command window, figure, and all variables.
4
5      %% Get the user input  for the ellipse and point.
6  -   disp('Welcome to Ellipse Collision Detection')
7  -   rx = input('what is the x-radius?');
8  -   ry = input('what is the y-radius?');
9  -   t = linspace(0,2*pi,100);          % t is the parameter to make the ellipse
10 -   x = rx * cos(t);                    % the x-values in the ellipse
11 -   y = ry * sin(t);                    % the y-values in the ellipse
12 -   plot(x,y,'-k','linewidth',2);      % Plots the ellipse.
13 -   hold on;                            % Do not erase it.
14 -   axis([-rx-1,rx+1, -ry-1,ry+1]);    % usage: axis([xmin, xmax, ymin, ymax])
15 -   axis equal     % Equal scalings on x and y axes.  Circles look like circles.
16 -   disp('click a point on the graph')  % display a message to command window.
17 -   [x_point, y_point] = ginput(1);    % ginput gets a point from the graph.
18 -   plot(x_point, y_point,'ok','MarkerFaceColor','yellow')        % plot point
19 -   fprintf('your point is (%1.2f,%1.2f) \n', x_point, y_point);
20 -   disp('you take it from here and determine')
21 -   disp('if the point is inside the ellipse or not')
22
23      %% Now determine whether the point (x_point,y_point) is in the ellipse or not.
```

1.7 Matrix Transformations

Here we look at how to move points and shapes around in 2 and 3 space by using matrix transformations. When I say a matrix transformation what I mean is that the new object (point, vector, geometric shape) can be obtained from the original by multiplying each point (expressed in vector form) of the object by a matrix T.

$$\left[\begin{array}{c} x' \\ y' \end{array}\right] = T \left[\begin{array}{c} x \\ y \end{array}\right] \quad \text{or} \quad \left[\begin{array}{c} x' \\ y' \\ z' \end{array}\right] = T \left[\begin{array}{c} x \\ y \\ z \end{array}\right]$$

In 2D, $[x, y]$ is the original point and $[x', y']$ is the transformed point. In 3D, $[x, y, z]$ is the original point and $[x', y', z']$ is the transformed point

The following table gives an incomplete list of various types of transformations and their associated matrices (T). We will spend more time with the 3D versions of these transformations after we have studied 3D math in the next chapter.

The nice thing about matrix transformations is how easily you can conduct a series of transformations. If you start with T_1, then T_2, then T_3 you can combine these into a single transformation matrix

$$T = T_3 \, T_2 \, T_1$$

and then hit all of the objects in your space with this single matrix. This saves time.

The other nice thing is how easy this makes it to go back and forth between transformations. Suppose you transfer a vector $\mathbf{v}$ into a new vector $\mathbf{v}_{new}$ by the transformation

$$\mathbf{v}_{new} = T\mathbf{v} = T_3 \, T_2 \, T_1 \, \mathbf{v}$$

then going back is just a matter of taking the inverse of the matrix:

$$\mathbf{v} = T^{-1} \, \mathbf{v}_{new} = T_1^{-1} \, T_2^{-1} \, T_3^{-1} \, \mathbf{v}_{new}.$$

Table 1: Scaling and Rotation Transformations

type	Description	T-Matrix (2D)	T-Matrix (3D)	Properties
Scaling	Scales along the x, y and z axes by S. We used this in transforming to *ellipse space*.	$\left[\begin{array}{cc} S_x & 0 \\ 0 & S_y \end{array}\right]$	$\left[\begin{array}{ccc} S_x & 0 & 0 \\ 0 & S_y & 0 \\ 0 & 0 & S_z \end{array}\right]$	B
Rotation	Rotates by an angle θ **clockwise** about the origin. In 3D - rotates around the z-axis.	$\left[\begin{array}{cc} \cos\theta & \sin\theta \\ -\sin\theta & \cos\theta \end{array}\right]$	$\left[\begin{array}{ccc} \cos\theta & \sin\theta & 0 \\ -\sin\theta & \cos\theta & 0 \\ 0 & 0 & 1 \end{array}\right]$	A, B, C

Properties Key: A: preserves angles between vectors. **B:** preserves interior and exterior points of closed curves. **C:** Preserves distances between points.

Table 2: More Matrix Transformations

type	Description	T-Matrix (2D)	T-Matrix (3D)	Properties
Reflection across y-axis.	Reflects across the y-axis. In 3D across the yz-plane.	$\begin{bmatrix} -1 & 0 \\ 0 & 1 \end{bmatrix}$	$\begin{bmatrix} -1 & 0 & 0 \\ 0 & 1 & 0 \\ 0 & 0 & 1 \end{bmatrix}$	A, B, C
Reflection across x-axis.	Reflects across the x-axis. In 3D across the xz-plane.	$\begin{bmatrix} 1 & 0 \\ 0 & -1 \end{bmatrix}$	$\begin{bmatrix} 1 & 0 & 0 \\ 0 & -1 & 0 \\ 0 & 0 & 1 \end{bmatrix}$	A, B, C
Reflection across a line.	Reflect across the line $y = mx$.	$\frac{1}{m^2+1}\begin{bmatrix} 1-m^2 & 2m \\ 2m & m^2-1 \end{bmatrix}$		A, B, C
Translations Matrix Form	Move all points a distance of $[d_x, d_y, d_z]$. You must *cheat* by expressing all vectors with one extra term. Put a 1 in the last position.	$\begin{bmatrix} 1 & 0 & d_x \\ 0 & 1 & d_y \\ 0 & 0 & 1 \end{bmatrix}$	$\begin{bmatrix} 1 & 0 & 0 & d_x \\ 0 & 1 & 0 & d_y \\ 0 & 0 & 1 & d_z \\ 0 & 0 & 0 & 1 \end{bmatrix}$	A, B, C
Translations Non-Matrix Form	Move all points a distance of $[d_x, d_y, d_z]$. **Warning:** Not a matrix transformation.	$\begin{bmatrix} x' \\ y' \end{bmatrix} = \begin{bmatrix} x \\ y \end{bmatrix} + \begin{bmatrix} d_x \\ d_y \end{bmatrix}$	$\begin{bmatrix} x' \\ y' \\ z' \end{bmatrix} = \begin{bmatrix} x \\ y \\ z \end{bmatrix} + \begin{bmatrix} d_x \\ d_y \\ d_z \end{bmatrix}$	A, B, C
Horizontal Shearing	Shears (slants) all points parallel to the x-axis: $x' = x + ky$. In 3D - proportional to y.	$\begin{bmatrix} 1 & k \\ 0 & 1 \end{bmatrix}$	$\begin{bmatrix} 1 & k_y & 0 \\ 0 & 1 & 0 \\ 0 & k_z & 1 \end{bmatrix}$	B
Vertical Shearing	Shears (slants) all points parallel to the y-axis: $y' = y + kx$. In 3D - proportional to x.	$\begin{bmatrix} 1 & 0 \\ k & 1 \end{bmatrix}$	$\begin{bmatrix} 1 & 0 & 0 \\ k_y & 1 & 0 \\ k_z & 0 & 1 \end{bmatrix}$	B

Properties Key: A: preserves angles between vectors. **B:** preserves interior and exterior points of closed curves. **C:** Preserves distances between points.

Here is a demonstration of three of the previously mentioned transformations. We start with a picture of a house (quit simple). The *house* in this case is just a list of points which represent the vertices of the polygon. This list of points is entered in MATLAB® as a vector of x-values, and a vector of corresponding y-values. Then you just plot x, y for a graph of the points with lines connecting them. First the *house* is rotated clockwise 60°. Notice the point at the origin is unaffected by this rotation. Then we reflect it across the y-axis. Again, the origin is unaffected by this transformation. In the final frame the current figure is then translated by $[dx, dy] = [1, 2]$ (Ie. the graph is moved one unit to the right and 2 units up). Notice the origin is affected by this translation but its position with respect to the other points is unchanged.

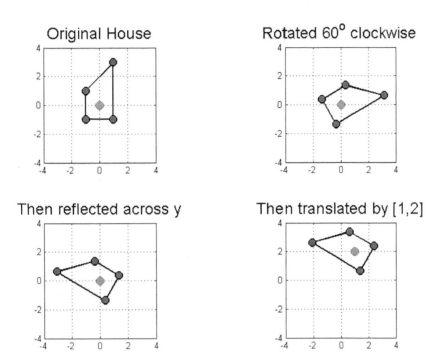

The code that generated this array of graphs is given on the next page.

Here is the code for rotating, reflecting, and translating the *house* from the last figure.

```
C:\_dropbox\Dropbox\_My Books\330-Book\Chapter-1\Chapter 1 MATLAB Examples\MatrixTransforms.m

File  Edit  Text  Go  Cell  Tools  Debug  Desktop  Window  Help

1    %% MatrixTransforms.m
2    % Tranforming shapes in 2-space
3  - clc; clf;     % clear console; clear figure;
4  - xHouse = [-1  1 1 -1 -1]; % x-values of the house points
5  - yHouse = [-1 -1 3  1 -1]; % y-values of the house points
6  - P = [0 0]';              % A point at the origin
7
8    %% original graph
9  - subplot(221)    % in a 2x2 array of graphs, start the 1st graph
10 - plot(xHouse,yHouse,'k-o','linewidth',2,'MarkerSize',10,'MarkerFace','r')
11 - hold on; grid on; axis equal; axis([-4,4,-4,4]);
12 - plot(P(1),P(2),'ro','MarkerSize',10,'MarkerFace','g')
13 - title('Original House','fontsize',18)
14
15   %% Rotate it 60 degrees
16 - subplot(222) % in a 2x2 array of graphs, start the 2nd graph.
17 - ThetaDegrees = 60;
18 - theta = ThetaDegrees*pi/180;  % CONVERT DEGREES TO RADIANS!!
19 - T1 = [cos(theta) sin(theta); -sin(theta) cos(theta)];
20 - xyHouse1 = T1*[xHouse;yHouse];
21 - xHouse1 = xyHouse1(1,:); yHouse1 = xyHouse1(2,:);
22 - P1 = T1*P;
23 - plot(xHouse1,yHouse1,'k-o','linewidth',2,'markersize',10,'markerfac','r')
24 - hold on; grid on; axis equal; axis([-4,4,-4,4]);
25 - plot(P1(1),P1(2),'ro','markersize',10,'markerface','g')
26 - title('Rotated 60^o clockwise','fontsize',18)
27
28   %% Reflect Across the y-axis
29 - subplot(223) % in a 2x2 array of graphs, start the 3rd graph
30 - T2 = [-1 0; 0 1];
31 - xyHouse2 = T2*[xHouse1;yHouse1];
32 - xHouse2 = xyHouse2(1,:); yHouse2 = xyHouse2(2,:);
33 - P2 = T1*P1;
34 - plot(xHouse2,yHouse2,'k-o','linewidth',2,'markersize',10,'markerface','r')
35 - hold on; grid on; axis equal; axis([-4,4,-4,4]);
36 - plot(P2(1),P2(2),'ro','markersize',10,'markerfac','g')
37 - title('Then reflected across y','fontsize',18)
38
39   %% Translated by [dx,dy] = [1,2]
40 - subplot(224) % in a 2x2 array of graphs, start the 4th graph
41 - dx = 1; dy = 2;
42 - xHouse3 = xHouse2 + dx;  yHouse3 = yHouse2 + dy;
43 - P3 = P2 + [dx dy]';
44 - plot(xHouse3,yHouse3,'k-o','linewidth',2,'markersize',10,'markerface','r')
45 - hold on; grid on; axis equal; axis([-4,4,-4,4]);
46 - plot(P3(1),P3(2),'ro','markersize',10,'markerfac','g')
47 - title('Then translated by [1,2]','fontsize',18)

                                                    script        Ln 1    Col 22   OVR
```

- **Animations:** Here we graph a *'guy'* (just an ellipse) skiing down a hill. Halfway down, he falls and starts to roll down the hill. Here are some clips from this simple animation:

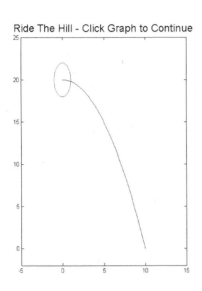 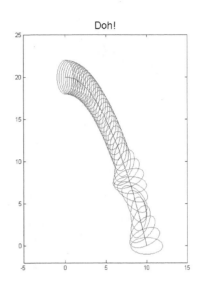

Game Plan

1. **The Hill:** I just took the downward parabola $y = -x^2$ and made some alterations.

   starting graph: $y = -x^2$

   bump it up 100 units: $y = 100 - x^2$

   too tall and skinny - squish it down: $y = .2\left(100 - x^2\right)$ for $x \in [0, 10]$

   MATLAB®   **Note:** When you want x^2 but x is a vector, you probably want to square every term in x. In MATLAB® this is accomplished by using a period before the operation. So, to square every term in the vector x you use the command:

   ```
   y = x.^2
   ```

2. **The Guy:** Now we'll define the 'guy' as an ellipse twice as tall as he is wide. To define the set of x and y values for this ellipse, we start with a parameter t which we will let range from 0 to 2π. So the x and y values are defined by

$$x = \cos(t) \quad y = 2\cos(t) \quad \text{for} \quad t \in [0, 2\pi]$$

   Unfortunately this ellipse is centered at (0,0). We'll worry about moving (translating) him next.

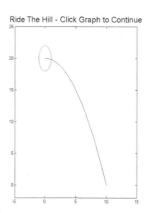
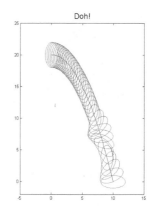

3. Now we have to move our 'guy' along the trajectory. We'll do this with a simple translation. For each frame of the movie, we'll translate each x-value of the ellipse by $dx = x$, and each y-value by $dy = y(x)$.

4. When the *guy* gets about half-way down the hill (at $y = 10$), we want to start rotating him in the clockwise direction. **IMPORTANT:** We must rotate him before the translation otherwise the translated guy will rotate around the origin and that will be bad.

5. Now we have to code it. The complete code is given on the next page. But there are some specifics worth noting.

   - If you want to write a quick function in MATLAB® , a good choice is something called an *anonymous* function such as the one in our program:

     ```
     F = @(x)[.2*(100-x.^2)]
     ```

     Here, F is the name of the function, the @ symbol is the command that MATLAB® recognizes, the first set of parentheses contains the independent (input) variable(s), and the square brackets contain the dependent (return) variable(s).

   - linspace(a,b,n) creates a vector of n values starting at a and ending at b. The values are equally spaced. You can create vectors like this by hand, but this function makes it so much easier.

   - In the animation it is best to give each graph a name so that you can delete the desired objects as needed. This way you do not have to erase and redraw the entire environment for each frame.

   - Don't be afraid to change the **pause** time. Depending the number of frames you might want to increase or decrease this value. If you have no pauses, the animation will go so fast that you might not even see it. Then you could spend forever trying to figure out what's wrong.

6. Read through the code carefully. Make sure you understand what each line does and why we need it. Minor deviations can cause major problems.

7. Here is the code for the animation of the *guy* skiing then falling down the hill.

```matlab
%%    This is Wipe_out.m
clc; clf; clear; % clears console, figure, and all variables respectively

%% Make the hill.
F = @(x)[.2*(100 - x.^2)];              % Defines an 'anonymous' function of x called F.
x_hill = linspace(0,10,200);            % 200 x-values of the hill graph from 0 to 10.
y_hill = F(x_hill);                      % y-values of the hill graph

%% Make the guy.
t = linspace(0,2*pi,100);               % 100 t-values for the ellipse from 0 to 2 pi
x_guy = cos(t); y_guy = 2*sin(t);       % The x and y values for the ellipse (guy).

%% Original plot with guy on top of hill
hill_plot = plot(x_hill,y_hill,'-b');   % plot the hill.
axis equal; hold on;                     % make axes equal scaling and don't erase.
guy_plot = plot(x_guy, y_guy+20, '-r'); % plot the guy on top of the hill.
axisbounds = [-5,15,-2,25];             % axis limits [xmin,xmax,ymin,ymax].
axis(axisbounds);                        % set the axis bounds.
title('Ride The Hill - Click Graph to Continue','fontsize',18) % title

%% Prompt to start and intial values.
w = waitforbuttonpress;  % waits for a button push or mouse click.
title('Ride On!','fontsize',18)          % change the title.
theta = 0;                               % original rotation angle.

%% Start the Animation.
for dx = 0:.1:10           % x goes from 0 to 10 by steps of .1
    delete(guy_plot);      % deletes the plot of the guy called guy_plot.
    dy = F(dx);            % sets dy
    if dy > 10;            % Dont' fall until dy < 10.
        guy_plot = plot(x_guy+dx, y_guy+dy, '-r');
    else                   % If the guy goes below y = 10, he starts to rotate.
        title('Doh!','fontsize',18)
        theta = theta + pi/8;  % increment the rotation angle theta.
        T_rotate = [cos(theta) sin(theta); -sin(theta) cos(theta)]; % rotation matrix
        rotated_guy = T_rotate*[x_guy;y_guy];  % Rotate all points in guy.
        rotated_x_guy = rotated_guy(1,:);      % get the x-values.
        rotated_y_guy = rotated_guy(2,:);      % get the y-values.
        guy_plot = plot(rotated_x_guy + dx, rotated_y_guy + dy, '-r');  %plot him
    end
    axis(axisbounds); % set the axis bounds.
    pause(.01);       % slow down the animation by pausing .01 seconds
end
```

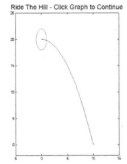

Ride The Hill - Click Graph to Continue

Doh!

Chapter 1.7 Problem Set

Numbers with an asterisk[*] have solutions in the back of the book.

1. **(Written/MATLAB®)** Suppose the point (0,3) is translated 2 units up (in the y-direction) and 1 unit to the right (in the x-direction) and **then** rotated **counter-clockwise** by 60°.

   (a)[*] Where would this point go? (**Round your answer to one decimal place**)

   (b) Suppose you did the operations in the reverse order. First you translated then rotated. Now where would this point go? (**Round your answer to one decimal place**)

2. **(Written/MATLAB®)** Suppose the point (x, y) is first rotated clockwise by $\theta = \dfrac{\pi}{6}$ radians and then reflected across the x-axis. After this sequence of transformations, the point (x,y) is now (-2,3). What was the original point (x, y) rounded to two decimal place?

   (a)[*] What was the original point (x, y) rounded to two decimal places?

   (b) Suppose the operations were done in reverse order. Now what would be the original point?

3. **(MATLAB®) Improved Wipe out:**

   Take the skiing Wipe Out program and make it look a little better. Two good places to start are:

   (a) Make the guy (ellipse) stand on the ground. Currently the middle of the ellipse is at ground level. That looks bad.

   (b) Give him skis that rotate appropriately after he wipes out.

   Below are some screen shots.

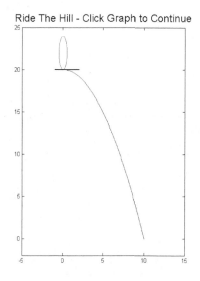
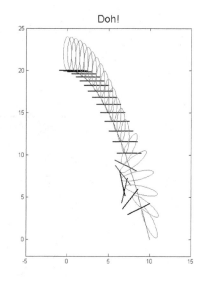

4. (MATLAB®) **Kick-Off!**

In this assignment you are to create an animation of a football being kicked across a trajectory that starts at $(0,0)$ and ends somewhere down the field at the point $(x_{end}, 0)$. The football should be an ellipse that looks like an ellipse in the final animation. It should also rotate counter-clockwise as it moves along it's trajectory. Below are a few shots from an animation I made with these requirements. You can figure out the trajectory below or you can create your own. You can start with the *Wipe-Out* code which already has the animation commands. You should change the variable names so as to make sense with respect to this problem.

You would be wise to take the code from the previous example and alter it instead of writing it from scratch.

Required Features:

(a) The ball must look like a football (elliptical).

(b) The ball must start at the origin.

(c) The ball must land on the ground.

(d) The trajectory must be visible in the animation.

(e) The trajectory must be smooth. (no sharp turns).

(f) The ball must rotate counter-clockwise as it follows it's trajectory.

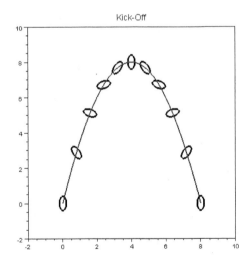

Chapter 1 Project: Real-Time Collision Detection

Here we combine the collision detection from Chapter 1.4 and the matrix transforms/animations from Chapter 1.5 to perform what is known as *Real-Time Collision Detection*.

Summary: You are to recreate your football kick-off animation. This time, before the ball is set in motion, you must prompt the user to place a bird somewhere on the plane. Then the ball is to fly along it's trajectory and the program must determine if the bird gets hit by the ball. You do this by performing a collision detection at every rendering of the figure. This is called **Real-Time Collision Detection**. If there is a collision, the bird should fall to the ground in some fashion while the ball continues on its trajectory. If there is no collision the bird should remain in it's initial location throughout the animation.

Required Features:

1. The ball must start by resting on the ground at the (0,0) location in the vertical position.

2. The trajectory must be visible by the viewer at this screen-shot.

3. The user is then prompted to place a bird on the figure by clicking on a point. The bird will remain stationary. The bird should just be a visible point on the graph.

4. When the ball is kicked. It must rotate counter-clockwise as it follows it's trajectory.

5. Erase the trajectory curve once the ball starts on its way. Only the ball and the bird should be visible in the animation.

6. At every screen-shot (or properly chosen subset of screen-shots) you must determine if the ball has hit the bird.

7. If the bird is hit, it should fall to the ground in some fashion while the ball continues on its trajectory. The title of the graph should mention this.

8. If the bird is never hit, it should remain in its initial location throughout the flight of the ball.

Here are some screen-shots from a miss and a hit.

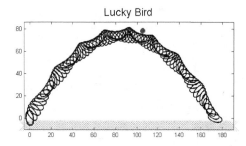 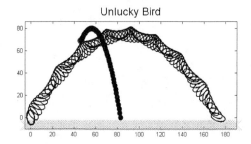

Hints

1. **Step size matters:** Make sure the animation loop takes small enough steps so that the ball does not go through the bird without a collision being detected. Don't make the steps so small that each pass during the debugging process takes forever.

2. **Perform the collision detection back at the origin.** We have only done collision detection with a non-rotated ellipse centered at the origin. So we have to perform the collision detection in that scenario. Before every frame is made, the ball starts like that anyway. So, we have to translate the bird back to the origin and un-rotate it. **The order makes all the difference.**

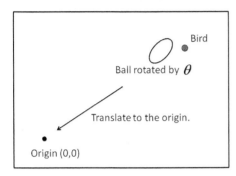

Assume the ball is currently centered at (x_{ball}, y_{ball}) and rotated by θ.

Perform the collision detection back at the origin, keeping the relative positions the same.

The bird's translated position will be
$(x_{bird} - x_{ball}, y_{bird} - y_{ball})$.
The ball starts centered at the origin anyway.

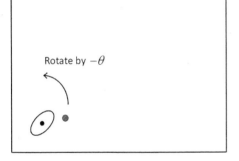

The ball will be rotated by θ.
You need to **un-rotate** the situation here.

So, rotate the bird by $-\theta$.
The ball starts in the un-rotated position anyway.

Perform the collision detection
as per Chapter 1.4.

Chapter 2

Vectors and the Geometry of Space

In this chapter we formalize our study of the mathematical geometry of space. It starts with some material that should be familiar to you from the last chapter. Specifically, we start with vectors. Previously when we discussed vectors, we considered a vector as an ordered list of numbers. We demonstrated how these vectors can be used to describe points in 2 and 3 dimensional space. Now we will consider a vector as a directed line segment that has a length and a direction. This vector can be situated anywhere in 2 or 3 space. As such, a single vector actually describes infinitely many possible directed line segments starting at any location in our geometry. Because of this ambiguity we generally consider the vector to start at the origin. Once this assumption is made, our definition of a vector results in our previous notion of a specific point in 2 or 3 space. By creating a vector-valued function we can trace out the endpoints of these vectors which makes a curve in space. We introduced dot products in the last chapter. In this chapter we will expand on this and describe what a dot product produces from a geometric perspective. We also introduce a different type of vector product called the cross product and describe this in geometric terms. Once we have these operations in our toolbox, we can go on to describe lines and planes in 3-space and investigate how and when these geometric objects intersect.

2.1 Vectors in the Plane

In this section we investigate vectors in the context of 2-dimensional geometry (vectors in the plane).

1. A **directed line segment** from an initial point P to a terminal point Q is denoted $\overrightarrow{PQ}$. It has a length (or magnitude) denoted by $||\overrightarrow{PQ}||$. Directed line segments with the same length and direction are called **equivalent**. For any directed line segment there are infinitely many equivalent directed line segments.

2. A **vector** is a standardized representation of all equivalent line segments.

3. **Component Form of a Vector**

If $\vec{v}$ is a vector with initial point at the origin (0,0) and terminal point (x, y) then the component form of $\vec{v}$ is $\vec{v} = \langle x, y \rangle$.

If $\vec{v}$ is a vector defined by the directed line segment with initial point $P = (P_1, P_2)$ and terminal point $Q = (Q_1, Q_2)$, then the component form of this vector is defined by $\vec{v} = \langle Q_1 - P_1, Q_2 - P_2 \rangle$. This has the geometric effect of taking the original directed line segment and translating it to an equivalent one with initial point at the origin.

Example: given $P = (-1, 3)$ and $Q = (3, -5)$ find $\vec{v} = \overrightarrow{PQ}$.

The vector is $\overrightarrow{PQ} = \langle 3 - (-1), -5 - 3 \rangle = \langle 4, -8 \rangle = \vec{v}$.

4. **Notation:**

- Vectors are denoted in two different ways. In typeset material a vector is generally denoted by a lower case, bold-faced letter such as **u**, **v**, or **w**. When written by hand the arrow notation is used such as $\vec{u}$, $\vec{v}$, or $\vec{w}$. I will try to stick with the bold-faced notation in this text but may occasionally use the arrow notation in some situations involving a vector representation of a directed line segment such as $\overrightarrow{PQ}$.

- Components of a vector are generally given in terms of the vector variable.

$$\mathbf{u} = \langle u_1, u_2 \rangle \qquad \text{and} \qquad \mathbf{v} = \langle v_1, v_2 \rangle$$

5. **Equivalent Vectors:** Two vectors are considered equivalent if they have the same length and direction. This reduces to the two vectors having identical components when written in component form.

If $\mathbf{u} = \langle u_1, u_2 \rangle$ and $\mathbf{v} = \langle v_1, v_2 \rangle$ then

$$\mathbf{u} = \mathbf{v} \iff u_1 = v_1 \text{ and } u_2 = v_2$$

Example: Verify that the three vectors in the figure below are equivalent.

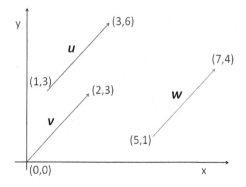

The vectors in component form are

$$\mathbf{u} = \langle 3 - 1, 6 - 3 \rangle = \langle 2, 3 \rangle$$
$$\mathbf{v} = \langle 2 - 0, 3 - 0 \rangle = \langle 2, 3 \rangle$$
$$\mathbf{w} = \langle 7 - 5, 4 - 1 \rangle = \langle 2, 3 \rangle$$

Since the components are identical these vectors are equivalent.

6. **Scalar Multiplication:** If k is a scalar (real number) and $\mathbf{u} = \langle u_1, u_2 \rangle$ is a vector, then

$$k\mathbf{u} = \langle ku_1, ku_2 \rangle.$$

Geometric Interpretation: The length of the vector is multiplied by $|k|$ and if k is negative then the direction switches. If $k = -1$, $k\mathbf{u}$ looks just like $\mathbf{u}$ only pointing in the opposite direction.

7. **Parallel Vectors:** Two vectors are parallel if one of they are scalar multiples of each other. (I.e., $\mathbf{v} = k\mathbf{u}$). If $\mathbf{u} = \langle u_1, u_2 \rangle$ and $\mathbf{v} = \langle v_1, v_2 \rangle$ then

$$\mathbf{u} \text{ is parallel to } \mathbf{v} \iff v_1 = k\, u_1 \text{ and } v_2 = k\, u_2$$

Example: Verify that the two vectors in the figure below are parallel.

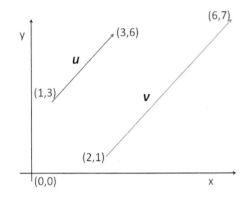

The vectors in component form are

$$\mathbf{u} = \langle 3 - 1, 6 - 3 \rangle = \langle 2, 3 \rangle$$
$$\mathbf{v} = \langle 6 - 2, 7 - 1 \rangle = \langle 4, 6 \rangle.$$

Notice

$$\frac{v_1}{u_1} = \frac{4}{2} = 2 \text{ and } \frac{v_2}{u_2} = \frac{6}{3} = 2$$

So $\mathbf{v} = 2\mathbf{u}$ and they are parallel.

8. **Application, Collinear Points:** To determine if three points P, Q and R are collinear (lie in a line), check to see if the vectors $\overrightarrow{PQ}$ and $\overrightarrow{PR}$ are parallel. If they are, then the three points are collinear.

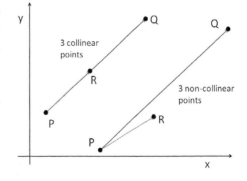

Example: Verify that the points $P(1,3)$, $Q(3,6)$, and $R(9, 15)$ are collinear.

Answer:
$\overrightarrow{PQ} = \langle 3 - 1, 6 - 3 \rangle = \langle 2, 3 \rangle$
$\overrightarrow{PR} = \langle 9 - 1, 15 - 3 \rangle = \langle 8, 12 \rangle.$
Since $\overrightarrow{PR} = 4\,\overrightarrow{PQ}$, these vectors are parallel and the points are collinear.

9. **Length (Magnitude or Norm) of a Vector**   A vector in component form $\mathbf{v} = \langle v_1, v_2 \rangle$ has length (or magnitude or norm) given by

$$||\mathbf{v}|| = \sqrt{v_1^2 + v_2^2} \tag{2.1}$$

A vector of zero length is called the **zero vector**; $\mathbf{0} = \langle 0, 0 \rangle$.

Example: Find the length of the vector from $P = (-1, 3)$ to $Q = (4, 15)$
Answer: $\overrightarrow{PQ} = \langle 5, 12 \rangle$, and $||\overrightarrow{PQ}|| = \sqrt{5^2 + 12^2} = \sqrt{169} = 13$.

10. **Vector Addition:** $\mathbf{u} + \mathbf{v} = \langle u_1 + v_1, u_2 + v_2 \rangle$

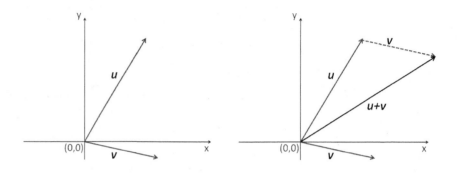

Geometric Interpretation (*Tip-to-Tail*) Align the tip of $\mathbf{u}$ with the tail of $\mathbf{v}$ then connect the tail of $\mathbf{u}$ with the tip of $\mathbf{v}$.
If $\mathbf{u}$ and $\mathbf{v}$ represent forces then $\mathbf{u} + \mathbf{v}$ is called the **resultant force**.

11. **Vector Subtraction**: $\mathbf{u} - \mathbf{v} = \langle u_1 - v_1, u_2 - v_2 \rangle$.

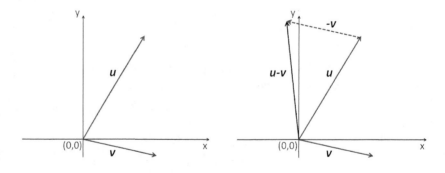

Geometric Interpretation: (*Tip-to-Tip*) Align the tip of $\mathbf{u}$ with the tip of $\mathbf{v}$, then connect the tail of $\mathbf{u}$ to the tail of $\mathbf{v}$. It might be easier just to picture $\mathbf{u} - \mathbf{v}$ as $\mathbf{u} + (-\mathbf{v})$.

12. **Unit Vectors and Normalizing a Vector**

A **unit vector** has length 1. The unit vector **u** in the direction of **v** is given by

$$\mathbf{u} = \frac{1}{||\mathbf{v}||}\,\mathbf{v} = \frac{\mathbf{v}}{||\mathbf{v}||}$$

When you do this it is called **normalizing** the vector **v**.

Example: Find the unit vector (**u**) in the direction of $\mathbf{v} = \langle -3, 2 \rangle$. I.e., Normalize **v**.

Answer: $||\mathbf{v}|| = \sqrt{(-3)^2 + 2^2} = \sqrt{13}$. So, $\mathbf{u} = \frac{1}{\sqrt{13}}\mathbf{v} = \left\langle \frac{-3}{\sqrt{13}}, \frac{2}{\sqrt{13}} \right\rangle$

Application: Given the points $P(2,3)$ and $Q(7,12)$ find the point S such that S is 4 units from P in the direction of Q.

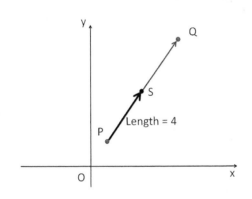

Strategy: Normalize $\overrightarrow{PQ}$ and multiply it by 4 to get $\overrightarrow{PS}$, then *add*** this to the point P.

$$\overrightarrow{PQ} = \langle 7 - 2, 12 - 3 \rangle = \langle 5, 9 \rangle$$

$$||\overrightarrow{PQ}|| = \sqrt{5^2 + 9^2} = \sqrt{106}$$

$$\mathbf{u} = \frac{1}{||\overrightarrow{PQ}||}\overrightarrow{PQ} = \frac{1}{\sqrt{106}}\langle 5, 9 \rangle$$

$$\overrightarrow{PS} = \frac{4}{\sqrt{106}}\langle 5, 9 \rangle$$

$$S = P + \overrightarrow{PS} = (2,3) + \frac{4}{\sqrt{106}}\langle 5, 9 \rangle \approx (3.94, 6.50)^{**}$$

** Mathematically speaking, you can't add a vector to a point (without defining a new operation) but we will allow it here for practical purposes.

13. Properties: Let **u**, **v** and **w** be vectors, and let c and d scalars.

(a) Commutative: $\mathbf{u} + \mathbf{v} = \mathbf{v} + \mathbf{u}$.

(b) Associative: $\mathbf{u} + (\mathbf{v} + \mathbf{w}) = (\mathbf{u} + \mathbf{v}) + \mathbf{w}$.

(c) Additive Identity: $\mathbf{0} = \langle 0, 0 \rangle$ is called the zero vector and $\mathbf{u} + \mathbf{0} = \mathbf{u}$.

(d) Additive Inverse $\mathbf{u} + (-\mathbf{u}) = \mathbf{0}$.

(e) $c(d\,\mathbf{u}) = cd\,\mathbf{u}$.

(f) Distributive Properties
  - $(c + d)\,\mathbf{u} = c\,\mathbf{u} + d\,\mathbf{u}$
  - $c(\mathbf{u} + \mathbf{v}) = c\,\mathbf{u} + c\,\mathbf{v}$

(g) $1\,\mathbf{u} = \mathbf{u}$ and $0\,\mathbf{u} = \mathbf{0}$

(h) $||k\mathbf{u}|| = |k|\,||\mathbf{u}||$

(i) Triangle inequality: $||\mathbf{u} + \mathbf{v}|| \leq ||\mathbf{u}|| + ||\mathbf{v}||$

14. **Basis Vectors** or **Standard Unit Vectors in 2D**

The standard unit vectors in 2-space are
$\mathbf{i} = \langle 1, 0 \rangle$ and $\mathbf{j} = \langle 0, 1 \rangle$.

Any vector $\mathbf{u} = \langle u_1, u_2 \rangle$ can be expressed as a linear combination of $\mathbf{i}$ and $\mathbf{j}$ by

$$\mathbf{u} = u_1 \, \mathbf{i} + u_2 \, \mathbf{j}$$

here, u_1 is called the **horizontal** component of $\mathbf{u}$ and u_2 is called the **vertical** component of $\mathbf{u}$.

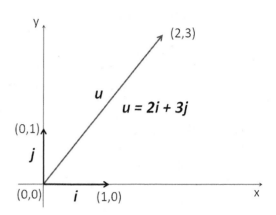

Example: Express the vector $\mathbf{u} = \langle 2, 3 \rangle$ as a linear combination of the standard unit vectors $\mathbf{i}$ and $\mathbf{j}$.

Answer: $\mathbf{u} = \langle 2, 3 \rangle = 2\,\mathbf{i} + 3\,\mathbf{j}$. Yes, it's that simple.

15. **Polar Representation of Vectors:**

If $\mathbf{u}$ is a vector with length $\|\mathbf{u}\|$ and makes a (counter-clockwise) angle of θ from the positive x-axis then

$$\mathbf{u} = \|\mathbf{u}\| \cos\theta \, \mathbf{i} + \|\mathbf{u}\| \sin\theta \, \mathbf{j} = \|\mathbf{u}\| \langle \cos\theta, \sin\theta \rangle$$

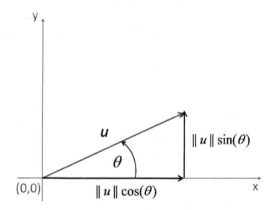

Example: Suppose the vector $\mathbf{u}$ has length 2 and makes an angle of 60° with the positive x axis. Express $\mathbf{u}$ as a linear combination of $\mathbf{i}$ and $\mathbf{j}$, then give the component form of $\mathbf{u}$.

Answer: Since the vector must have length 2, we know that $\|\mathbf{u}\| = 2$. Also, $60^o = \pi/3$ radians.

Expressed as a linear combination of $\mathbf{i}$ and $\mathbf{j}$

$\mathbf{u} = \|\mathbf{u}\| \cos\theta \, \mathbf{i} + \|\mathbf{u}\| \sin\theta \, \mathbf{j} = 2 \cos(\pi/3) \, \mathbf{i} + 2 \sin(\pi/3) \mathbf{j} = 2\frac{1}{2}\mathbf{i} + 2\frac{\sqrt{3}}{2}\mathbf{j} = \mathbf{i} + \sqrt{3}\,\mathbf{j}$

Expressed in component form $\mathbf{u} = \langle 1, \sqrt{3} \rangle$.

Chapter 2.1 Problem Set

Numbers with an asterisk[*] have solutions in the back of the book.

1. The initial point and terminal points of a directed line segment are given. (1) Sketch the directed line segment. (2) Write the vector in component form. (3) Sketch the vector with its initial point at the origin.

    (a)[*] Initial Point: (1,3)   Terminal Point: (-2, -7).

    (b) Initial Point: (1,3)   Terminal Point: (2, 7).

2. Find the vectors $\mathbf{u} = \overrightarrow{PQ}$ and $\mathbf{v} = \overrightarrow{RS}$ for the given points P, Q, R and S. Then (1) determine if $\mathbf{u}$ and $\mathbf{v}$ are equivalent vectors and (2) determine if $\mathbf{u}$ and $\mathbf{v}$ are parallel vectors.

    (a)[*] $\mathbf{u}$: $P(-2,3), Q(-4,-2)$ $\mathbf{v}$: $R(2,4), S(-2,3)$.
    (b) $\mathbf{u}$: $P(0,2), Q(3,0)$ $\mathbf{v}$: $R(-1,5), S(2,3)$.
    (c)[*] $\mathbf{u}$: $P(2,2), Q(5,0)$ $\mathbf{v}$: $R(1,3), S(-5,7)$.

3. Use vectors to determine whether the points are collinear. Plot the points by hand or in MATLAB® to check your answers.

    (a)[*] P(0, -2), Q(3, 4), R(2, 2)
    (b) P(1, 2), Q(2, 5), R(4, 8)

4. (**MATLAB®**) Write a program that plots two points on the plane. Now prompt the user to click somewhere on the graph. The program must determine whether the third point lies on the line created by the initial two points. This is far more complicated than you might think because remember: **you can't divide by zero.** Now, it will be almost impossible to click a point exactly on the line. How could you include a *close enough* option?

5.[*] Find the value of w needed to make the points P, Q, and R collinear.

    (a)[*] $P(-1,3)$ $Q(2,7)$ $R(7,w)$
    (b)[*] $P(-1,3)$ $Q(w,7)$ $R(7,4)$

6.[*] Given the vectors $\mathbf{u} = \langle 2,3 \rangle$ and $\mathbf{v} = \langle -2,-4 \rangle$ find

    (a) $\mathbf{u} + \mathbf{v}$
    (b) $\mathbf{u} - \mathbf{v}$
    (c) $||\mathbf{u}||$ and $||\mathbf{v}||$.
    (d) $||\mathbf{u} + \mathbf{v}||$
    (e) Verify the triangle inequality in this case: $||\mathbf{u} + \mathbf{v}|| \leq ||\mathbf{u}|| + ||\mathbf{v}||$
    (f) $-2\mathbf{u} + 3\mathbf{v}$

7. Find the unit vector in the direction of v for each of the following.

  (a)* $\mathbf{v} = \langle 3, -4 \rangle$

  (b) $\mathbf{v} = \langle -5, 2 \rangle$

8. Find the unit vector in the direction of $\overrightarrow{PQ}$ where P is the point $(1, 2)$ and Q is the point $(4, 10)$.

9.* Find a vector of length 2 in the direction of $\overrightarrow{PQ}$ where P is the point $(1, 2)$ and Q is the point $(4, 10)$.

10. Here we try to line up the terminal point of a *gun* in such a way that it is pointing in the direction of a given point in space. Assume the initial point (the handle of the gun) is $H(0, 2)$ and the point in space is $(4, 22)$. Make the length of the gun 2. Find the tip of the gun $T(t_1, t_2)$.

11.* Express the following vectors as linear combinations of the standard unit vectors.

  (a) $\mathbf{u} = \langle 2, 3 \rangle$

  (b) $\mathbf{v} = \langle \sqrt{3}, -7 \rangle$

12.* Consider the vector with the initial point at the origin, is 3 units in length, and makes an angle of -120° with the positive x-axis. Express this vector as a linear combination of the standard basis vectors and in component form. Round your answers to two decimal places.

13. Give the component form of the vector $\mathbf{v}$ depicted below.
Give your answer exactly or rounded to 2 decimal places

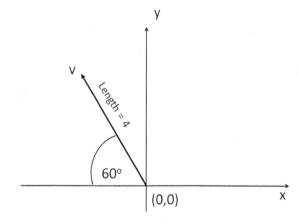

2.2   Vectors in Space

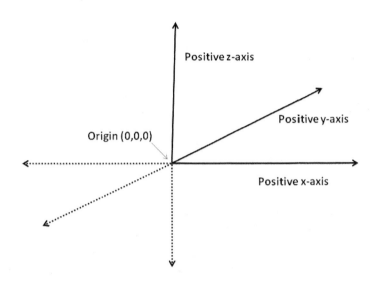

1. The **Three Dimensional Coordinate System** is created by passing a z-axis perpendicular to the usual x and y axes of the cartesian coordinate system. When depicting this system there are two orientations. The one illustrated above represents a *Right-Handed System*. Imagine you are standing at the origin with your arms along the positive x and y axes. The orientation of the system is determined by which hand points along the x-axis. This text will use the right-handed system exclusively but some software programs may use a left-handed system. The default orientation for MATLAB® is also a right-handed system.

2. Taken as pairs these axes determine 3 **coordinate planes**; the xy-plane, the xz-plane, and the yz-plane. Visualize these planes in the figure above. These three planes divide 3-space into 8 octants. Unlike 2-space, there is no agreed-upon numbering system for these 8 octants.

3. A **point** in 3 dimensional space (or just space) is determined by an ordered triplet (x, y, z). You start by moving x units along the x-axis, then proceed y units parallel to the y-axis, and finally move z units parallel to the z-axis.

4. **Perspective:** Draw your own coordinate axes or using the those on the top of this page. Sketch and label the points $P = (2, 3, 4)$, $Q = (-4, 1, 3)$, $R = (-3, -3, 4)$, and $S = (-1, -1, -4)$. Now sketch the directed line segments $\overrightarrow{PQ}$ and $\overrightarrow{RS}$. Try to make them *look real*. What lines are behind other? Using a pencil helps.

5. **Distance**

The **Distance** from any point (x, y, z) to the origin is given by

$$d = \sqrt{x^2 + y^2 + z^2}$$

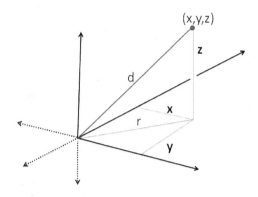

Mini-Proof: (See Figure)
$r^2 = x^2 + y^2$, and
$d^2 = r^2 + z^2$, so
$d = \sqrt{r^2 + z^2} = \sqrt{x^2 + y^2 + z^2}$.

6. The **Distance** between points (x_1, y_1, z_1) and (x_2, y_2, z_2) is

$$d = \sqrt{(x_2 - x_1)^2 + (y_2 - y_1)^2 + (z_2 - z_1)^2} \tag{2.2}$$

7. The **midpoint** between points (x_1, y_1, z_1) and (x_2, y_2, z_2) is

$$\left(\frac{(x_2 + x_1)}{2}, \frac{(y_2 + y_1)}{2}, \frac{(z_2 + z_1)}{2} \right) \tag{2.3}$$

8. Standard equation of a **sphere** with center (x_0, y_0, z_0) and radius r is:

$$(x - x_0)^2 + (y - y_0)^2 + (z - z_0)^2 = r^2 \tag{2.4}$$

Example: Find the standard equation of a sphere with (4,-2,2) and (0,5,-2) as endpoints of a diameter.

Answer: The diameter is given by the distance between the two points.

$$\text{diameter} = \sqrt{(0 - 4)^2 + (5 - (-2))^2 + (-2 - 2)^2} = \sqrt{16 + 49 + 16} = \sqrt{81} = 9$$

so the radius is half of this: $r = 4.5$. Now, the midpoint (center) is given by

$$\left(\frac{(4 + 0)}{2}, \frac{(-2 + 5)}{2}, \frac{(2 - 2)}{2} \right) = \left(2, \frac{3}{2}, 0 \right)$$

Now that we have the radius and center, the equation of the desired sphere is given by equation (2.4),

$$(x - 2)^2 + \left(y - \frac{3}{2} \right)^2 + z^2 = (4.5)^2$$

9. Vectors in 3-space are defined equivalently to those defined previously for 2-space only now we have three components for each vector. Specifically, a **vector in space** is a standardized representation of all equivalent directed line segments in space.

10. **Component Form:** If **v** is represented by the line directed line segment from $P = (p_1, p_2, p_3)$ to $Q = (q_1, q_2, q_3)$ then the component form of **v** is given by

$$\mathbf{v} = \langle q_1 - p_1, q_2 - p_1, q_3 - p_3 \rangle$$

11. Operations and Properties: Vectors in Space

   Most of the operations and properties from vectors in the plane extend naturally to space. Review them from the previous lists. Below are a few. Let $\vec{u} = \langle u_1, u_2, u_3 \rangle$, $\vec{v} = \langle v_1, v_2, v_3 \rangle$, and k be a scalar.

   - **Equality:** $\mathbf{u} = \mathbf{v}$ only if $u_1 = v_1$, $u_2 = v_2$ and $u_3 = v_3$.
   - **Parallel:** Two vectors **u** and **v** are parallel only if $\mathbf{u} = k\,\mathbf{v}$ for some scalar k.
   - **Length**, Norm, or Magnitude $= ||\mathbf{v}|| = \sqrt{v_1^2 + v_2^2 + v_3^2}$.
   - **Sum:** $\mathbf{u} + \mathbf{v} = \langle u_1 + v_1, u_2 + v_2, u_3 + v_3 \rangle$
   - **scalar multiplication.** $k\mathbf{u} = \langle ku_1, ku_2, ku_3 \rangle$ Note: $||k\mathbf{u}|| = |k|\,||\mathbf{u}||$
   - The **Unit vector** in the direction of **v** is given by $\mathbf{u} = \dfrac{\mathbf{v}}{||\mathbf{v}||}$.

12. **Example, Collinear Points:**

   Are the points $P(1, -2, 3)$, $Q(2, 1, 0)$, and $R(4, 7, -4)$ collinear?

   $\overrightarrow{PQ} = \langle 1, 3, -3 \rangle$ and $\overrightarrow{PR} = \langle 3, 9, -7 \rangle$. It starts to look like $\overrightarrow{PR} = 3\overrightarrow{PQ}$ but the last term messes this up $\left(\dfrac{3}{1} = \dfrac{9}{3} \neq \dfrac{-7}{-3} \right)$. So, the vectors are not parallel and thus the points are not collinear.

13. **Example, Unit Vector:**

   Find the unit vector in the opposite direction of $v = \langle -1, 2, 3 \rangle$.

   $$\mathbf{u} = \frac{-1}{||\mathbf{v}||}\mathbf{v} = \frac{-1}{\sqrt{14}}\mathbf{v} = \left\langle \frac{1}{\sqrt{14}}, \frac{-2}{\sqrt{14}}, \frac{-3}{\sqrt{14}} \right\rangle.$$

14. **Example, Point the Arrow**

Given the points $P(2,3,3)$ and $Q(7,12,-2)$ find the point S such that S is 4 units from P in the direction of $\overrightarrow{PQ}$.

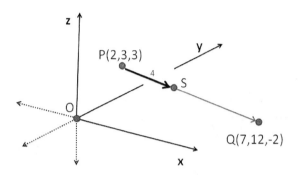

Same strategy as in 2D: First find the unit vector in the direction of $\overrightarrow{PQ}$, then multiply this by 4 so that it has length 4, then the terminal point of the sum of this vector and $\overrightarrow{OP}$ is the point we seek.

- The vector $\overrightarrow{PQ} = \langle 7-2, 12-3, -2-3 \rangle = \langle 5, 9, -5 \rangle$.

- The vector in the direction of $\overrightarrow{PQ}$ of length 4 is $\overrightarrow{PS} = \dfrac{4}{||\overrightarrow{PQ}||}\overrightarrow{PQ} = \dfrac{4}{\sqrt{131}}\langle 5, 9, -5 \rangle$.

- The terminal point of $\overrightarrow{OP} + \overrightarrow{PS} = \langle 2,3,3 \rangle + \dfrac{4}{\sqrt{131}}\langle 5,9,-5 \rangle \approx \langle 3.75, 6.15, 1.25 \rangle$.
  $S \approx (3.75, 6.15, 1.25)$.

15. The **Standard Unit Vectors** in space are $\mathbf{i} = \langle 1,0,0 \rangle$, $\mathbf{j} = \langle 0,1,0 \rangle$, and $\mathbf{k} = \langle 0,0,1 \rangle$.

Any vector $\mathbf{u} = \langle u_1, u_2, v_3 \rangle$ can be expressed as a linear combination of $\mathbf{i}$, $\mathbf{j}$, and $\mathbf{k}$ by

$$\mathbf{u} = u_1\,\mathbf{i} + u_2\,\mathbf{j} + u_3\,\mathbf{k}.$$

Examples:

Express $\mathbf{u} = 3\mathbf{i} - 2\mathbf{k}$ in component form.

$\qquad 3\mathbf{i} - 2\mathbf{k} = 3\mathbf{i} + 0\mathbf{j} - 2\mathbf{k} = \langle 3, 0, -2 \rangle$.

Express $\mathbf{u} = \langle 1, 2, -3 \rangle$ as a linear combination of the standard unit vectors.

$\qquad \langle 1, 2, -3 \rangle = \mathbf{i} + 2\mathbf{j} - 3\mathbf{k}$

16. **MATLAB®** **Demonstration:** Plotting line segments, vectors, and points in 2 and 3D.

Code is on the next page.

- MATLAB® has many ways to graph 2 and 3 dimensional curves and surfaces that we will investigate in later sections. It does not have a great way of plotting directed line segments and vectors (making the arrow is hard for some reason). The MATLAB® program called `vectarrow.m` is available from the book's supplemental web site at

  http://cosmos.champlain.edu/people/stevens/MV3D/index.html

  Usage: `vectarrow(P1,P1,'color')`

- It uses the `plot3` command which is good for plotting points and curves in 3D.

  Usage: `plot3(x-values,y-values,z-values, ...)`

- The program `vectarrow.m` allows you to draw directed line segments from one point to the other with an arrow indicating the terminal point. It is also good at drawing vectors. In this case you let P1 = [0,0,0].

  This program file is available on the internet. Please don't try and rewrite it from scratch.

- Graphs:

  Figure(a) depicts the 3-dimensional graph of the directed line segment from P1(-2, -1, 2) to the P2(0,1,4) using the command `vectarrow(P1, P2, 'red')`.

  Figure (b) depicts the associated vector, $\mathbf{u} = \langle 2, 2, 2 \rangle$, which has the origin as the initial point. This is created using the same function only now use `vectarrow([0,0,0], u, 'blue')`.

  Figure (c) depicts the point at the end of this vector as a large dot in 3-space and is created using the built in `plot3` function.

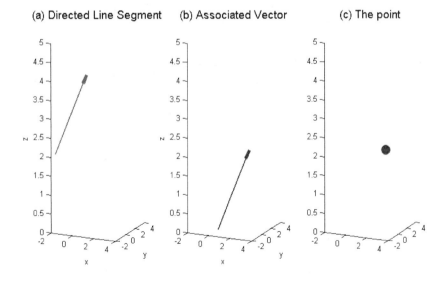

(a) Directed Line Segment   (b) Associated Vector   (c) The point

MATLAB® code for creating the previous figures.

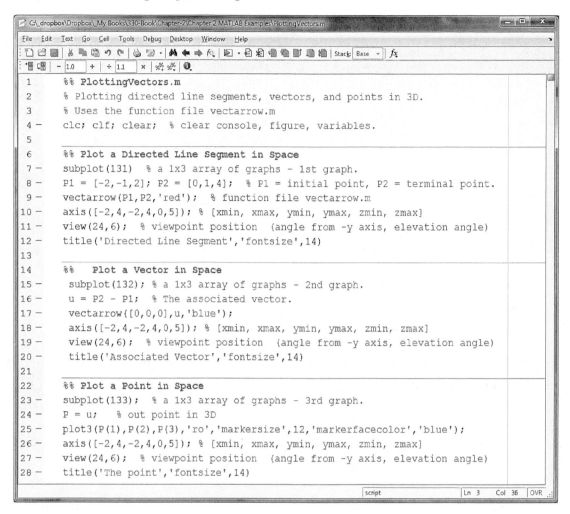

```
1    %% PlottingVectors.m
2    % Plotting directed line segments, vectors, and points in 3D.
3    % Uses the function file vectarrow.m
4  - clc; clf; clear;  % clear console, figure, variables.
5
6    %% Plot a Directed Line Segment in Space
7  - subplot(131)  % a 1x3 array of graphs - 1st graph.
8  - P1 = [-2,-1,2]; P2 = [0,1,4];  % P1 = initial point, P2 = terminal point.
9  - vectarrow(P1,P2,'red');  % function file vectarrow.m
10 - axis([-2,4,-2,4,0,5]); % [xmin, xmax, ymin, ymax, zmin, zmax]
11 - view(24,6);  % viewpoint position  (angle from -y axis, elevation angle)
12 - title('Directed Line Segment','fontsize',14)
13
14   %%   Plot a Vector in Space
15 -  subplot(132); % a 1x3 array of graphs - 2nd graph.
16 -  u = P2 - P1;  % The associated vector.
17 -  vectarrow([0,0,0],u,'blue');
18 -  axis([-2,4,-2,4,0,5]); % [xmin, xmax, ymin, ymax, zmin, zmax]
19 -  view(24,6);  % viewpoint position  (angle from -y axis, elevation angle)
20 -  title('Associated Vector','fontsize',14)
21
22   %% Plot a Point in Space
23 - subplot(133);  % a 1x3 array of graphs - 3rd graph.
24 - P = u;    % out point in 3D
25 - plot3(P(1),P(2),P(3),'ro','markersize',12,'markerfacecolor','blue');
26 - axis([-2,4,-2,4,0,5]); % [xmin, xmax, ymin, ymax, zmin, zmax]
27 - view(24,6);  % viewpoint position  (angle from -y axis, elevation angle)
28 - title('The point','fontsize',14)
```

Chapter 2.2 Problem Set

Numbers with an asterisk[*] have solutions in the back of the book.

1. Find the standard equation of the sphere that

    (a)[*] is centered at (0, -4, 7) with radius = 4.

    (b) has the points (3,0,0) and (0,4,0) as endpoints of a diameter.

    (c)[*] is centered at (-2,3,4) and is tangent to the xz plane.

2. The initial point and terminal points of a directed line segment are given. (1) Sketch the directed line segment. (2) Write the vector in component form. (3) Sketch the vector with its initial point at the origin.

    (a)[*] Initial Point: (1,3,-2)   Terminal Point: (-2, -7, 8).

    (b) Initial Point: (1,3,0)   Terminal Point: (2, 7, 0).

3. Find the vectors $\mathbf{u} = \overrightarrow{PQ}$ and $\mathbf{v} = \overrightarrow{RS}$ for the given points P, Q, R and S. Then (1) determine if $\mathbf{u}$ and $\mathbf{v}$ are equivalent vectors and (2) determine if $\mathbf{u}$ and $\mathbf{v}$ are parallel vectors.

    (a)[*] $\mathbf{u}$: $P(-2,3,7)$, $Q(-4,-2,9)$ $\mathbf{v}$: $R(2,4,4)$, $S(-2,3,4)$.

    (b) $\mathbf{u}$: $P(0,2,-4)$, $Q(3,0,4)$ $\mathbf{v}$: $R(-1,5,0), S(2,3,8)$.

    (c)[*] $\mathbf{u}$: $P(2,2,1)$, $Q(5,0,4)$ $\mathbf{v}$: $R(1,3,3), S(-5,7,-3)$.

4. Use vectors to determine whether the points are collinear. Plot the points to confirm your answers.

    (a)[*] (0, -2, -5), (3, 4, 4), (2, 2, 1)

    (b) (1, 2, 4), (2, 5, 0), (0, 1, 5)

5.[*] Find the values of x and y needed to make the points P, Q, and R collinear.

    (a)[*] $P(-1,3,4)$ $Q(2,7,0)$ $R(x,y,7)$

    (b) $P(1,1,-2)$ $Q(2,y,1)$ $R(3,5,z)$

6.[*] Given the vectors $\mathbf{u} = \langle 2,3,-5 \rangle$ and $\mathbf{v} = \langle -2,-4,0 \rangle$ find

    (a) $\mathbf{u} + \mathbf{v}$

    (b) $\mathbf{u} - \mathbf{v}$

    (c) $||\mathbf{u}||$ and $||\mathbf{v}||$.

    (d) $||\mathbf{u} + \mathbf{v}||$

    (e) Verify the triangle inequality in this case: $||\mathbf{u} + \mathbf{v}|| \leq ||\mathbf{u}|| + ||\mathbf{v}||$

    (f) $-2\mathbf{u} + 3\mathbf{v}$

    (g) The unit vector in the direction of $\mathbf{v}$.

7. Find the unit vector in the direction of $\overrightarrow{HP}$ where H is the point $(0,0,2)$ and P is the point $(4,10,8)$.

8.* Here we try to line up the tip of an arrow in such a way that it is pointing in the direction of a given point in space. Assume the initial point (the tail of the arrow) is $H(0,0,2)$ and the point in space is $(4,10,8)$. Make the arrow have length 2. Find the tip of the arrow $T(t_1,t_2,t_3)$.

9. **MATLAB® Version of Previous Problem:** Write a program that gets the answers to the previous two problems and graphs the point and the arrow in 3D.

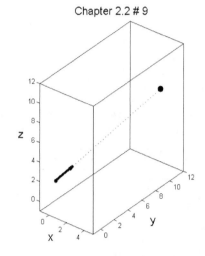

- Plot the points $H(0,0,2)$ and $P(4,10,8)$ with a dashed line connecting them.

- Find the point T (arrow tip) which is 2 units from H in the direction of P. Getting a unit vector in MATLAB® is easily done with the **norm** command: **u = v/norm(v);**, then $T = 2\mathbf{u} + H$.

- Plot the directed line segment from H to T. You may want to use the **vectarrow.m** program (available from the textbook's program repository).

- Format the plot so it looks like the arrow is pointing toward P.

10.* (**MATLAB**®)Create a program which does the following:

(a) Plots $\mathbf{u} = \langle -2, 5, 7 \rangle$ and $\mathbf{v} = \langle 4, 3, -3 \rangle$ in red and green respectively.

(b) Plots $u + v$ in blue and $u - v$ in black.

(c) Make sure you can *see* what is happening with vector addition (tip to tail) and vector subtraction (tip to tip). You may need to rotate the screen to help visualize these. You should end up with a graph similar to the one below.

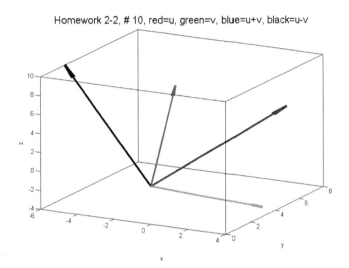

Homework 2-2, # 10, red=u, green=v, blue=u+v, black=u-v

11. Using the points P and Q depicted in the figure, find the point S which is three units from the point P in the direction of Q.

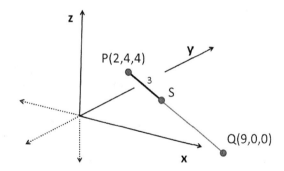

2.3   The Dot Product

In the previous chapter the **dot product** of two vectors was introduced. It played a critical role in describing how matrix multiplication worked and, as such, how one might solve a system of equations or perform transformations of various types. Here we use the dot product again. In the vector space of $\mathbb{R}^2$ and $\mathbb{R}^3$ (2D and 3D) the dot product is used for many practical purposes such as projecting a vector onto another vector or plane. In my opinion, the dot product is the most important operation in 3D mathematics. Another important operation is the **cross product**, which also has some very practical uses and properties. In this section we investigate the dot product and save the cross product for the next section.

We will start right off with vectors in 3-space. The dot product of $\mathbf{u}$ and $\mathbf{v}$ is defined by

$$\mathbf{u} \cdot \mathbf{v} = \langle u_1, u_2, u_3 \rangle \cdot \langle v_1, v_2, v_3 \rangle = u_1 v_1 + u_2 v_2 + u_3 v_3 \tag{2.5}$$

which should be familiar to you from the previous chapter. The dot product described here satisfies the same properties as the dot product described in the previous chapter. For example: $\mathbf{u} \cdot (\mathbf{v} + \mathbf{w}) = \mathbf{u} \cdot \mathbf{v} + \mathbf{u} \cdot \mathbf{w}$. While we are reviewing stuff, it is worth noting that the dot product can help us get the length of a vector by the equation

$$||\mathbf{u}||^2 = \mathbf{u} \cdot \mathbf{u} \tag{2.6}$$

because $||\mathbf{u}||^2 = \left(\sqrt{u_1^2 + u_2^2 + u_3^2} \right)^2 = u_1^2 + u_2^2 + u_3^2 = \mathbf{u} \cdot \mathbf{u}$.

Before continuing, it is worth noting that two distinct vectors in space define a plane in that space. In that plane, there is an angle created by the two vectors $\mathbf{u}$ and $\mathbf{v}$. We will call that angle θ and assume that $0 \le \theta \le \pi$ ($0 \le \theta \le 180^o$). What makes the dot product so special is the equivalent definition which can be derived using the law of cosines:

$$\mathbf{u} \cdot \mathbf{v} = ||\mathbf{u}||\,||\mathbf{v}||\,\cos(\theta). \tag{2.7}$$

♣ **Mini-Proof:**

By the *Law of Cosines*

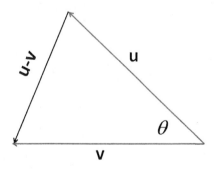

$$
\begin{aligned}
||\mathbf{u}||^2 + ||\mathbf{v}||^2 - 2\,||\mathbf{u}||\,||\mathbf{v}||\,\cos\theta &= ||\mathbf{u} - \mathbf{v}||^2 \\
&= (\mathbf{u} - \mathbf{v}) \cdot (\mathbf{u} - \mathbf{v}) \\
&= \mathbf{u} \cdot \mathbf{u} - 2\,\mathbf{u} \cdot \mathbf{v} + \mathbf{v} \cdot \mathbf{v} \\
&= ||\mathbf{u}||^2 - 2\,\mathbf{u} \cdot \mathbf{v} + ||\mathbf{v}||^2
\end{aligned}
$$

and subtracting $||\mathbf{u}||^2 + ||\mathbf{v}||^2$ from both sides

$$
\begin{aligned}
-2\,||\mathbf{u}||\,||\mathbf{v}||\,\cos\theta &= -2\,\mathbf{u} \cdot \mathbf{v} \\
||\mathbf{u}||\,||\mathbf{v}||\,\cos\theta &= \mathbf{u} \cdot \mathbf{v} \qquad ♣
\end{aligned}
$$

Equation (2.7) allows us to easily determine the angle between vectors by

$$\cos(\theta) = \frac{\mathbf{u} \cdot \mathbf{v}}{||\mathbf{u}|| \, ||\mathbf{v}||} \quad \text{or} \quad \theta = \arccos\left(\frac{\mathbf{u} \cdot \mathbf{v}}{||\mathbf{u}|| \, ||\mathbf{v}||}\right). \tag{2.8}$$

Note: The arccosine function is denoted arccos in text. On calculators it is often denoted $\cos^{-1}$ (cosine inverse). In software, is it usually called with a function like `acos`.

In addition to getting the angle between vectors, equation (2.8) allows us to learn a lot about the angle between two vectors without any trigonometry. The following sequence of graphs depicts this information.

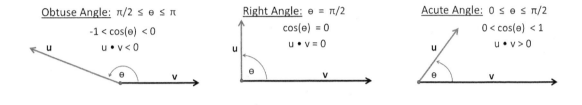

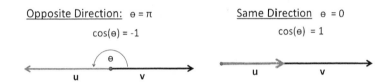

Example: Consider the two vectors, $\mathbf{u} = \langle 1, 2, 3 \rangle$ and $\mathbf{v} = \langle -1, 3, 5 \rangle$.

- Using only the dot product. Determine if the angle between the two vectors less than, more than, or equal to 90°.

  Answer: $\mathbf{u} \cdot \mathbf{v} = -1 + 6 + 15 = 20$. Since this is greater than zero, we know the angle is acute and therefore less 90°.

- Determine the angle between the two vectors.

  Answer: $\cos(\theta) = \dfrac{\mathbf{u} \cdot \mathbf{v}}{||\mathbf{u}|| \, ||\mathbf{v}||} = \dfrac{20}{\sqrt{14}\sqrt{35}}$. Using software, $\theta = \arccos\left(\frac{20}{\sqrt{14}\sqrt{35}}\right) \approx 0.443$ radians or 25.4^o.

1. **Definition of Orthogonal Vectors:** The vectors $\mathbf{u}$ and $\mathbf{v}$ are **orthogonal** if $\mathbf{u} \cdot \mathbf{v} = 0$

   Example: Prove that the vectors $\mathbf{u} = \langle 1, -2, 3 \rangle$ and $\mathbf{v} = \langle 2, -2, -2 \rangle$ are orthogonal.

   Answer: $\mathbf{u} \cdot \mathbf{v} = 2 + 4 - 6 = 0$ and the vectors are orthogonal.

2. **Projections:** The projection of $\mathbf{u}$ onto $\mathbf{v}$, denoted $\text{Proj}_{\mathbf{v}}\mathbf{u}$, is given by

$$\text{Proj}_{\mathbf{v}}\mathbf{u} = \left(\frac{\mathbf{u} \cdot \mathbf{v}}{||\mathbf{v}||^2} \right) \mathbf{v}. \qquad (2.9)$$

   This will prove to be very useful. We are able to do projections without any trigonometry!

   ♣ **Mini-Proof:** This must be done in two separate situations: $0 \le \theta \le \pi/2$ and $\pi/2 \le \theta < \pi$. If $\theta = \pi/2$ (90°) then the projection equals the zero vector.

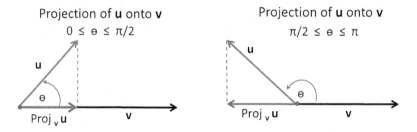

$$\text{Proj}_{\mathbf{v}}\mathbf{u} = ||\mathbf{u}|| \cos(\theta) \frac{\mathbf{v}}{||\mathbf{v}||} = ||\mathbf{u}|| \frac{\mathbf{u} \cdot \mathbf{v}}{||\mathbf{u}|| \, ||\mathbf{v}||} \frac{\mathbf{v}}{||\mathbf{v}||} = \left(\frac{\mathbf{u} \cdot \mathbf{v}}{||\mathbf{v}||^2} \right) \mathbf{v} \qquad ♣$$

3. **Examples:**

   (a) Let $\mathbf{u} = \langle -2, 2 \rangle$ and $\mathbf{v} = \langle 0, 3 \rangle$ find $\text{Proj}_{\mathbf{v}}\mathbf{u}$ and $\text{Proj}_{\mathbf{u}}\mathbf{v}$.

   $\text{Proj}_{\mathbf{v}}\mathbf{u} = \left(\frac{\mathbf{u} \cdot \mathbf{v}}{||\mathbf{v}||^2} \right) \mathbf{v} = \left(\frac{6}{9} \right) \langle 0, 3 \rangle = \langle 0, 2 \rangle.$ Notice: $\text{Proj}_{\mathbf{v}}\mathbf{u}$ is parallel to $\mathbf{v}$.

   $\text{Proj}_{\mathbf{u}}\mathbf{v} = \left(\frac{\mathbf{v} \cdot \mathbf{u}}{||\mathbf{u}||^2} \right) \mathbf{u} = \left(\frac{6}{8} \right) \langle -2, 2 \rangle = \langle -1.5, 1.5 \rangle.$ Notice: $\text{Proj}_{\mathbf{u}}\mathbf{v}$ is parallel to $\mathbf{u}$.

   $\text{Proj}_{(-\mathbf{u})}\mathbf{v} = \left(\frac{\mathbf{v} \cdot (-\mathbf{u})}{||-\mathbf{u}||^2} \right) (-\mathbf{u}) = \left(\frac{-6}{8} \right) \langle 2, -2 \rangle = \langle -1.5, 1.5 \rangle.$ Notice: $\text{Proj}_{(-\mathbf{u})}\mathbf{v} = \text{Proj}_{\mathbf{u}}\mathbf{v}$

   (b) Let $\mathbf{u} = \langle -2, 2, 1 \rangle$ and $\mathbf{v} = \langle 1, 0, 3 \rangle$ find $\text{Proj}_{\mathbf{v}}\mathbf{u}$ and $\text{Proj}_{\mathbf{u}}\mathbf{v}$.

   $\text{Proj}_{\mathbf{v}}\mathbf{u} = \left(\frac{\mathbf{u} \cdot \mathbf{v}}{||\mathbf{v}||^2} \right) \mathbf{v} = \left(\frac{1}{10} \right) \langle 1, 0, 3 \rangle = \langle 0.1, 0, 0.3 \rangle.$ Notice: $\text{Proj}_{\mathbf{v}}\mathbf{u}$ is parallel to $\mathbf{v}$.

   $\text{Proj}_{\mathbf{u}}\mathbf{v} = \left(\frac{\mathbf{v} \cdot \mathbf{u}}{||\mathbf{u}||^2} \right) \mathbf{u} = \left(\frac{1}{9} \right) \langle -2, 2, 1 \rangle = \langle \frac{-2}{9}, \frac{2}{9}, \frac{1}{9} \rangle.$ Notice: $\text{Proj}_{\mathbf{u}}\mathbf{v}$ is parallel to $\mathbf{u}$.

   $\text{Proj}_{\mathbf{u}}(-\mathbf{v}) = \left(\frac{-\mathbf{v} \cdot \mathbf{u}}{||\mathbf{u}||^2} \right) \mathbf{u} = \left(\frac{-1}{9} \right) \langle -2, 2, 1 \rangle = \langle \frac{2}{9}, \frac{-2}{9}, \frac{-1}{9} \rangle.$ Notice: $\text{Proj}_{\mathbf{u}}(-\mathbf{v}) = -\text{Proj}_{\mathbf{u}}\mathbf{v}$.

4. **Application:** As an object moves through 2 or 3 space it will run into other objects. Let's consider the case where an object hits a wall. There are two standard responses to hitting a wall. The object can *slide* along the wall in a way indicative of the way how it hit the wall. On the other hand, if we are talking about a ball or some projectile, it may bounce off the wall at an appropriate angle (angle of incidence = angle of reflection). For now we stick with 2D because in 3D we will look at collisions with planes and we haven't studied these yet. Let M represent the initial point of the object. Let the vector $\mathbf{v} = \overrightarrow{MQ}$ represent the velocity vector which tells us the direction and distance of motion. At point P, the object hits the wall defined by the vector $\mathbf{w}$.

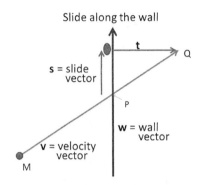

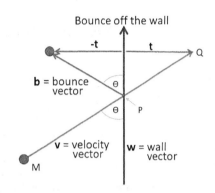

Slide Response:

The slide vector is $\mathbf{s} = \text{Proj}_{\mathbf{w}} \overrightarrow{PQ}$.

The final location of the ball is then $P + \mathbf{s}$.

Bounce Response:

Well $\mathbf{t} = \overrightarrow{PQ} - \mathbf{s}$ and $\mathbf{b} = \mathbf{s} - \mathbf{t}$.

So the bounce vector is $\mathbf{b} = 2\mathbf{s} - \overrightarrow{PQ}$.

The final location of the ball is $P + \mathbf{b}$.

5. **Example:.** Determine the final location of the guy (or ball) for a slide and a bounce if $M = (0,0)$, $\mathbf{v} = \langle 12, 9 \rangle$, and a wall is at $x = 8$.

Answers: First you need P at the intersection of $\mathbf{v}$ and $x = 8$. The line containing $\mathbf{v}$ is $y = 9/12x$. When $x = 8$, $y = 6$. So $P = (8, 6)$.

$\mathbf{w} = \langle 0, k \rangle$ for any $k > 0$.

$\overrightarrow{PQ} = Q(12, 9) - P(8, 6) = \langle 4, 3 \rangle$

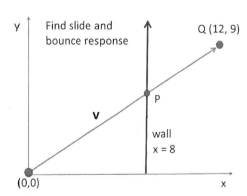

Slide: $\quad \mathbf{s} = \text{Proj}_{\mathbf{w}} \overrightarrow{PQ} = \left(\dfrac{\mathbf{w} \cdot \overrightarrow{PQ}}{||\mathbf{w}||^2} \right) \mathbf{w} = \dfrac{3k}{k^2} \langle 0, k \rangle = \langle 0, 3 \rangle$, and the final point is $(8, 9)$.

Bounce: $\quad \mathbf{b} = 2\mathbf{s} - \overrightarrow{PQ} = 2 \langle 0, 3 \rangle - \langle 4, 3 \rangle = \langle -4, 3 \rangle$, and the final point is $(4, 9)$.

6. **MATLAB®️ Demonstration:** Here we use MATLAB®️ to perform the last example.

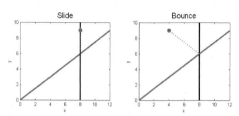

```
function [w] = ProjUV(u,v)
% Project the vector u in the direction of v
% Vectors u and v must be the same length.
% This returns w - same dimensions as v.
[nu,mu] = size(u);
[nv,mv] = size(v);
if max(size(u)) ~= max(size(v)) | min(size(u)) ~= min(size(v))
    error('must be vectors of the same length')
    abort;
end
w = dot(u,v)/(norm(v))^2 * v;
```

```
%% Plotting_Projections.m
% Calculating projections with ProjUV function and plotting in 2D.
clc; clf; clear;  % clear console, figure, and all variables

%% Start
M = [0 0]; % origin
P = [8 6];  % collision point (you have to determine this)
Q = [12 9]; % terminal point of v
w1 = [8 0];  % bottom of the wall
w2 = [8 10]; % top of the wall
PQ = Q - P;  % vector PQ
w = w2 - w1;  % wall vector
s = ProjUV(PQ,w);  % slide vector = Projection of PQ onto w.
b = 2*s - PQ;     % bounce vector
SlidePoint = P + s; % endpoint of slide
BouncePoint = P + b; % endpoint of bounce

subplot(121)
plot([M(1),Q(1)],[M(2),Q(2)],'r-','linewidth',3); hold on;
plot([w1(1),w2(1)],[w1(2),w2(2)], 'k-','linewidth',3);
plot([SlidePoint(1)],[SlidePoint(2)], 'r.','markersize',30);
plot([P(1),SlidePoint(1)],[P(2),SlidePoint(2)], 'r:','linewidth',3);
xlabel('x'); ylabel('y'); title('Slide','fontsize',16);
axis equal; axis([0,12,0,10]);

subplot(122)
plot([M(1),Q(1)],[M(2),Q(2)],'r-','linewidth',3); hold on;
plot([w1(1),w2(1)],[w1(2),w2(2)], 'k-','linewidth',3);
plot([BouncePoint(1)],[BouncePoint(2)], 'r.','markersize',30);
plot([P(1),BouncePoint(1)],[P(2),BouncePoint(2)], 'r:','linewidth',3);
xlabel('x'); ylabel('y'); title('Bounce','fontsize',16);
axis equal; axis([0,12,0,10]);
```

Chapter 2.3 Problem Set

Numbers with an asterisk[*] have solutions in the back of the book.

1. For the following vectors, find a) $\mathbf{u} \cdot \mathbf{v}$,   b) $\mathbf{u} \cdot \mathbf{u}$,   c) $||\mathbf{u}||^2$,   d) $2(\mathbf{u} \cdot \mathbf{v})\,\mathbf{v}$

    (a)[*] $\mathbf{u} = \langle 3, 4 \rangle$ and $\mathbf{v} = \langle 2, -3 \rangle$

    (b) $\mathbf{u} = \langle 2, -3, 4 \rangle$ and $\mathbf{v} = \langle 1, 0, -1 \rangle$

2. Find $\mathbf{u} \cdot \mathbf{v}$

    (a)[*] $||\mathbf{u}|| = 8$, $||\mathbf{v}|| = 3$, and the angle between $\mathbf{u}$ and $\mathbf{v}$ is 35°.

    (b) $||\mathbf{u}|| = 2$, $||\mathbf{v}|| = 6$, and the angle between $\mathbf{u}$ and $\mathbf{v}$ is $\frac{\pi}{2}$.

3. Find the angle θ between the vectors.

    (a)[*] $\mathbf{u} = \langle 1, 1 \rangle$ and $\mathbf{v} = \langle 2, -2 \rangle$

    (b) $\mathbf{u} = \langle 1, 1, 1 \rangle$ and $\mathbf{v} = \langle 2, 1, -1 \rangle$

4. Find the cosine of the angle between the given vectors. Determine whether $\mathbf{u}$ and $\mathbf{v}$ are orthogonal, parallel (same direction or opposite), or neither. If neither, determine whether the angle between them is acute or obtuse.

    (a)[*] $\mathbf{u} = \langle 4, 0 \rangle$ and $\mathbf{v} = \langle 1, 1 \rangle$

    (b) $\mathbf{u} = \langle 2, 18 \rangle$ and $\mathbf{v} = \left\langle \frac{3}{2}, \frac{-1}{6} \right\rangle$

    (c)[*] $\mathbf{u} = \langle 2, -3, 1 \rangle$ and $\mathbf{v} = \langle -1, 1, -1 \rangle$

    (d) $\mathbf{u} = \langle \cos(\theta), \sin(\theta), -1 \rangle$ and $\mathbf{v} = \langle \sin(\theta), -\cos(\theta), 0 \rangle$

5.[*] Determine the value of w needed to make $\mathbf{u}$ and $\mathbf{v}$ orthogonal.

    (a) $\mathbf{u} = \langle 3, -2, 1 \rangle$ is orthogonal to $\mathbf{v} = \langle 1, 2, w \rangle$.

    (b) $\mathbf{u} = \langle 3, w, 1 \rangle$ is orthogonal to $\mathbf{v} = \langle w, 5, 4 \rangle$.

6. Find $\mathrm{Proj}_{\mathbf{v}}\mathbf{u}$ for the following vectors.

    (a)[*] $\mathbf{u} = \langle 4, 0 \rangle$ and $\mathbf{v} = \langle 1, 1 \rangle$

    (b) $\mathbf{u} = \langle 2, 18 \rangle$ and $\mathbf{v} = \left\langle \frac{3}{2}, \frac{-1}{6} \right\rangle$

    (c)[*] $\mathbf{u} = \langle 2, -3, 1 \rangle$ and $\mathbf{v} = \langle -1, 1, -1 \rangle$

7. Determine the point R from the figure.
Give your answer exactly or round to two decimal places.

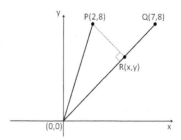

8.* Determine which of the following are well-defined for nonzero vectors **u**, **v**, and **w** of equal length.

    (a) $\mathbf{u} \cdot (\mathbf{v} + \mathbf{w})$

    (b) $\mathbf{u} \cdot \mathbf{v} + \mathbf{w}$

    (c) $(\mathbf{u} \cdot \mathbf{v})\, \mathbf{w}$

    (d) $(\mathbf{u} \cdot \mathbf{v}) \cdot \mathbf{w}$

    (e) $\|\mathbf{u}\|(\mathbf{v} + \mathbf{w})$

9.* (**MATLAB®**): Given $\mathbf{u} = \langle 3, -1, 2 \rangle$ and $\mathbf{v} = \langle 2, 2, 3 \rangle$. Use MATLAB® to plot both vectors in 3D. On the same graph plot the the projection of **u** onto **v**. Title the graph to distinguish which vector is which. Finally, use the `acos` (MATLAB® 's arccosine function) to determine the angle between **u** and **v** in **degrees**.

10. (**MATLAB®**): A ball starts at (0,0) and follows the velocity vector shown in the figure. It eventually hits the wall at point P. Use MATLAB® to demonstrate a slide response and a bounce response to the collision. Return the endpoint of each type of response. Use `axis equal;` to make sure these responses *look* right.

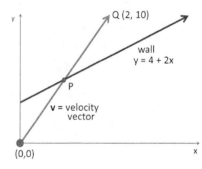

11.* Use the definition of the $\text{Proj}_{\mathbf{v}}\mathbf{u}$ to prove the following identities.

    (a)* $\text{Proj}_{(-\mathbf{v})}\mathbf{u} = \text{Proj}_{\mathbf{v}}\mathbf{u}$
    (b) $\text{Proj}_{\mathbf{v}}(-\mathbf{u}) = -\text{Proj}_{\mathbf{v}}\mathbf{u}$.

12.* Suppose you are given 2 distinct points P and Q in 2D or 3D. Write an algorithm that would determine whether a given point R lies on the line determined by the points P and Q. You don't have to code this up, just map the flow-chart or write pseudo-code describing the process. Hint: Find the cosine of the angle between $\overrightarrow{PQ}$ and $\overrightarrow{PR}$. These vectors are parallel if the cosine of the angle is $\pm\, 1$.

2.4 The Cross Product

The cross product is very different from the dot product. First, the cross product is used almost exclusively for vectors in $\mathbb{R}^3$. Second, the dot product returns a scalar while the cross product returns a vector. The important feature of this vector is that it is perpendicular (normal or orthogonal) to both of the original vectors. We start with the formal definition of the cross-product.

1. **Definition:** If $\mathbf{u} = \langle u_1, u_2, u_3 \rangle$ and $\mathbf{v} = \langle v_1, v_2, v_3 \rangle$ then the **cross product** of $\mathbf{u}$ and $\mathbf{v}$ is

$$\mathbf{u} \times \mathbf{v} = \langle (u_2 v_3 - u_3 v_2), \ -(u_1 v_3 - u_3 v_1), \ (u_1 v_2 - u_2 v_1) \rangle \tag{2.10}$$

2. The above definition is difficult (or impossible) to remember. Here is another way of describing it when the vectors are written in terms of the standard unit vectors and the cross product is described by the determinant of a special matrix.

   Let $\mathbf{u} = u_1 \mathbf{i} + u_2 \mathbf{j} + u_3 \mathbf{k}$ and $\mathbf{v} = v_1 \mathbf{i} + v_2 \mathbf{j} + v_3 \mathbf{k}$

   then

$$\mathbf{u} \times \mathbf{v} = \begin{vmatrix} \mathbf{i} & \mathbf{j} & \mathbf{k} \\ u_1 & u_2 & u_3 \\ v_1 & v_2 & v_3 \end{vmatrix}$$

   or

$$\mathbf{u} \times \mathbf{v} = (u_2 v_3 - u_3 v_2)\mathbf{i} - (u_1 v_3 - u_3 v_1)\mathbf{j} + (u_1 v_2 - u_2 v_1)\mathbf{k}$$

3. **Algebraic Properties:** If $\mathbf{u}$, $\mathbf{v}$, and $\mathbf{w}$ are vectors and c is a scalar

   - $\mathbf{u} \times \mathbf{v} = -(\mathbf{v} \times \mathbf{u})$
   - $\mathbf{u} \times (\mathbf{v} + \mathbf{w}) = \mathbf{u} \times \mathbf{v} + \mathbf{u} \times \mathbf{w}$
   - $c\,(\mathbf{u} \times \mathbf{v}) = c\,\mathbf{u} \times \mathbf{v} = \mathbf{u} \times c\,\mathbf{v}$
   - $\mathbf{u} \times \mathbf{0} = \mathbf{0} \times \mathbf{u} = \mathbf{0}$
   - $\mathbf{u} \times \mathbf{u} = \mathbf{0}$
   - $\mathbf{u} \cdot (\mathbf{v} \times \mathbf{w}) = (\mathbf{u} \times \mathbf{v}) \cdot \mathbf{w}$

4. **Geometric Properties:** If $\mathbf{u}$ and $\mathbf{v}$ are vectors, θ is the angle between them, and c is a scalar:

   - $\mathbf{u} \times \mathbf{v}$ is orthogonal to both $\mathbf{u}$ and $\mathbf{v}$.
   - $\|\mathbf{u} \times \mathbf{v}\| = \|\mathbf{u}\| \, \|\mathbf{v}\| \, \sin \theta$
   - $\|c\mathbf{u} \times \mathbf{v}\| = \|\mathbf{u} \times c\mathbf{v}\| = |c| \, \|\mathbf{u} \times \mathbf{v}\|$
   - $\mathbf{u} \times \mathbf{v} = \mathbf{0}$ if and only if $\mathbf{u}$ and $\mathbf{v}$ are scalar multiples of each other.
   - $\|\mathbf{u} \times \mathbf{v}\| =$ the area of the parallelogram having $\mathbf{u}$ and $\mathbf{v}$ as adjacent sides.
   - $|\mathbf{w} \cdot (\mathbf{u} \times \mathbf{v})| =$ the volume of the parallelepiped spanned by $\mathbf{u}$, $\mathbf{v}$, and $\mathbf{w}$.

5. **Example:** Given $\mathbf{u} = \langle 0, 1, 5 \rangle$ and $\mathbf{v} = \langle -1, 0, -2 \rangle$, find $\mathbf{u} \times \mathbf{v}$ and $\mathbf{v} \times \mathbf{u}$. Then verify (a) that $\mathbf{u} \times \mathbf{v} = -\mathbf{v} \times \mathbf{u}$, (b) that $\mathbf{u} \times \mathbf{v}$ is orthogonal to both $\mathbf{u}$ and $\mathbf{v}$, and (c) that $\mathbf{v} \times \mathbf{u}$ is orthogonal to $\mathbf{u}$ and $\mathbf{v}$.

$$\text{Let } \mathbf{w}_1 = \mathbf{u} \times \mathbf{v} = \begin{vmatrix} \mathbf{i} & \mathbf{j} & \mathbf{k} \\ 0 & 1 & 5 \\ -1 & 0 & -2 \end{vmatrix} = -2\mathbf{i} - 5\mathbf{j} + 1\mathbf{k} = \langle -2, -5, 1 \rangle.$$

$$\text{Let } \mathbf{w}_2 = \mathbf{v} \times \mathbf{u} = \begin{vmatrix} \mathbf{i} & \mathbf{j} & \mathbf{k} \\ -1 & 0 & -2 \\ 0 & 1 & 5 \end{vmatrix} = 2\mathbf{i} + 5\mathbf{j} - 1\mathbf{k} = \langle 2, 5, -1 \rangle.$$

(a) Notice from above that $\mathbf{u} \times \mathbf{v} = -\mathbf{v} \times \mathbf{u}$.

(b) Recall, two vectors are orthogonal if their dot product is zero. Notice $\mathbf{w}_1 \cdot \mathbf{u} = 0$ and $\mathbf{w}_1 \cdot \mathbf{v} = 0$, therefore $\mathbf{u} \times \mathbf{v}$ is orthogonal to both $\mathbf{u}$ and $\mathbf{v}$.

(c) Likewise, $\mathbf{w}_2 \cdot \mathbf{u} = 0$ and $\mathbf{w}_2 \cdot \mathbf{v} = 0$, therefore $\mathbf{v} \times \mathbf{u}$ is orthogonal to both $\mathbf{u}$ and $\mathbf{v}$.

6. **The right-hand rule:** We know that $\mathbf{u} \times \mathbf{v}$ is orthogonal to both $\mathbf{u}$ and $\mathbf{v}$. Consider the plane containing $\mathbf{u}$ and $\mathbf{v}$. There are two possible vectors that are orthogonal to both $\mathbf{u}$ and $\mathbf{v}$. They point in opposite directions. Which one is $\mathbf{u} \times \mathbf{v}$? We use the right-hand rule to make this determination. Hold out your right hand and curl your fingers from $\mathbf{u}$ to $\mathbf{v}$ via the smaller angle. Now, your thumb is pointing in the direction of $\mathbf{u} \times \mathbf{v}$.

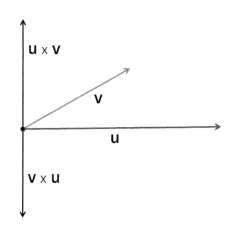

7. **Application in Physics:**
The **moment M** of a force $\mathbf{F}$ about a point P applied at the point Q is given by

$$\mathbf{M} = \overrightarrow{PQ} \times \mathbf{F}.$$

This is also called the **torque vector** and $\|\mathbf{M}\|$ is called the **torque** which is a measure of the tendency for the vector $\overrightarrow{PQ}$ to rotate counterclockwise (using the right hand rule) about the axis directed along the vector $\mathbf{M}$.

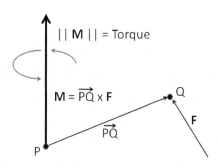

Notice, if $\overrightarrow{PQ}$ is longer (longer wrench) or the force $\mathbf{F}$ is increased, then the torque is increased.

8. **Application in Graphics:** Back-face culling $\rightarrow$ Clockwise or Counter-Clockwise

When rendering images on a computer, you may only want to render the surfaces facing the camera. The vertices of objects can be ordered in such a way that only those appearing (from the camera's perspective) in a clockwise order will be rendered. So the question becomes; How can we take a set of points and a given camera position and determine whether or not the ordered points *appear* in a clockwise or counter-clockwise fashion from the camera's perspective?

Getting Started:

- Let A, B, and C represent the vertices in question

- $\overrightarrow{AB} \times \overrightarrow{AC}$ produces a vector orthogonal to both $\overrightarrow{AB}$ and $\overrightarrow{AC}$.

- Using the *right-hand-rule*, the vertices A, B, and C appear in a *counter-clockwise* fashion from the perspective of any point on $\overrightarrow{AB} \times \overrightarrow{AC}$

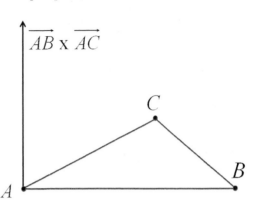

Now we introduce a point P representing the camera position. Recall from the previous section

- If $\mathbf{u} \cdot \mathbf{v} > 0$ the angle between $\mathbf{u}$ and $\mathbf{v}$ is acute ($< 90^o$).

- If $\mathbf{u} \cdot \mathbf{v} < 0$ the angle between $\mathbf{u}$ and $\mathbf{v}$ is obtuse ($> 90^0$).

Let θ be the angle between $\overrightarrow{AP}$ and $\overrightarrow{AB} \times \overrightarrow{AC}$.

If $\overrightarrow{AP} \cdot \left(\overrightarrow{AB} \times \overrightarrow{AC} \right) > 0$ then $\theta < 90^o$

If $\overrightarrow{AP} \cdot \left(\overrightarrow{AB} \times \overrightarrow{AC} \right) < 0$ then $\theta > 90^o$

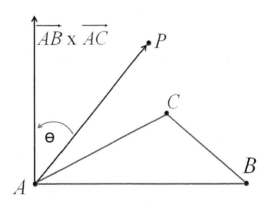

With respect to P, the orientation of A, B, and C is

$$\begin{aligned} \text{counter-clockwise} \quad &\Longleftrightarrow \quad \overrightarrow{AP} \cdot \left(\overrightarrow{AB} \times \overrightarrow{AC} \right) > 0 \\ \text{clockwise} \quad &\Longleftrightarrow \quad \overrightarrow{AP} \cdot \left(\overrightarrow{AB} \times \overrightarrow{AC} \right) < 0 \end{aligned}$$

9. **Demonstration:** Calculating Cross Products and Graphing Them.

MATLAB® has a built-in Cross Product function called `cross`. Here again, we use the `vectarrow` function to graph the vectors.

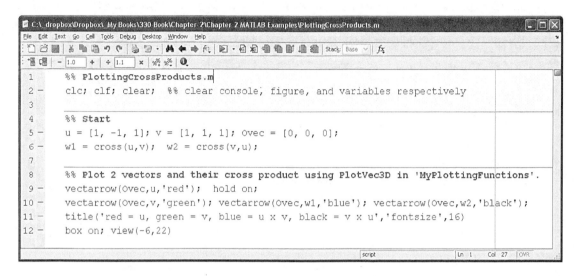

```matlab
%% PlottingCrossProducts.m
clc; clf; clear;  %% clear console, figure, and variables respectively

%% Start
u = [1, -1, 1]; v = [1, 1, 1]; Ovec = [0, 0, 0];
w1 = cross(u,v);  w2 = cross(v,u);

%% Plot 2 vectors and their cross product using PlotVec3D in 'MyPlottingFunctions'.
vectarrow(Ovec,u,'red');  hold on;
vectarrow(Ovec,v,'green'); vectarrow(Ovec,w1,'blue'); vectarrow(Ovec,w2,'black');
title('red = u, green = v, blue = u x v, black = v x u','fontsize',16)
box on; view(-6,22)
```

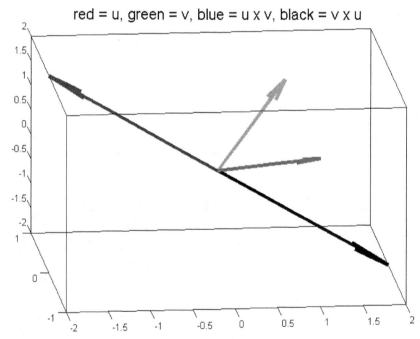

Chapter 2.4 Problem Set

Numbers with an asterisk* have solutions in the back of the book.

1.* Suppose $\mathbf{u} \times \mathbf{v} = \mathbf{w}$. What can be said about the following?

    (a) $\mathbf{v} \times \mathbf{u}$

    (b) $-\mathbf{u} \times \mathbf{v}$

    (c) $\|2\,\mathbf{u} \times 2\,\mathbf{v}\|$

    (d) $\mathbf{w} \cdot \mathbf{u}$

2. Given the vectors $\mathbf{u}$ and $\mathbf{v}$ below, find two **unit** vectors that are orthogonal to both.

    (a)* $\mathbf{u} = \langle 1, -1, 1 \rangle$ and $\mathbf{v} = \langle -2, 3, 0 \rangle$.

    (b) $\mathbf{u} = \langle 2, -1, 1 \rangle$ and $\mathbf{v} = \langle -2, 3, 6 \rangle$.

3. (**MATLAB**®): Given $\mathbf{u} = \langle 3, -1, 2 \rangle$ and $\mathbf{v} = \langle 2, 2, 3 \rangle$. Use MATLAB® to plot both vectors in 3D. On the same graph plot $\mathbf{u} \times \mathbf{v}$ and $\mathbf{v} \times \mathbf{u}$. Be sure to set the camera so that it is clear to the viewer that both are orthogonal to the original vectors. They point in opposite direction. Verify the right hand rule visually. Print up the resulting figure and attach it to the homework.

4. (**MATLAB**®): Grab the MATLAB® file `Culling.m` from the Chapter 2 program repository. Run it. It will give you the points A, B, and C which form a triangle. It also plots a camera point. Your task is to edit the program so that the title of the graph tells whether the points appear in a clockwise or counter-clockwise fashion from the perspective of the camera.

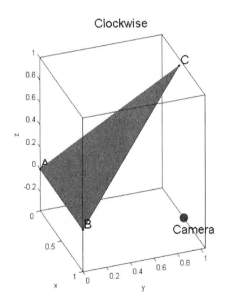 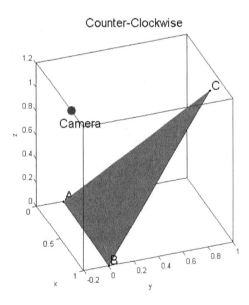

The *starter-code* is depicted on the next page. It can be found at
http://cosmos.champlain.edu/people/stevens/MV3D/index.html

C:_dropbox\Dropbox_My Books\MV3D-Book\Chapter-2\Chapter 2 MATLAB Examples\Culling.m

File   Edit   Text   Go   Cell   Tools   Debug   Desktop   Window   Help

```
1        %% This is Culling.m
2          % You complete the program and title the figure as to whether or not
3          % the points A,B,C appear clockwise or counter-clockwise from the
4          % perspective of the camera.
5 -      clc; clf; clear;  % clear console, figure, variables.
6
7        %% The Vertices under consideration
8 -      A = [0,0,0];
9 -      B = [1,0,0];
10 -     C = [.5,1,1];
11
12       %% The Camera P
13 -     den = randi([1,3],1); r = (1- 2*randi([0,1],1))
14 -     P = 1/den*(A+B+C) + r*cross(B-A,C-A)/norm(cross(B-A,C-A));
15
16       %% Plotting Stuff
17 -     X = [A(1),B(1),C(1)];  Y = [A(2),B(2),C(2)];  Z = [A(3),B(3),C(3)];
18 -     plot3(X,Y,Z,'k.','markersize',10); hold on;    % Plots the vertices
19 -     fill3(X,Y,Z,'r');                              %% fills the triangle
20 -     plot3(P(1),P(2),P(3),'b.','markersize',40);    % places the camera
21 -     text(A(1)+.01,A(2)+.01,A(3)+.05,'A','fontsize',16)
22 -     text(B(1)+.01,B(2)+.01,B(3)+.05,'B','fontsize',16)
23 -     text(C(1)+.01,C(2)+.01,C(3)+.05,'C','fontsize',16)
24 -     text(P(1)+.01,P(2)-.1,P(3)-.08,'Camera','fontsize',16)
25 -     axis equal; box on; xlabel('x'); ylabel('y'); zlabel('z');
26 -     view(70,30);
27
28       %%  You take it from here and label accordingly
29 -     if 1 > 0   %% A dummy test to choose the title.
30 -         title('Clockwise or Counter-Clockwise','fontsize',16)
31 -     else
32 -         title('Clockwise or Counter-Clockwise','fontsize',16)
33 -     end
```

script   Ln 33   Col 4   OVR

2.5   Lines and Curves in Space

Here we study **parametric equations** or **vector-valued functions**. We used these types of functions when we plotted circles and ellipses in past exercises. We start with lines and move on to curves and trajectories later in this section.

2.5.1   Lines in 3-Space

Equations for a Line in Space: When seeking the equation for a line in 3D we need a point and a direction vector.

A line L parallel to the vector $\mathbf{v} = \langle a, b, c \rangle$ and passing through the point $P(x_1, y_1, z_1)$ is represented by the **parametric equations**

$$x = x_1 + at, \quad y = y_1 + bt, \quad z = z_1 + ct \quad \text{for} \quad t \in (-\infty, \infty). \tag{2.11}$$

The vector $\mathbf{v}$ is called the **direction vector** and a, b, c are called the **direction numbers**.

♣ *Mini-Proof:* If $Q(x, y, z)$ is a point on L then $\overrightarrow{PQ} = \langle x - x_1, y - y_1, z - z_1 \rangle$ is parallel to $\mathbf{v} = \langle a, b, c \rangle$. This means that $\overrightarrow{PQ} = t\mathbf{v}$ where t is a scalar. Therefore,

$$
\begin{aligned}
x - x_1 = at &\iff x = x_1 + at \\
y - y_1 = bt &\iff y = y_1 + bt \\
z - z_1 = ct &\iff z = z_1 + ct
\end{aligned}
$$

and the second column gives us the equations in (2.11) for all points on the line.   ♣.

- **Example, Finding a line from a point and a direction vector:** Find the parametric equations for the line through the point (3, -2, 0) parallel to the vector $\mathbf{v} = \langle -2, 0, -1 \rangle$.

  Answer: $x = 3 - 2t, \quad y = -2, \quad z = -t$

- **Example, Finding a line from two points:** Find the parametric equations for the line through $P(-2, 1, 0)$ and $Q(1, 3, 5)$.

  You have two points on the line (you only need one) but you also need a direction vector $\mathbf{v}$. In this case $\mathbf{v} = \overrightarrow{PQ} = \langle 1, 3, 5 \rangle - \langle -2, 1, 0 \rangle = \langle 3, 2, 5 \rangle$. Choosing the point (-2, 1, 0) as the point for describing the line, the parametric equations are

  $$x = -2 + 3t, \quad y = 1 + 2t, \quad z = 5t.$$

Note: You can use either of the two points and get an equivalent set of equations for the line. You could also use $\overrightarrow{QP}$ and the direction numbers would switch sign resulting in still another equivalent set of equations for the same line.

Parallel Lines: Two lines are parallel if their direction vectors are parallel.

- **Example, Determining if two lines are parallel.** Find the direction vectors of the two lines and determine whether the lines are parallel or not.

  1. $L_1:$ $x = 3 - 4t$, $y = 3$, $z = 1 - t$
     $L_2:$ $x = 2 + 2s$, $y = 3 + 2s$, $z = 1 - s$
     The direction vector for L_1 is $\langle -4, 0, -1 \rangle$ and the direction vector for L_2 is $\langle 2, 2, -1 \rangle$. Since these direction vectors are not scalar multiples of each other, the lines are not parallel.

  2. $L_1:$ $x = 3$, $y = 3 + t$, $z = 4 - 2t$
     $L_2:$ $x = 7$, $y = 8 + 3s$, $z = 1 - 6s$
     The direction vector for L_1 is $\langle 0, 1, -2 \rangle$ and the direction vector for L_2 is $\langle 0, 3, -6 \rangle$. Since the second is three times the first, these direction vectors are parallel and the lines are parallel.

Intersection of Lines in Space: Unlike 2D, it is quite possible that two lines in 3D do not intersect and are not parallel. They could just lie in different planes. When seeking to find the intersection of two lines in space, we need to solve a system of 3 equations in 2 unknowns. As such, you have to get pretty lucky to get a valid solution.

- **Example:** Two lines that **do not intersect**.

  Determine if the lines intersect, if so, find the point of intersection and the angle of intersection.

  $L_1:$ $x = 2 + t$, $y = 3$, $z = 1 + 4t$

  $L_2:$ $x = 5 - s$, $y = 3 + 2s$, $z = 9 + 2s$

  You need to determine if there are values for t and s where (x, y, z) are the same for both lines. So we need to solve these three equations for the two unknown values of s and t.

$$
\begin{array}{lrcl}
\text{for x:} & 2 + t & = & 5 - s \\
\text{for y:} & 3 & = & 3 + 2s \\
\text{for z:} & 1 + 4t & = & 9 + 2s
\end{array}
\sim
\begin{array}{rcl}
t + s & = & 3 \\
-2s & = & 0 \\
4t - 2s & = & 8
\end{array}
\sim
\begin{bmatrix} 1 & 1 \\ 0 & -2 \\ 4 & -2 \end{bmatrix}
\begin{bmatrix} t \\ s \end{bmatrix}
=
\begin{bmatrix} 3 \\ 0 \\ 8 \end{bmatrix}
$$

Expressing these equations in augmented matrix form, you can use Gaussian Elimination to solve for the variables (or have software do it for you but be careful of the *no solution* problems that can occur).

$$
\begin{bmatrix} 1 & 1 & | & 3 \\ 0 & -2 & | & 0 \\ 4 & -2 & | & 8 \end{bmatrix}
\sim
\begin{bmatrix} 1 & 1 & | & 3 \\ 0 & -2 & | & 0 \\ 0 & -6 & | & -4 \end{bmatrix}
\sim
\begin{bmatrix} 1 & 1 & | & 3 \\ 0 & 1 & | & 0 \\ 0 & -6 & | & -4 \end{bmatrix}
\sim
\begin{bmatrix} 1 & 1 & | & 3 \\ 0 & 1 & | & 0 \\ 0 & 0 & | & -4 \end{bmatrix}
$$

The last equation says that $0t + 0s = -4$. There are no solutions to such an equation so the lines **do not intersect**. Notice, however, the lines are not parallel.

Warning: If you try to solve this system in MATLAB® , it will not give you a warning and will produce a *least squares solution*. This is not a real solution it is just the best of all non-solutions. There will be no warning so you should check that the solution you get is actually a solution by plugging it into the original system of equations.

- **Example:** Two lines that **do intersect**.

Determine if the lines intersect, if so, find the point of intersection and the angle of intersection.

L_1: $x = 2 + t$, $y = 3$, $z = 1 + 4t$

L_2: $x = 4 - s$, $y = 3 + 2s$, $z = 9 + 2s$

You need to determine if there are values for t and s where (x, y, z) are the same for both lines. So we need to solve these three equations for the two unknown values of s and t.

$$
\begin{array}{llll}
\text{for x:} & 2 + t = 4 - s & t + s = 2 \\
\text{for y:} & 3 = 3 + 2s & \sim \quad -2s = 0 & \sim \\
\text{for z:} & 1 + 4t = 9 + 2s & 4t - 2s = 8
\end{array}
\quad
\begin{bmatrix} 1 & 1 \\ 0 & -2 \\ 4 & -2 \end{bmatrix}
\begin{bmatrix} t \\ s \end{bmatrix}
=
\begin{bmatrix} 2 \\ 0 \\ 8 \end{bmatrix}
$$

Expressing these equations in augmented matrix form, you can use Gaussian Elimination to solve for the variables (or have software do it for you but be careful of the *no solution* problems that can occur).

$$
\left[\begin{array}{cc|c} 1 & 1 & 2 \\ 0 & -2 & 0 \\ 4 & -2 & 8 \end{array}\right]
\sim
\left[\begin{array}{cc|c} 1 & 1 & 2 \\ 0 & -2 & 0 \\ 0 & -6 & 0 \end{array}\right]
\sim
\left[\begin{array}{cc|c} 1 & 1 & 2 \\ 0 & 1 & 0 \\ 0 & -6 & 0 \end{array}\right]
\sim
\left[\begin{array}{cc|c} 1 & 1 & 2 \\ 0 & 1 & 0 \\ 0 & 0 & 0 \end{array}\right]
$$

The second equation says that $s = 0$, plugging this into the first equation gives $t = 2$. Notice when $t = 2$ and $s = 0$ in the parametric equations of the lines, they both result in $x = 4$, $y = 3$, and $z = 9$. **The point of intersection is (4,3,9).**

Note: If you try to solve this system in MATLAB® it will produce a valid solution. The solution can be verified by plugging it into the original system of equations.

To find the angle of intersection, you must find the angle between the two direction vectors $\mathbf{u} = \langle 1, 0, 4 \rangle$ and $\mathbf{v} = \langle -1, 2, 2 \rangle$. Using equation (2.8) for the angle between two vectors, you get

$$
\cos(\theta) = \frac{\mathbf{u} \cdot \mathbf{v}}{\|\mathbf{u}\|\,\|\mathbf{v}\|} = \frac{7}{\sqrt{17}\,\sqrt{9}} = \frac{7}{3\sqrt{17}}.
$$

Therefore $\theta = \arccos\left(\frac{7}{3\sqrt{17}}\right) \approx 0.97$ radians or 55.5^o.

Distance Between a point and a line. Given a line with direction vector $\mathbf{v}$ and a point Q not on the line, then the distance between Q and the line is given by

$$D = \frac{||\overrightarrow{PQ} \times \mathbf{v}||}{||\mathbf{v}||} \tag{2.12}$$

where P is a any point on the line.

♣ *Mini-Proof:* As seen in the figure below, the distance from Q to the line is given by $D = ||\overrightarrow{PQ}|| \sin(\theta)$. Since $||\overrightarrow{PQ} \times \mathbf{v}|| = ||\overrightarrow{PQ}|| \, ||\mathbf{v}|| \, \sin(\theta)$, then $\dfrac{||\overrightarrow{PQ} \times \mathbf{v}||}{||\mathbf{v}||} = ||\overrightarrow{PQ}|| \, \sin(\theta) = D$.   ♣

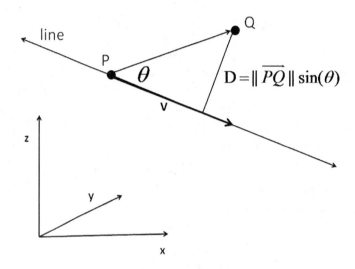

- **Example:** Find the distance from the point $Q(-1, 0, 3)$ to the line defined by

$$x = 3 - t, \quad y = -2 + t, \quad z = 5 - 3t$$

The direction vector of the line is given by $\mathbf{v} = \langle -1, 1, -3 \rangle$ and a point on the line is $P(3, -2, 5)$. Therefore, $\overrightarrow{PQ} = \langle -4, 2, -2 \rangle$, and

$$\overrightarrow{PQ} \times \mathbf{v} = \begin{vmatrix} \mathbf{i} & \mathbf{j} & \mathbf{k} \\ -4 & 2 & -2 \\ -1 & 1 & -3 \end{vmatrix} = -4\mathbf{i} - 10\mathbf{j} - 2\mathbf{k} = \langle -4, -10, -2 \rangle,$$

then using equation (2.12),

$$D = \frac{||\overrightarrow{PQ} \times \mathbf{v}||}{||\mathbf{v}||} = \frac{|| \langle -4, -10, -2 \rangle ||}{|| \langle -1, 1, -3 \rangle ||} = \frac{\sqrt{120}}{\sqrt{11}} \approx 3.303$$

MATLAB® Demonstration: Plotting Lines

Here we use the `plot3` to create a function called `Plotline3d`. Then we use it to plot some lines given a point and a direction vector.

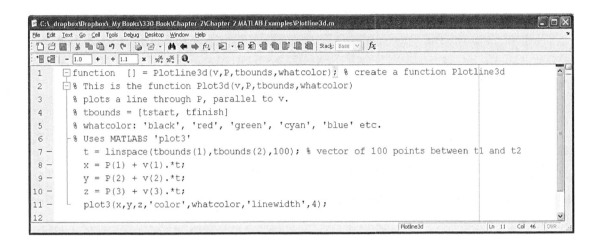

```matlab
1  function  [] = Plotline3d(v,P,tbounds,whatcolor); % create a function Plotline3d
2  % This is the function Plot3d(v,P,tbounds,whatcolor)
3  % plots a line through P, parallel to v.
4  % tbounds = [tstart, tfinish]
5  % whatcolor: 'black', 'red', 'green', 'cyan', 'blue' etc.
6  % Uses MATLABS 'plot3'
7      t = linspace(tbounds(1),tbounds(2),100); % vector of 100 points between t1 and t2
8      x = P(1) + v(1).*t;
9      y = P(2) + v(2).*t;
10     z = P(3) + v(3).*t;
11     plot3(x,y,z,'color',whatcolor,'linewidth',4);
12
```

```matlab
1  %% PlottingLines.m
2  % Here we plot a line in 3D using the
3  % Plotline3d function we wrote
4  clc; clf; clear;
5
6  %% Let's plot some lines.
7  v1 = [1 2 3]; P1 = [0 0 0];
8  v2 = [-1 2 3]; P2 = [2 2 2];
9  v3 = [-1 -2 3]; P3 = [-2 0 0];
10 tbounds = [0, 10];
11 Plotline3d(v1,P1,tbounds,'red'); hold on;
12 Plotline3d(v2,P2,tbounds,'blue');
13 Plotline3d(v3,P3,tbounds,'green');
14 title('Some Lines in 3D','fontsize',16);
15 xlabel('x'); ylabel('y'); zlabel('z');
16 box on; view(17,18);
```

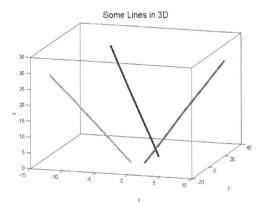

2.5.2   Curves in 2D and 3D

A curve (of which a line is one) is a one dimensional object within 2D or 3D. These curves can be described as parametric functions by

$$x = f(t), \quad y = g(t), \quad z = h(t) \tag{2.13}$$

where t is called the *parameter*. Parametric equations can be expressed equivalently as a vector-valued function by

$$\mathbf{v}(t) = \langle x(t), y(t), z(t) \rangle. \tag{2.14}$$

The curves traced out by equations (2.13) and (2.14) are the same if $x(t)$, $y(t)$, and $z(t)$ from equation (2.14) are equal to $f(t)$, $g(t)$, and $h(t)$ from equation (2.13). The curves described by these functions are best visualized by tracing out the terminal point of $\mathbf{v}$ as the parameter t passes through it's domain.

- **Example in 2D:** An ellipse in 2D with x radius $= 4$ and y radius $= 2$ can be described in either format.

$$x = 4\cos(t), \quad y = 2\sin(t), \quad \text{for} \quad t \in [0, 2\pi]$$

or

$$\mathbf{v}(t) = \langle 4\cos(t),\, 2\sin(t) \rangle \quad \text{for} \quad t \in [0, 2\pi]$$

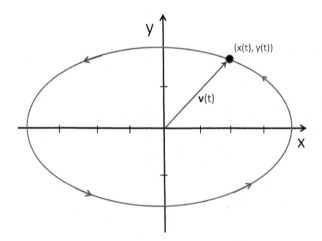

Notice: The curve does have a direction with increasing t. In this case, the ellipse is traced out in the counter-clockwise direction.

- **Example in 3D:** A helix in 3D can be traced out by the vector-valued function

$$\mathbf{v}(t) = \langle \cos(t), \sin(t), t \rangle \quad \text{for} \quad t \in [0, 6\pi]$$

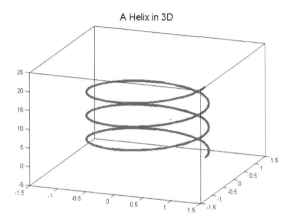

Notice, if you let $z = 0$, the trace of this curve projected onto the $z = 0$ plane is just the unit circle. However, as t increases, so does z, and as this happens the trajectory moves up the z-axis while tracing out the circle and forms the helix in 3D. In this case, the circle is traced out three times (each 2π produces a complete revolution). The code used to generate this curve is given below.

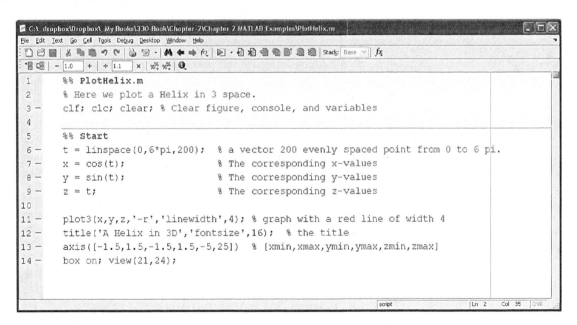

```matlab
%% PlotHelix.m
% Here we plot a Helix in 3 space.
clf; clc; clear; % Clear figure, console, and variables

%% Start
t = linspace(0,6*pi,200);  % a vector 200 evenly spaced point from 0 to 6 pi.
x = cos(t);                % The corresponding x-values
y = sin(t);                % The corresponding y-values
z = t;                     % The corresponding z-values

plot3(x,y,z,'-r','linewidth',4); % graph with a red line of width 4
title('A Helix in 3D','fontsize',16);  % the title
axis([-1.5,1.5,-1.5,1.5,-5,25])   % [xmin,xmax,ymin,ymax,zmin,zmax]
box on; view(21,24);
```

A Projectile in Motion: Here we model a projectile in motion according the laws of Newtonian physics in the absence of air resistance. We will restrict ourselves to the 2D case for now. The position of a projectile from an initial height of h with an initial velocity of v_o, and an angle of elevation of θ is given by the vector-valued function

$$\mathbf{r}(t) = \left\langle [v_o \cos(\theta)]t, \quad h + [v_o \sin(\theta)]t - \frac{1}{2}gt^2 \right\rangle = \langle x(t),\ y(t) \rangle. \tag{2.15}$$

In this equation, g is the acceleration due to gravity = 32 feet per second per second (or 9.8 meters per second per second). To find how far (in the x direction) the ball will travel, you must set $y(t) = 0$, from equation (2.15), and solve for t using the quadratic formula.

$$\text{projectile hits the ground at } t^* = \frac{v_o \sin(\theta) + \sqrt{v_o^2 \sin^2(\theta) + 2gh}}{g} \text{ seconds.} \tag{2.16}$$

The distance the projectile travels is found by substituting t^* into the equation for $x(t)$.

$$\text{total distance } = \frac{v_o^2 \cos(\theta)}{g} \left(\sin(\theta) + \sqrt{\sin^2(\theta) + \frac{2gh}{v_o^2}} \right). \tag{2.17}$$

The time t of maximum height is found by differentiating $y(t)$, from equation (2.15), with respect to t, then setting this equal to zero and solving for t.

$$y'(t) = v_o \sin(\theta) - gt = 0 \quad \rightarrow \quad \tilde{t} = \frac{v_o \sin(\theta)}{g} \tag{2.18}$$

Then, to get the actual maximum height, you must insert $\tilde{t}$ into the equation for $y(t)$.

$$\text{maximum height} = h + \frac{v_o^2 \sin^2(\theta)}{2g} \tag{2.19}$$

- **Example: Football Trajectory** Suppose a football is kicked from the ground at an initial angle of 30° with an initial velocity of 80 feet per second. Neglecting the effects of wind or air resistance, (a) Determine the vector-valued function that describes the trajectory of the ball. (b) How far will the ball travel? (c) How high will it go? Give your answers in feet (Ie. Use $g = 32$ ft/sec^2).

  Answers: Here, $h = 0$, $\theta = \pi/6$, and $v_o = 80$ ft/sec. Note: $\sin(\pi/6) = \frac{1}{2}$ and $\cos(\pi/6) = \frac{\sqrt{3}}{2}$. We want to plug these into equation (2.15) but that equation is only valid until the ball hits the ground. So we must first determine when this happens via equation (2.16). Plugging h, θ, v_o, and g into equation (2.16) yields

$$t^* = \frac{v_o \sin(\theta) + \sqrt{v_o^2 \sin^2(\theta) + 2gh}}{g} = \frac{80\frac{1}{2} + \sqrt{80^2 \left(\frac{1}{2}\right)^2}}{32} = 2.5 \text{ seconds}$$

Now that we have the total time the ball is in the air, we use equation (2.15) for the actual trajectory:

$$\begin{aligned}
\mathbf{r}(t) &= \left\langle [v_o \cos(\theta)]t, \quad h + [v_o \sin(\theta)]t - \frac{1}{2}gt^2 \right\rangle \\
&= \left\langle [80 \cos(\pi/6)]t, \quad 0 + [80 \sin(\pi/6)]t - \frac{1}{2}32t^2 \right\rangle \\
&= \left\langle \left(80\frac{\sqrt{3}}{2}\right)t, \quad \left(80\frac{1}{2}\right)t - \frac{1}{2}32t^2 \right\rangle \\
&= \left\langle 40\sqrt{3}\, t, \quad 40t - 16t^2 \right\rangle \qquad \text{for} \quad t \in [0, 2.5]
\end{aligned}$$

To get the total distance traveled we can plug our values into the total distance formula (equation (2.17)) or just plug our ending time $t^* = 2.5$ into $x(t)$ (the first term in $\mathbf{r}(t)$).

$$\text{total disance} = 40\sqrt{3}\, 2.5 = 100\sqrt{3} \approx 173.2 \text{ feet}$$

To get the maximum height we plug the same values into equation (2.19) which yields

$$\text{maximum height} = h + \frac{v_o^2 \sin^2(\theta)}{2g} = \frac{80^2 \sin^2(\pi/6)}{64} = 25 \text{ feet.}$$

Note: In general you will need to use software to perform these types of calculations.

- **Example: Max height and distance for a given v_o.**

  If you are given an initial velocity and h, what angle produces the maximum height (y-value), and what angle produces the maximum distance (x-value)?

  1. The maximum height occurs if $\theta = 90^o$ where $\sin(\theta) = 1$. Thus, the maximum possible height for a given initial velocity is given by equation (2.19) where $\theta = 90^o = \pi/2$ radians.

  $$\begin{aligned}
  \text{maximum height} &= h + \frac{v_o^2 \sin^2(\theta)}{2g} \\
  \text{maximum possible height} &= h + \frac{v_o^2}{2g}.
  \end{aligned}$$

  2. The maximum possible distance occurs if $\theta = 45^o$ (a little calculus can produce this result). Plugging this value of θ into the formula for the total distance yields

  $$\begin{aligned}
  \text{total distance} &= \frac{v_o^2 \cos(\theta)}{g}\left(\sin(\theta) + \sqrt{\sin^2(\theta) + \frac{2gh}{v_o^2}}\right) \\
  \text{maximum possible distance} &= \frac{v_o^2 \sqrt{2}}{2g}\left(\frac{\sqrt{2}}{2} + \sqrt{\frac{1}{2} + \frac{2gh}{v_o^2}}\right)
  \end{aligned}$$

Chapter 2.5 Problem Set

Numbers with an asterisk[*] have solutions in the back of the book.

1. **Parametric Equations for Lines in 3D:**
   Find the parametric equations for the line with the given properties.

   (a) The line passes through the point (2,3,4) and is parallel to the vector $\mathbf{v} = \langle 1, -2, 3 \rangle$.

   (b)[*] The line passes through the points (2,3,4) and (-1, 0, 4).

   (c) The line passes through the point (2,3,4) and is parallel to the xz-plane and the yz-plane.

   (d)[*] The line passes through the point (2,3,4) and is perpendicular to $\mathbf{u} = \langle 1, -1, 1 \rangle$ and $\mathbf{v} = \langle -2, 3, 0 \rangle$.
   Hint: Find $\mathbf{u} \times \mathbf{v}$ to get a vector that is perpendicular to both $\mathbf{u}$ and $\mathbf{v}$.

   (e) The line that passes through (1,3,5) and is normal to the plane $2x - 3y + 7z - 12 = 0$.

2. **Intersection of Lines in 3D:**
   Determine if the two lines intersect. If they do, find the angle of intersection.

   (a)[*] $x = 4t + 2$, $y = 3$, $z = -t + 1$
   $x = 2s + 2$, $y = 2s + 3$, $z = s + 1$

   (b) $x = 3t$, $y = -t + 2$, $z = t - 1$
   $x = 4s + 1$, $y = s - 2$, $z = -3s - 3$

3. **Intersection of Lines in 2D:**
   Determine if the two lines intersect. If they do, where do they intersect and what is the angle of intersection?

   (a)[*] $x = 4t + 2$, $y = 6t + 3$
   $x = s + 1$, $y = 2s + 4$,

   (b) $x = t - 2$, $y = -t + 5$
   $x = 2s + 1$, $y = s - 4$,

   (c)[*] $x = t - 2$, $y = -t + 5$
   $x = -3s + 1$, $y = 3s - 4$,

   (d) $x = t - 2$, $y = -t + 5$
   $x = -3s - 2$, $y = 3s + 5$,

4. **Directed Line Segments from P to Q:**

The parametric equations for a directed line segment that starts at $P(p_1, p_2)$ and ends at $Q(q_1, q_2)$ are determined by the set of points defined by

$$\text{line}: \quad P + t\,\overrightarrow{PQ} \quad \text{or} \quad P + t\,(Q - P) \quad \text{for} \quad t \in [0, 1]$$

Notice: When $t = 0$, the line starts at P, and when $t = 1$, the line ends at Q. The actual parametric equations look like

$$x = p_1 + t(q_1 - p_1) \quad \text{and} \quad y = p_2 + t(q_2 - p_2) \quad \text{for} \quad t \in [0, 1].$$

(a)* Find the parametric equations for the directed line segment from $P(1, 2)$ to $Q(-2, 5)$.

(b) Find the parametric equations for the directed line segment from $P(-1, -2)$ to $Q(2, 7)$.

5. **Intersection of 2 Line Segments:**

Here we check to see if two lines intersect between two given points. Suppose there is a wall from point P to point Q and you have a *ball* going from point R to point S. You want to know if the ball hits the wall. Equivalently, you want to know if the directed line segment $\overrightarrow{RS}$ intersects the directed line segment $\overrightarrow{PQ}$. It is not sufficient to know whether the lines defined by P & Q and R & S intersect. We want to know if the lines intersect between P & Q and R & S. And, if they intersect, where does the intersection occur?

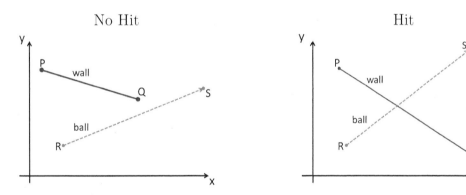

There are a few ways to do this and here is one way. The directed line segments $\overrightarrow{PQ}$ and $\overrightarrow{RS}$ can be defined as follows.

$$\overrightarrow{PQ} = P + t\,\overrightarrow{PQ} = P + t(Q - P) \quad \text{for} \quad t \in [0, 1]$$
$$\overrightarrow{RS} = R + s\,\overrightarrow{RS} = R + s(S - R) \quad \text{for} \quad s \in [0, 1]$$

If you can solve these equations for t and s and both are between 0 and 1, then the line segments intersect. If either one is (t or s) is not between 0 and 1, then they do not intersect.

(a)* Determine if, and where, the ball going from $R(3, 1)$ to $S(5, 11)$ hits the wall defined by $P(1, 8)$ and $Q(10, 2)$.

(b) Determine if, and where, the ball going from $R(-2, 8)$ to $S(6, 4)$ hits the wall defined by $P(2, 2)$ and $Q(14, 4)$.

6. **Distance between a point and a line:**

   (a)[*] Find the distance between the point $Q(1, 5, -2)$ and the line $L : x = 4t - 2$, $y = 3$, $z = -t + 1$.

   (b) Find the distance between the point $Q(1, 5, -2)$ and the line with direction vector $\mathbf{v} = \langle 1, 2, -3 \rangle$ through the point $(0, 2, 4)$.

7. **Curves in 2D:**

   (a)[*] **Lower Half of Ellipse:**
   The vector-valued function $\langle x(t), y(t) \rangle$ traces out the bottom half of an ellipse centered at (2,3) that starts at the point (0,3), moves counter-clockwise through passes through (2,2), and terminates at the point (4,3).

   Give $x(t)$, $y(t)$, and the interval for the parameter t.

   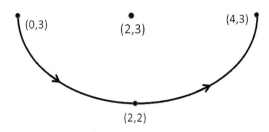

   (b) **Spiral:**
   The vector-valued function $\langle x(t), y(t) \rangle$ traces out the spiral depicted in the figure. The curve should start at (0,0) and go through the points (1,0), (2,0), (3,0), (4,0), and end at (5,0).

   Give $x(t)$, $y(t)$, and the interval for the parameter t.

   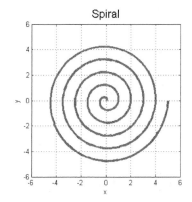

8. **MATLAB® Curves in 3D**

   (a)[*] **Double Helix**
   Plot a double helix in 3D using the `plot3` function in MATLAB® by making two plots in the same figure. It should look something like the one in the figure.

   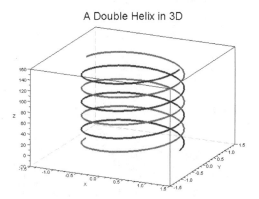

(b) **Twister!**

Plot a twister in 3D using the `plot3` function in MATLAB® . It should look something like the one in the figure.

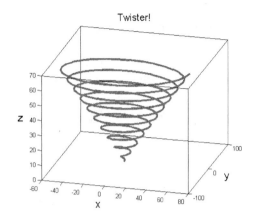

Twister!

9. (**MATLAB® Kick-Off**) Here we visit the kick-off problem from Chapter 1.7 only this time the football should follow a realistic trajectory. Write a program that prompts the user for an initial angle of kick-off (in degrees) and initial velocity (in feet/second). Then have the football follow the trajectory defined by equation (2.15) while rotating in the counter-clockwise direction. Be sure to set your graph bounds so that the trajectory never leaves the graph bounds and takes up most of the graph area. These bounds should be determined by first calculating the maximum distance (*x*-value) and the maximum height (*y*-value). You can force MATLAB® to obey your graph bounds with `axis([xmin, xmax, ymin, ymax])` and maintain equal scaling with `axis equal`. Sample *kick* animations are displayed below.

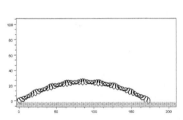

theta = 30.0 (degrees) and vo = 80.0 (feet per second)

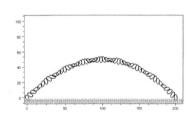

theta = 45.0 (degrees) and vo = 80.0 (feet per second)

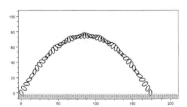

theta = 60.0 (degrees) and vo = 80.0 (feet per second)

10.[*] **Trajectory in 2D:**

A ball is kicked from the top of a 400-foot building at an angle of 0° from horizontal with an initial velocity of 60 feet/second. (see figure).

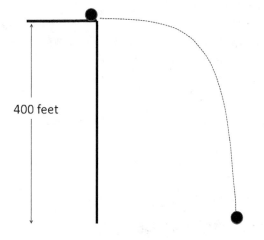

(a) Find the parametric equations for x (distance from the building) and y (height).

(b) How high is the ball after 2 seconds?

(c) How far from the building does it land?

11. **Trajectory in 2D:**

A projectile is launched from the edge of a building 40 feet tall. The initial velocity is 50 feet/second and the angle of elevation is 60°. (figure not necessarily drawn to scale)

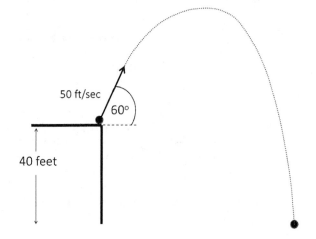

(a) Find the parametric equations for the trajectory where
$x(t)$ = horizontal distance from the building and
$y(t)$ = height above ground.

(b) Determine the height (y) when $x = 75$.

2.6 Planes in 3D

Terminology: When two lines meet at a right angle, they are called perpendicular. When two vectors are perpendicular, they are called orthogonal. When a vector is perpendicular to a plane (or surface) it is called a **normal** vector. When defining a plane we use a normal vector (**n**) to help describe it.

Equations for a plane: A normal vector and a point.

If a plane goes through the point $P(x_1, y_1, z_1)$ and has a normal vector $\mathbf{n} = \langle a, b, c \rangle$, then for any other point $Q(x, y, z)$ on the plane, it must be true that $\mathbf{n} \cdot \overrightarrow{PQ} = 0$. This requirement leads to the equations that describe a plane.

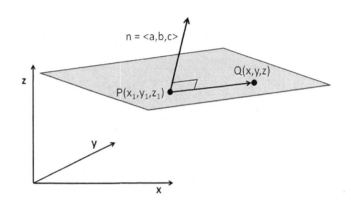

$$
\begin{aligned}
\mathbf{n} \cdot \overrightarrow{PQ} &= 0 & \\
a(x - x_1) + b(y - y_1) + c(z - z_1) &= 0 & \text{standard equation} \\
ax + by + cz + d &= 0 & \text{general equation} \\
z &= (-d - ax - by)/c & \text{function form } z = f(x, y) \\
y &= (-d - ax - cz)/b & \text{function form } y = g(x, z) \\
x &= (-d - by - cz)/a & \text{function form } x = h(y, z)
\end{aligned}
\tag{2.20}
$$

In these equations, $d = -ax_1 - by_1 - cz_1$.

- **Example, Finding a plane from a point and a normal vector:** Find the general equation for a plane that goes through the point (1,-2,3) with normal vector $\mathbf{n} = \langle 4, 5, -6 \rangle$.

We start with the standard form and then convert it to general form:

$$
\begin{aligned}
4(x - 1) + 5(y + 2) - 6(z - 3) &= 0 & \text{standard equation} \\
4x - 4 + 5y + 10 - 6z + 18 &= 0 & \text{intermediate step} \\
4x + 5y - 6z + 24 &= 0 & \text{general equation}
\end{aligned}
$$

- **Example, Finding a plane from 3 points:** Find the standard form of the plane through $P(2,1,1)$, $Q(0,4,1)$, $R(-2,1,4)$.

We need a point on the plane (we have three) and a normal vector. To get the normal vector $\mathbf{n}$ we set $\mathbf{n} = \overrightarrow{PQ} \times \overrightarrow{PR}$ which will be orthogonal to both vectors that form the plane. In our case, $\overrightarrow{PQ} = \langle -2, 3, 0 \rangle$, $\overrightarrow{PR} = \langle -4, 0, 3 \rangle$, and

$$\overrightarrow{PQ} \times \overrightarrow{PR} = \begin{vmatrix} \mathbf{i} & \mathbf{j} & \mathbf{k} \\ -2 & 3 & 0 \\ -4 & 0 & 3 \end{vmatrix} = 9\mathbf{i} + 6\mathbf{j} + 12\mathbf{k} = \langle 9, 6, 12 \rangle = \mathbf{n}.$$

Using the point $P(2,1,1)$ as the point,

$$\begin{array}{rcll} 9(x-2) + 6(y-1) + 12(z-1) & = & 0 & \text{standard equation} \\ 9x - 18 + 6y - 6 + 12z - 12 & = & 0 & \text{intermediate step} \\ 9x + 6y + 12z - 36 & = & 0 & \text{general equation} \end{array}$$

Using the point $Q(0,4,1)$ as the point,

$$\begin{array}{rcll} 9(x-0) + 6(y-4) + 12(z-1) & = & 0 & \text{standard equation} \\ 9x + 6y - 24 + 12z - 12 & = & 0 & \text{intermediate step} \\ 9x + 6y + 12z - 36 & = & 0 & \text{general equation} \end{array}$$

Using the point $R(-2,1,4)$ as the point,

$$\begin{array}{rcll} 9(x+2) + 6(y-1) + 12(z-4) & = & 0 & \text{standard equation} \\ 9x + 18 + 6y - 6 + 12z - 48 & = & 0 & \text{intermediate step} \\ 9x + 6y + 12z - 36 & = & 0 & \text{general equation} \end{array}$$

Notice: It doesn't matter which point you choose, you get the same general equation.

- **Another Example:** Find the plane through the point $P(2,1,-4)$ and perpendicular to the line described by the parametric equations

$$L: \quad x = 2 - t, \quad y = 3, \quad z = 3t.$$

We have a point, so all we need is a normal vector. The direction vector for the given line is $\langle -1, 0, 3 \rangle$. Letting this be the normal vector to the plane we get

$$\begin{array}{rcll} -1(x-2) + 0(y-1) + 3(z+4) & = & 0 & \text{standard equation} \\ -x + 2 + 3z + 12 & = & 0 & \text{intermediate step} \\ -x + 3z + 14 & = & 0 & \text{general equation} \end{array}$$

Notice: The line is parallel to the xz-plane because y is constant. Therefore the plane is parallel to the y-axis. (There is no y-intercept). Try to picture this in your head.

Drawing a plane by hand using intercepts: Sketch $4x + 2y + 2z - 12 = 0$ by finding the intercepts.

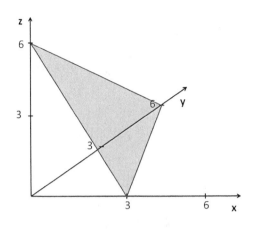

- The x intercept is where both y, and z are zero. This results in the equation $4x - 12 = 0$ or $x = 3$.

- The y intercept is where both x, and z are zero. This results in the equation $2y - 12 = 0$ or $y = 6$.

- The z intercept is where both x, and y are zero. This results in the equation $2z - 12 = 0$ or $z = 6$.

The angle between two planes: If two planes have normal vectors given by $\mathbf{n_1}$ and $\mathbf{n_2}$, then the angle of intersection $(0 \leq \theta \leq \pi/2)$[1] is given by

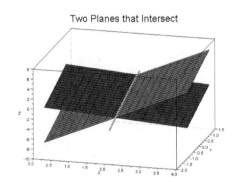

Two Planes that Intersect

$$\cos(\theta) = \frac{|\mathbf{n_1} \cdot \mathbf{n_2}|}{||\mathbf{n_1}|| \, ||\mathbf{n_2}||} \qquad (2.21)$$

$$\theta = \arccos\left(\frac{|\mathbf{n_1} \cdot \mathbf{n_2}|}{||\mathbf{n_1}|| \, ||\mathbf{n_2}||}\right) \qquad (2.22)$$

- The planes are perpendicular if $\mathbf{n_1} \cdot \mathbf{n_2} = 0$.

- The planes are parallel if $\mathbf{n_2} = c \, \mathbf{n_1}$.

- **Example:** Given the two planes defined below, find the angle of intersection.

$$\text{Plane 1:} \quad 3x - y + 2z - 12 = 0 \qquad \text{Plane 2:} \quad x - 2z + 3 = 0$$

The two normal vectors are given by $\mathbf{n_1} = \langle 3, -1, 2 \rangle$ and $\mathbf{n_2} = \langle 1, 0, -2 \rangle$. The angle of intersection is given by

$$\theta = \arccos\left(\frac{|\mathbf{n_1} \cdot \mathbf{n_2}|}{||\mathbf{n_1}|| \, ||\mathbf{n_2}||}\right) = \arccos\left(\frac{1}{\sqrt{14}\,\sqrt{5}}\right) = \arccos\left(\frac{1}{\sqrt{70}}\right) \approx 1.45 \text{ radians or } 83.1^o$$

---

[1] In these equations, the absolute value of the dot product $(|\mathbf{n_1} \cdot \mathbf{n_2}|)$ is used to ensure that we get the smaller of the two angles of intersection.

The line of the intersection of two planes: If two planes intersect, they intersect in a line. There are a couple of ways to find the equations for that line.

Method 1: By finding the general solution to a system of linear equations.

Method 2: By finding one particular solution and getting a direction vector: $\mathbf{v} = \mathbf{n_1} \times \mathbf{n_2}$.

- **Example:** Given the two planes below, find the parametric equations for the line of intersection.

$$\text{Plane 1:}\quad x + 3z - 10 = 0 \qquad \text{Plane 2:}\quad 2x + y + 5z + 3 = 0$$

Method 1: We must find all points on the intersection of both planes. This means we must find values of x, y and z that satisfy both plane equations or

$$
\begin{array}{rcl}
x + 3z - 10 & = & 0 \\
2x + y + 5z + 3 & = & 0
\end{array}
\quad\sim\quad
\begin{array}{rcl}
x + 3z & = & 10 \\
2x + y + 5z & = & -3
\end{array}
\quad\sim\quad
\begin{bmatrix} 1 & 0 & 3 \\ 2 & 1 & 5 \end{bmatrix}
\begin{bmatrix} x \\ y \\ z \end{bmatrix}
=
\begin{bmatrix} 10 \\ -3 \end{bmatrix}
$$

Expressing these equations in augmented matrix form, you can use Gaussian Elimination to solve for the variables. You will get infinitely many solutions provided the planes actually intersect.

$$
\left[\begin{array}{ccc|c} 1 & 0 & 3 & 10 \\ 2 & 1 & 5 & -3 \end{array}\right]
\quad\sim\quad
\left[\begin{array}{ccc|c} 1 & 0 & 3 & 10 \\ 0 & 1 & -1 & -23 \end{array}\right]
$$

The second equation states that $y - z = -23$. If we let z be the free variable, then $y = -23 + z$ and the first equation becomes $x = 10 - 3z$. Letting $z = t$ be the free variable, the general solution is given by

$$x = 10 - 3t, \qquad y = -23 + t, \qquad z = t, \quad \text{for} \quad t \in (-\infty, \infty)$$

This general solution represents the parametric equations for the line.

Method 2: Repeat most of the calculations from Method 1 except you only need one particular solution such as (10,-23,0). The normal vectors for the planes are given by $\mathbf{n_1} = \langle 1, 0, 3 \rangle$ and $\mathbf{n_2} = \langle 2, 1, 5 \rangle$. The direction vector for the line of intersection $\mathbf{v}$ is

$$
\mathbf{v} = \mathbf{n_1} \times \mathbf{n_2} =
\begin{vmatrix} \mathbf{i} & \mathbf{j} & \mathbf{k} \\ 1 & 0 & 3 \\ 2 & 1 & 5 \end{vmatrix}
= -3\mathbf{i} + \mathbf{j} + \mathbf{k} = \langle -3, 1, 1 \rangle
$$

Now we have a direction vector $\mathbf{v} = \langle -3, 1, 1 \rangle$ and a point (10, -23, 0). So the parametric equations for the line of intersection are

$$x = 10 - 3t, \qquad y = -23 + t, \qquad z = t, \quad \text{for} \quad t \in (-\infty, \infty)$$

The two methods won't always have identical parametric equations. However, they will always trace out the same line and have parallel direction vectors.

Distance between a point and a plane:

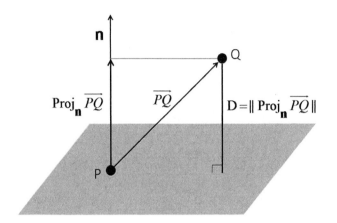

The distance between a plane through P with $\mathbf{n} = \langle a, b, c \rangle$ and a point Q is

$$D = ||\text{proj}_{\mathbf{n}} \overrightarrow{PQ}|| = \frac{|\overrightarrow{PQ} \cdot \mathbf{n}|}{||\mathbf{n}||} \qquad (2.23)$$

where P is a point in the plane.

♣ *Mini-Proof:* As seen in the figure above, $D = ||\text{Proj}_{\mathbf{n}} \overrightarrow{PQ}|| = ||\frac{\overrightarrow{PQ} \cdot \mathbf{n}}{||\mathbf{n}||^2} \mathbf{n}|| = \frac{|\overrightarrow{PQ} \cdot \mathbf{n}|}{||\mathbf{n}||^2} ||\mathbf{n}|| = \frac{|\overrightarrow{PQ} \cdot \mathbf{n}|}{||\mathbf{n}||}$.

Note on Collision Detection: If you want to see if Q has hit the plane, you want to check if $D = 0$. Unfortunately, the point Q might pass through the plane in a given time step without $D = 0$. However, if this happens, $\text{Proj}_{\mathbf{n}} \overrightarrow{PQ}$ will change sign. So, in addition to checking if $D = 0$ it also worth checking whether the sign of $\overrightarrow{PQ} \cdot \mathbf{n}$ changes during a given time step. If it has, then a collision has occurred.

- **Example, The distance between a point and a plane:** Find the distance between the point $Q(1, 2, 3)$ and the plane $4x - 2y + z - 6 = 0$.

  The normal to the plane is given by $\mathbf{n} = \langle 4, -2, 1 \rangle$. To find a point on the plane, let $x = y = 0$, then $z = 6$ and $P = (0, 0, 6)$. Now, the vector $\overrightarrow{PQ} = \langle 1, 2, -3 \rangle$. So

$$D = ||\text{proj}_{\mathbf{n}} \overrightarrow{PQ}|| = \frac{|\overrightarrow{PQ} \cdot \mathbf{n}|}{||\mathbf{n}||} = \frac{3}{\sqrt{21}}$$

- **Example, The distance between two parallel planes** Given the equations for two parallel planes, find the distance between them.

$$\text{Plane 1:} \quad 3x - y + 2z - 6 = 0 \qquad \text{Plane 2:} \quad 3x - y + 2z + 5 = 0$$

  Let Q be a point on Plane 2, $Q = (0, 5, 0)$. Now just find the distance from Q to Plane 1. The normal vector is given by $\mathbf{n} = \langle 3, -1, 2 \rangle$ and a point on Plane 1 is $P(0, -6, 0)$. Now, the vector $\overrightarrow{PQ} = \langle 0, -11, 0 \rangle$. So

$$D = ||\text{proj}_{\mathbf{n}} \overrightarrow{PQ}|| = \frac{|\overrightarrow{PQ} \cdot \mathbf{n}|}{||\mathbf{n}||} = \frac{11}{\sqrt{14}}$$

MATLAB® Demonstration: Plotting Planes

The `surf` command can be used to build a function called `PlotPlaneFunction` which plots planes given a point and a normal vector.

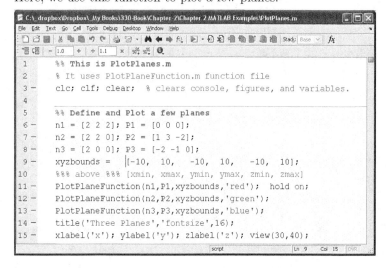

Here, we use this function to plot a few planes.

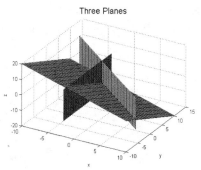

MATLAB® Demonstration: Plotting Planes and Normal Vectors

Here we combine graphs using functions defined earlier to produce the the graph of a plane and it's unit normal emanating from a given point.

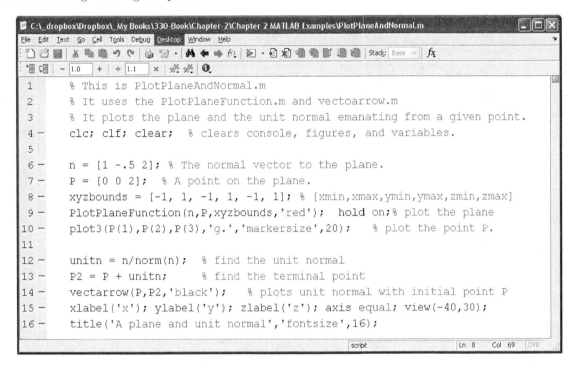

```matlab
% This is PlotPlaneAndNormal.m
% It uses the PlotPlaneFunction.m and vectoarrow.m
% It plots the plane and the unit normal emanating from a given point.
clc; clf; clear;  % clears console, figures, and variables.

n = [1 -.5 2]; % The normal vector to the plane.
P = [0 0 2];  % A point on the plane.
xyzbounds = [-1, 1, -1, 1, -1, 1]; % [xmin,xmax,ymin,ymax,zmin,zmax]
PlotPlaneFunction(n,P,xyzbounds,'red');  hold on;% plot the plane
plot3(P(1),P(2),P(3),'g.','markersize',20);    % plot the point P.

unitn = n/norm(n);  % find the unit normal
P2 = P + unitn;     % find the terminal point
vectarrow(P,P2,'black');   % plots unit normal with initial point P
xlabel('x'); ylabel('y'); zlabel('z'); axis equal; view(-40,30);
title('A plane and unit normal','fontsize',16);
```

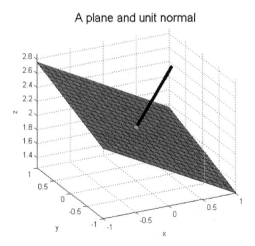

Chapter 2.6 Worksheet

Way back when solving systems of equations we came across the 3 x 3 system:

$$\begin{aligned} x_2 - 4x_3 &= 8 \\ 2x_1 - 3x_2 + 2x_3 &= 1 \\ 5x_1 - 8x_2 + 7x_3 &= 1 \end{aligned}$$

and we determined that there were no solutions. Allowing each equation to represent the graph of a plane, you can see that the planes are not parallel. Graph the 3 planes in such a way that you can ascertain why there is no point of intersection.

Chapter 2.6 Problem Set

Numbers with an asterisk[*] have solutions in the back of the book.

You are welcome to let MATLAB® do a lot of the work for these problems but you will have to do some of the preliminary work by hand. It might also be useful to plot the objects to visualize what is being requested. In some of the problems this is required.

1. (**Written**) Find the equation for the plane with the given properties.

   (a)[*] The plane goes through the points $P(0, 1, 2)$, $Q(1, 0, 3)$, and $R(-2, 3, 4)$.

   (b) The plane goes through the point (0,0,6) and is perpendicular to the line given by $x = 1 - t$, $y = 2 + t$, $z = 4 - 2t$.

   (c)[*] The plane goes through the point (1,2,3) and is parallel to the xy-plane.

   (d) The plane passes through the points (2,2,1) and (-1,1,-1) and is perpendicular to the plane $2x - 3y + z = 3$.

2. (**Written**) Sketch the given plane using intercepts.

   (a)[*] $6x + 4y - 3z + 24 = 0$

   (b) $x + y - 2z - 6 = 0$

3.[*] (**Written**) Consider the two planes $x + 2y - 2z = 4$ and $3x - 3z = 6$.

   (a) Find the angle of intersection.

   (b) Find the parametric equations for the line of intersection of the planes.

4. (**Written/MATLAB®**) Consider the two planes $3x + 2y - z = 7$ and $x - 4y + 2z = 0$.

   (a) Find the angle of intersection.

   (b) Find the parametric equations for the line of intersection of the planes.

   (c) Use MATLAB® to plot both planes and the line you found in part (b). Does the line follow the intersection? Your graph should look something like the one below.

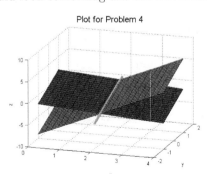

Plot for Problem 4

5. Calculate the distance between the given point and the given plane.

   (a)* The point is $Q(1, -1, 1)$ and the plane is defined by $6x - 3y + 2z - 8 = 0$.

   (b) The point is $Q(1, 2, 3)$ and the plane is defined by $3x + 2y - 5z + 8 = 0$.

6. (**Written**) Planes and Spheres

   (a)* Below are the equations for a sphere and a plane. Use the formula for the distance between a point and a plane to determine if the sphere intersects the plane.

   $$\text{sphere: } (x - 1)^2 + (y + 2)^2 + z^2 = 4 \qquad \text{plane: } 2x - 3y + z - 2 = 0$$

   (b) Find the standard equation of the sphere that is centered at $Q(8, -5, 7)$ and is tangent to the plane $2x - y - 2z + 8 = 0$.

7.* (**MATLAB®**) Find the distance between the point $(2,4,8)$ and the plane $2x + y + z = 5$. Use MATLAB® to plot the point and the plane then draw the directed line segment between the point and the plane that has this distance as its length.

Your plot should look like the one to the right.

In order to make sure orthogonal objects appear orthogonal it is necessary to use the command `axis equal;` following the plot command.

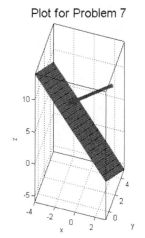

Plot for Problem 7

8.* (**MATLAB®**) Find the distance between the planes $x - 3y + 4z = 10$ and $x - 3y + 4z = 6$. Use MATLAB® to plot both planes and a directed line segment connecting the planes with length equal to this distance.

Your graph should look like the one to the right.

In order to make sure orthogonal objects appear orthogonal it is necessary to use the command `axis equal;` following the plot command.

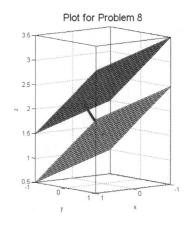

Plot for Problem 8

2.7 Collision Detection and Response: Lines and Planes

1. **Example: The intersection of a line and a plane.**

   Given the equation for a plane: $3x + 2y - 2z = 0$ and a line

   $$\text{Line:} \quad x = 1 - t, \quad y = 4t, \quad z = 9$$

   Find where the line intersects the plane.

   The answer is quite simple. Just put your expressions for x, y, and z, into the equation for the plane and solve to t.

   $$3x + 2y - 2z = 0 \tag{2.24}$$
   $$3(1 - t) + 2(4t) - 2(9) = 0 \tag{2.25}$$
   $$3 - 3t + 8t - 18 = 0 \tag{2.26}$$
   $$5t - 15 = 0 \tag{2.27}$$
   $$t = 3 \tag{2.28}$$

   So, when $t = 3$ the point on the line is also on the plane. That point is (-2, 12, 9).

2. **Shortcut for finding the point of intersection between a line and a plane.**

   If you solve everything symbolically and simplify, you can derive the following expression for the time (t) of collision between a straight line and a plane by

   $$t = \frac{\mathbf{n} \cdot \langle P_P - P_L \rangle}{\mathbf{n} \cdot \mathbf{v}} \tag{2.29}$$

   where $\mathbf{n}$ is the normal to the plane, P_P is a point on the plane, P_L is a point on the line, and $\mathbf{v}$ is the direction vector for the line. Notice, if the line and the plane are parallel then $\mathbf{n} \cdot \mathbf{v} = 0$ and there is no point of collision unless the line is in the plane, in which case $\mathbf{n} \cdot \langle P_P - P_L \rangle = 0$. Now, the point of collision is given by

   $$\text{Point of Collision} = P_L + t \, \mathbf{v} \tag{2.30}$$

   Example: Use this formula for the previous example.

   Here, $\mathbf{n} = \langle 3, 2, -2 \rangle$, $\mathbf{v} = \langle -1, 4, 0 \rangle$, $P_P = (0, 0, 0)$, and $P_L = (1, 0, 9)$. So, $P_P - P_L = (-1, 0, -9)$, and

   $$t = \frac{\mathbf{n} \cdot \langle P_P - P_L \rangle}{\mathbf{n} \cdot \mathbf{v}} = \frac{15}{5} = 3$$

   and

   $$\text{Point of Collision} = P_L + t \, \mathbf{v} = (1, 0, 9) + 3 \langle -1, 4, 0 \rangle = (-2, 12, 9)$$

   Note: Some abuse of notation here is used as I am treating points and vectors the same.

3. **A bounce response to a collision between a moving point and a plane.**

   Consider an object moving with a velocity vector from point M to point Q. However, it hits a plane at point P. How would the bounce response be modeled?

   Some Definitions and Assumptions:

   (a) The collision point is P.

   (b) The normal to the plane is given by $\mathbf{n}$ **.

   (c) Let B represent the final resting point after the ball has bounced.

   (d) We will assume the ball travels the same distance as it would if there was no collision. I.e., $||\overrightarrow{PQ}|| = ||\overrightarrow{PB}||$.

   (e) We will allow the addition of points and vectors. This addition will result in a point. For example, if P is the point (x, y, z) and $\mathbf{v}$ is the vector $\langle v_1, v_2, v_3 \rangle$, then $P + \mathbf{v}$ is the point given by

   $$P + \mathbf{v} = (x, y, z) + \langle v_1, v_2, v_3 \rangle = (x + v_1,\ y + v_2,\ z + v_2)$$

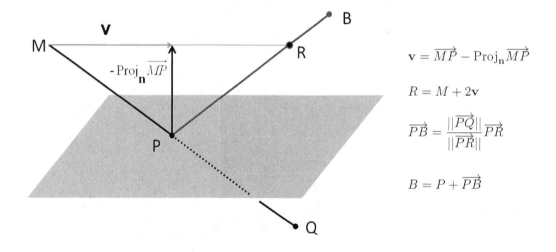

$$\mathbf{v} = \overrightarrow{MP} - \text{Proj}_{\mathbf{n}} \overrightarrow{MP}$$

$$R = M + 2\mathbf{v}$$

$$\overrightarrow{PB} = \frac{||\overrightarrow{PQ}||}{||\overrightarrow{PR}||} \overrightarrow{PR}$$

$$B = P + \overrightarrow{PB}$$

** **Note:** Since $\text{Proj}_{\mathbf{n}} \overrightarrow{MP} = \text{Proj}_{(-\mathbf{n})} \overrightarrow{MP}$ it doesn't matter which normal to the plane we use in the formula. In fact, any multiple of any normal will work.

4. Example: **A bounce response to a collision between a moving point and a plane.**

Consider the plane defined by $x + z - 2 = 0$. A ball starts at the point $M(-6, 0, 15)$ with a velocity vector that ends at the point $Q(0, 0, -5)$. Find where the ball hits the plane and determine the final location of the ball when a bounce response to this collision occurs.

First, the normal for our plane is $\mathbf{n} = \langle 1, 0, 1 \rangle$. Now we have to determine where the directed line segment $\overrightarrow{MQ}$ hits the plane. So we consider the line which contains this directed line segment. Using the point $M(-6, 0, 15)$ and the direction vector given by $\overrightarrow{MQ} = \langle 6, 0, -20 \rangle$.

$$\text{Line:} \quad x = -6 + 6t, \quad y = 0, \quad z = 15 - 20t$$

The line hits the plane when each expression for x, y, and z, of the line satisfies the equation for the plane or

$$x + z - 2 = 0 \;\rightarrow\; (-6 + 6t) + (15 - 20t) - 2 = 0 \;\rightarrow\; 7 - 14t = 0 \rightarrow t = \frac{1}{2}$$

So the line hits the plane where $t = \frac{1}{2}$ or at $P(-3, 0, 5)$.

We now have all the points we need.

$$\mathbf{v} = \overrightarrow{MP} - \text{Proj}_{\mathbf{n}} \overrightarrow{MP} = \langle 3, 0, -10 \rangle - \frac{\langle 3, 0, -10 \rangle \cdot \langle 1, 0, 1 \rangle}{|| \langle 1, 0, 1 \rangle ||^2} \langle 1, 0, 1 \rangle \tag{2.31}$$

$$= \langle 3, 0, -10 \rangle - \frac{-7}{2} \langle 1, 0, 1 \rangle = \left\langle \frac{13}{2}, 0, -\frac{13}{2} \right\rangle \tag{2.32}$$

$$R = M + 2\mathbf{v} = (-6, 0, 15) + 2 \left(\frac{13}{2}, 0, -\frac{13}{2} \right) = (7, 0, 2) \tag{2.33}$$

$$\overrightarrow{PB} = \frac{|| \overrightarrow{PQ} ||}{|| \overrightarrow{PR} ||} \overrightarrow{PR} = \frac{|| \langle 3, 0, -10 \rangle ||}{|| \langle 10, 0, -3 \rangle ||} \langle 10, 0, -3 \rangle = \langle 10, 0, -3 \rangle \tag{2.34}$$

$$B = P + \overrightarrow{PB} = (-3, 0, 5) + (10, 0, -3) = (7, 0, 2) \tag{2.35}$$

A Collision Occurs

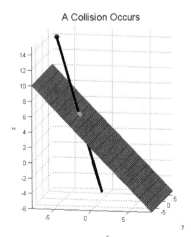

A Bounce Response

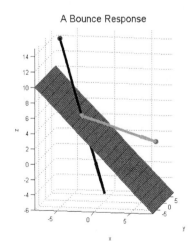

Chapter 2.7 Problem Set

Numbers with an asterisk[*] have solutions in the back of the book.

1.[*] Consider the plane defined by $2x + y + -z + 1 = 0$ and the line connecting the two points $M(-10, -10, -10)$ and $Q(10, 10, 10)$. Determine where the line intersects the plane. Call this point P.

2.[*] Consider the plane and two points defined in the previous problem. A ball starts at the point M with a velocity vector that ends at Q. It hits the plane at the point found in the previous problem. Determine the final location of the ball when a bounce response to this collision occurs. It can be done by hand but you should try to do this in MATLAB® as the calculations get pretty tricky.

3.[*] (**MATLAB®**) Plot the plane, $\overrightarrow{MQ}$, P, and the final location of the ball (B) after the bounce. It should look something like the graph to the right.

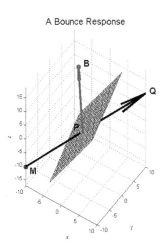

4. Find the point $P(x, y, z)$ where the line connecting the points $M(1, 2, 3)$ and $Q(-8, -5, -2)$ intersects the plane defined by $2x - 5y + 7z - 4 = 0$

5. (**MATLAB®**) Consider the plane and two points defined in the previous problem. A ball starts at the point M with a velocity vector that ends at Q. It hits the plane at P found in the previous problem. Determine the final location of the ball B when a bounce response to this collision occurs. You need to do this in MATLAB® as the calculations get very ugly.
Round your answers to 2 decimal places.

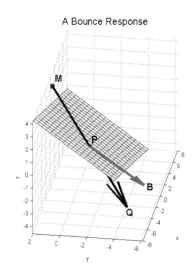

2.8   Polar, Cylindrical, and Spherical Coordinates

1. Polar Coordinates: 2D

In polar coordinates each point $(x,\ y)$ in the cartesian plane is described by $(r,\ \theta)$ where r is the distance from the point to the origin, and θ is the angle made by the ray connecting the origin to the point and the positive x-axis.

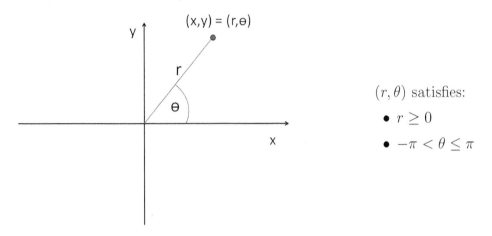

(r, θ) satisfies:

- $r \geq 0$
- $-\pi < \theta \leq \pi$

(a) **Uniqueness:** Since any point can be described infinitely many ways in polar coordinates we generally assume that $r \geq 0$, and $\theta \in (-\pi, \pi]$. With these constraints, each point in the plane has a unique polar representation.

(b) **Converting cartesian coordinates to polar coordinates:**. If a point (x, y) is given in cartesian coordinates then the polar coordinates $(r,\ \theta)$ are given by

$$r = \sqrt{x^2 + y^2} \quad \text{and} \quad \theta = \arctan\left(\frac{y}{x}\right) = \tan^{-1}\left(\frac{y}{x}\right) \tag{2.36}$$

The formula for θ can be problematic as the arctan function generally returns an angle between $-\pi/2$ and $\pi/2$. Since we will be using software (MATLAB®), it is best to use the function

$$\theta = \texttt{atan2}(y, x) \quad \text{yields} \quad \theta \in (-\pi, \pi].$$

(c) **Converting polar coordinates to cartesian coordinates** is much easier. If a point is described in polar coordinates by (r, θ) the cartesian coordinates (x, y) are given by

$$x = r\cos(\theta) \quad \text{and} \quad y = r\sin(\theta). \tag{2.37}$$

(d) Polar Coordinates are great for circles (centered at the origin).

The circle $x^2 + y^2 = 4^2$ is defined in polar coordinates as $r = 4$. Very easy.

(e) Polar Coordinates are also good for spirals and flowers.

2. ## Cylindrical Coordinates: 3D

The **cylindrical coordinate system** represents a point in space by an ordered triplet (r, θ, z). It is very similar to polar coordinates. In fact (r, θ) is the polar representation of the point projected onto the xy-plane.

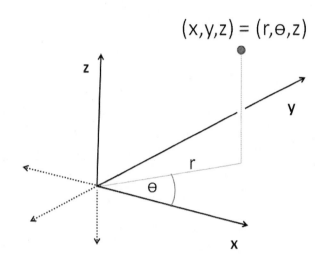

(r, θ, z) satisfies:

- $r \geq 0$
- $-\pi < \theta \leq \pi$

(a) Converting from cylindrical to rectangular coordinates: $(r, \theta, z) \to (x, y, z)$

$$x = r\cos(\theta) \qquad y = r\sin(\theta) \qquad z = z. \tag{2.38}$$

(b) Converting from rectangular to cylindrical coordinates: $(x, y, z) \to (r, \theta, z)$

$$r = \sqrt{x^2 + y^2} \qquad\qquad \theta = \tan^{-1}\left(\frac{y}{x}\right) \; ^2 \qquad\qquad z = z$$

(c) Surfaces described in cylindrical coordinates

- $x^2 + y^2 = 9$ or $r = 3$ both represent the same cylinder.
- $z = x^2 + y^2$ or $z = r^2$ both represent the same paraboloid
- $x^2 + y^2 = z^2$ or $r^2 = z^2$ both represent the same cone.
- vertical plane: $\theta = c$.

---

[2]In MATLAB® the $\tan^{-1}$ function (or arctangent) is called with $\theta = $ `atan2(y,x)`

3. **Spherical Coordinates: 3D**

   Any point in 3-space defined by (x, y, z), can be expressed in spherical coordinates. In the spherical coordinate system, each point is represented by an ordered triplet of the form (ρ, θ, α). The first term; ρ, (*rho*) is the distance from the point to the origin. The second term; θ, (*theta*) is the angle that the the vector $\langle x, y \rangle$ makes with the positive x-axis in the counter-clockwise direction. The third term; α, (*alpha*) represents the angle that the vector $\langle x, y, z \rangle$ makes with the positive z axis.

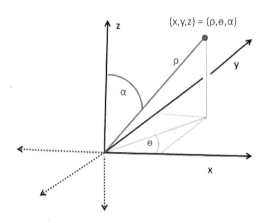

(ρ, θ, α) satisfies:

- $\rho \geq 0$
- $-\pi < \theta \leq \pi$
- $0 \leq \alpha \leq \pi$

   (a) Converting Rectangular to Spherical Coordinates: $(x, y, z) \to (\rho, \theta, \alpha)$.

$$\rho = \sqrt{x^2 + y^2 + z^2} \qquad \theta = \tan^{-1}\left(\frac{y}{x}\right) {}^{3} \qquad \alpha = \arccos\left(\frac{z}{\rho}\right)$$

   (b) Converting Spherical to Rectangular Coordinates: $(\rho, \theta, \alpha) \to (x, y, z)$

$$x = \rho \sin(\alpha) \cos(\theta), \qquad y = \rho \sin(\alpha) \sin(\theta), \qquad z = \rho \cos(\alpha)$$

   (c) Spherical Coordinates are great for spheres and ellipsoids centered at the origin.
   The sphere $x^2 + y^2 + z^2 = 4^2$ is defined in spherical coordinates as $\rho = 4$. Very easy.

   (d) Closed surfaces are often better described in spherical coordinates but it gets tricky.

---

[3]In MATLAB® the $\tan^{-1}$ function (or arctangent) is called with $\theta = $ `atan2(y,x)`

Chapter 3

Vector-Valued Functions

In this chapter we look at vector valued functions of the form:

2-Dimensional

$$\mathbf{r}(t) = \langle x(t), y(t) \rangle \tag{3.1}$$

3-Dimensional

$$\mathbf{r}(t) = \langle x(t), y(t), z(t) \rangle \tag{3.2}$$

We have already seen a little of this when we found the parametric equations for lines and curves in 3-space back in Chapter 2. This chapter will take it from there. Specifically we will now differentiate these functions and find tangent vectors which describe the direction in which an object is moving. We can go one step further, differentiating one more time, and get acceleration vectors. We will then use Euler's method to determine trajectories based only on the current position and velocity. This last trick is especially handy when animating objects in motion when forces act on the object as it moves around in space.

3.1 Vector-Valued Functions and Curves in Space

A curve is a one dimensional object within 2D or 3D. Previously we defined these curves in terms of parametric functions by

$$x = f(t), \quad y = g(t), \quad z = h(t) \tag{3.3}$$

where t is called the *parameter*. In this chapter we will describe these curves by vector-valued functions of the form

$$\mathbf{v}(t) = \langle x(t), y(t), z(t) \rangle . \tag{3.4}$$

The curves described by vector-valued functions are best visualized by tracing out the terminal point of $\mathbf{v}$ as the parameter t passes through it's domain.

You may recall these examples from Chapter 2.5.2.

Example in 2D: An ellipse in 2D with x radius $= 4$ and y radius $= 2$ can be described by the vector-valued function

$$\mathbf{v}(t) = \langle 4\cos(t),\, 2\sin(t) \rangle \quad \text{for} \quad t \in [0, 2\pi]$$

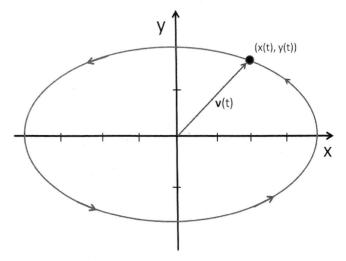

Notice: The curve does have a direction with increasing t. In this case, the ellipse is traced out in the counter-clockwise direction as t increase. This will become evident when we look at the associated velocity vectors.

Example in 3D: A helix in 3D can be traced out by the vector-valued function

$$\mathbf{r}(t) = \langle \cos(t), \sin(t), t \rangle \quad \text{for} \quad t \in [0, 6\pi]$$

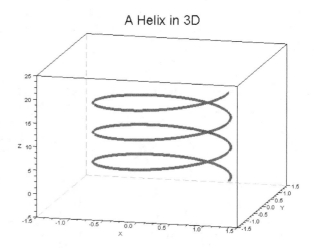

A Helix in 3D

Notice: The curve does have a direction with increasing t. In this case, the ellipsoid is traced out in the counter-clockwise direction moving upward at t increases. This will become evident when we look at the associated velocity vectors.

A Projectile in Motion: 3D

Here we model a projectile in motion according the laws of Newtonian physics in the absence of air resistance. We previously did this in 2D and so now we will study the same motion in 3D.

To start, we now have a couple of new terms: θ is now the angle in the xy-plane made by the initial launch, and ϕ is the elevation angle with respect to the xy-plane.

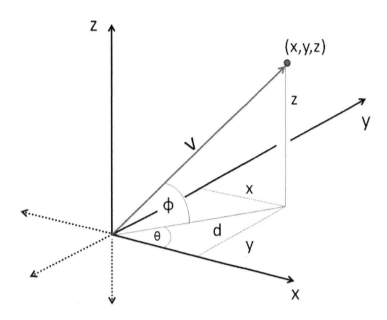

In this figure, $z = ||\mathbf{v}|| \sin(\phi)$ and $d = ||\mathbf{v}|| \cos(\phi)$. This makes $x = ||\mathbf{v}|| \cos(\phi) \cos(\theta)$ and $y = ||\mathbf{v}|| \cos(\phi) \sin(\theta)$. To summarize:

$$x = ||\mathbf{v}|| \cos(\phi) \cos(\theta) \tag{3.5}$$

$$y = ||\mathbf{v}|| \cos(\phi) \sin(\theta) \tag{3.6}$$

$$z = ||\mathbf{v}|| \sin(\phi) \tag{3.7}$$

Vector-Valued Function for a Projectile in 3D:

The position of a projectile from an initial height of h with an initial velocity of v_o, an angle with the positive x-axis of θ, and an angle of elevation given by ϕ is given by the vector-valued function $\mathbf{r}(t)$ defined by

$$\mathbf{r}(t) = \left\langle v_o \cos(\theta) \cos(\phi)\, t, \quad v_o \sin(\theta) \cos(\phi)\, t, \quad h + v_o \sin(\phi)\, t - \frac{1}{2} g\, t^2 \right\rangle = \langle x(t),\, y(t),\, z(t) \rangle. \qquad (3.8)$$

In this equation, g is the acceleration due to gravity $= 32$ feet per second per second (or 9.8 meters per second per second).

If we want to find out when the ball hits the ground, we just set $z(t) = 0$ and solve for t. We'll call this value of t, t^*

$$t^* = \frac{v_o \sin(\phi) + \sqrt{v_o^2 \sin^2(\phi) + 2gh}}{g} \quad \text{seconds.} \qquad (3.9)$$

The ball hits the ground at the point $(x(t^*), y(t^*), 0)$. If you want the distance the ball travels in the xy-plane,

$$\text{total distance in } xy\text{-plane} \;=\; \sqrt{[x(t^*)]^2 + [y(t^*)]^2} \qquad (3.10)$$

The time t of maximum height is found by differentiating $z(t)$, from equation (3.8), with respect to t, then setting this equal to zero and solving for t, we'll call this value of t, $\tilde{t}$.

$$z'(t) = v_o \sin(\phi) - gt = 0 \quad \rightarrow \quad \tilde{t} = \frac{v_o \sin(\phi)}{g} \qquad (3.11)$$

Then, to get the actual maximum height, you must insert $\tilde{t}$ into the expression for $z(t)$ in equation (3.8):

$$\text{maximum height} = h + \frac{v_o^2 \sin^2(\phi)}{2g} \qquad (3.12)$$

Note: These formulas look almost exactly as they do for a projectile in motion for 2D. The only difference is that ϕ now plays the role that θ did, and the total distance traveled is the distance from the landing point in the xy-plane to the origin.

- **Example: Projectile Trajectory:** Suppose a projectile is launched from the point (0,0,0). The angle of elevation is 30°, and the launcher is positioned to point 45° from the positive x-axis. The initial velocity is 80 feet/second. Neglecting the effects of wind or air resistance, (1) Determine when it hits the ground, (2) Determine the vector-valued function that describes the trajectory of the ball. (3) Where will it land? (4) How far will it travel in the xy-plane, and (5) How high will it go? Give your answers in feet. (Ie. Use $g = 32$ ft/sec^2).

Here, $h = 0$, $\phi = 30^o = \pi/6$, $\theta = 45^o = \pi/4$, $v_o = 80$ ft/sec, and $g = 32$ feet/sec^2.

Note: $\sin(\pi/6) = \frac{1}{2}$, $\cos(\pi/6) = \frac{\sqrt{3}}{2}$, and $\sin(\pi/4) = \cos(\pi/4) = \sqrt{2}/2$.

1. Plugging these values into equation (3.9) for when the ball hits the ground we get

$$t^* = \frac{v_o \sin(\phi) + \sqrt{v_o^2 \sin^2(\phi) + 2gh}}{g} = \frac{80\frac{1}{2} + \sqrt{80^2 \left(\frac{1}{2}\right)^2}}{32} = 2.5 \text{ seconds}$$

2. Now that we have the total time the ball is in the air, we use equation (3.8) for the actual trajectory:

$$
\begin{aligned}
\mathbf{r}(t) &= \left\langle v_o \cos(\theta)\cos(\phi)t, \quad v_o \sin(\theta)\cos(\phi)t, \quad h + v_o \sin(\phi)t - \frac{1}{2}gt^2 \right\rangle \\
&= \left\langle 80\cos(\pi/4)\cos(\pi/6)t, \quad 80\sin(\pi/4)\cos(\pi/6)t, \quad 0 + 80\sin(\pi/6)t - \frac{1}{2}gt^2 \right\rangle \\
&= \left\langle \left(80\frac{\sqrt{2}}{2}\frac{\sqrt{3}}{2}\right)t, \quad \left(80\frac{\sqrt{2}}{2}\frac{\sqrt{3}}{2}\right)t, \quad \left(80\frac{1}{2}\right)t - \frac{1}{2}32t^2 \right\rangle \\
&= \left\langle 20\sqrt{6}\,t, \quad 20\sqrt{6}\,t, \quad 40t - 16t^2 \right\rangle \qquad \text{for} \quad t \in [0, 2.5]
\end{aligned}
$$

3. To find where the ball lands in the xy-plane we just evaluate $x(t)$ and $y(t)$ at $t^* = 2.5$.

$$x(t^*) = 50\sqrt{6} \approx 122.5, \quad \text{and} \quad y(t^*) = 50\sqrt{6} \approx 122.5$$

4. To get the total distance traveled in the xy-plane we just determine the distance from

$$\text{total distance in } xy\text{-plane} = \sqrt{[50\sqrt{6}]^2 + [50\sqrt{6}]^2} = \sqrt{30000} = 100\sqrt{3} \approx 173.2$$

5. To get the maximum height we plug the same values into equation (3.12) which yields

$$\text{maximum height} = h + \frac{v_o^2 \sin^2(\phi)}{2g} = \frac{80^2 \sin^2(\pi/6)}{64} = 25 \text{ feet.}$$

Note: These answers match those obtained when we did a similar problem in 2D.

The code on the next page does most of this and animates the projectile.

C:_dropbox\Dropbox_My Books\MV3D-Book\Chapter-3\Chapter 3 MATLAB Examples\Projectile3D.m

File   Edit   Text   Go   Cell   Tools   Debug   Desktop   Window   Help

```
1        %% Projectile3D.m
2        % Plots an animated projectile in 3D example in Chapter 3.1
3  -     clc; clf; clear;
4
5        %% Initial Values
6  -     vo = 80; thetadegrees = 45; phidegrees = 30; h = 0; g = 32;
7  -     theta = thetadegrees*pi/180; phi = phidegrees*pi/180;
8
9        %% Plotting directives
10 -     xyzbounds = [-1.5, 150, -1.5, 150, -1, 30];  % graph bounds
11 -     tsteps = 50;    % number of points to plot
12
13       %%    create the trajectory points
14 -     tstar = (vo*sin(phi) + sqrt(vo^2 * (sin(phi))^2 + 2*g*h))/g;   %hit time
15 -     t = linspace(0,tstar,tsteps);    % the parameter t
16 -     x = vo * cos(theta) * cos(phi) * t;    % x(t)
17 -     y = vo * sin(theta) * cos(phi) * t;    % y(t)
18 -     z = h + vo*sin(phi)*t - 1/2*g*t.^2;    % z(t)
19
20       %% initial plot
21 -     trajplot = plot3(x,y,z);  hold on; grid on;
22 -     view(10,10); axis equal; axis(xyzbounds);
23 -     xlabel('x'); ylabel('y'); zlabel('z');
24 -     title('click to fire','fontsize',16);
25 -     waitforbuttonpress % waits for a click on the graph.
26 -     delete(trajplot);
27
28       %% Animation Loop
29 -     for i = 1:1:tsteps
30 -        pointplot = plot3(x(i), y(i), z(i),'b.','markersize',30);
31 -        pause(.05);
32 -     end
33 -     title('Projectile in 3D','fontsize',16)
```

script   Ln 2   Col 53   OVR

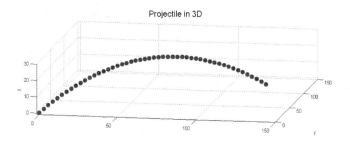

Chapter 3.1 Problem Set

Numbers with an asterisk* have solutions in the back of the book.

1.* Define a vector-valued function that creates something similar to the graphs depicted below. Use
    software to create the graphs.

(a)   (b)

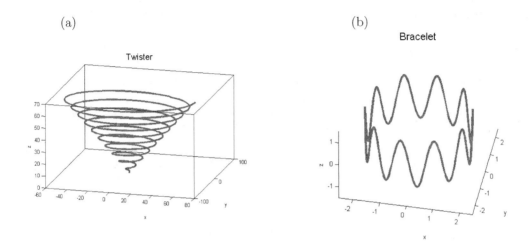

2. Define a vector-valued function that creates something similar to the graphs depicted below. Use
   software to create the graphs.

(a)   (b)   (c)

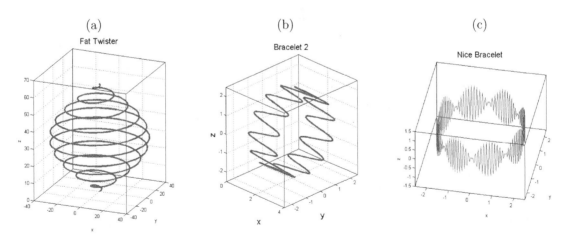

3.* **Projectile in 3D:** Consider the projectile that is launched from the point (0,0,60). The angle of elevation is 30°, and the launcher is positioned to point 45° from the positive x-axis. The initial velocity is 100 feet/second. Give your answers in feet and seconds. (Ie. Use $g = 32$ ft/sec^2). You are welcome to use software to complete these questions.

   (a) Determine when the ball hits the ground.

   (b) Determine the vector-valued function that describes the trajectory of the ball.

   (c) Where will it land?

   (d) How far will it travel in the xy-plane?

   (e) How high will it go?

4.* Use software to plot the trajectory described in the previous problem. It should look something like the plot below.

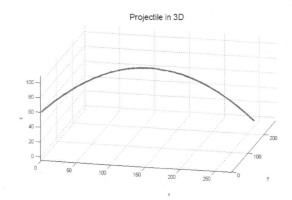

5. **Projectile in 3D:** Consider the projectile that is launched from the point (0,0,10). The angle of elevation is 60°, and the launcher is positioned to point 70° from the positive x-axis. The initial velocity is 100 feet/second. Give your answers in feet and seconds. (Ie. Use $g = 32$ ft/sec^2). You are welcome to use software to complete these questions.

   (a) Determine when the ball hits the ground.

   (b) Determine the vector-valued function that describes the trajectory of the ball.

   (c) Where will it land?

   (d) How far will it travel in the xy-plane?

   (e) How high will it go?

6. Use software to plot the trajectory described in the previous problem.

3.2 Differentiation of Vector-Valued Functions

Differentiation of vector valued functions requires no additional differentiation techniques! You should already know all of the differentiation methods you will need (provided you successfully completed one-variable Calculus). A review of some differentiation rules from Calculus I are found in Appendix B on page 173. The main difference now is the independent variable. In the past it was usually x, now it is usually t.

- One Variable Calculus: Differentiation

$$\text{the derivative of } f(x) = \frac{df}{dx} = f'(x)$$

- Multi-variable Calculus: Differentiation of Vector-Valued-Functions

$$\text{the derivative of } \mathbf{r}(t) = \frac{d\mathbf{r}}{dt} = \mathbf{r}'(t) = \langle x'(t), y'(t), z'(t) \rangle$$

1. **Differentiation: Formal Definition**

   Technically speaking, the derivative of a vector-valued function $\mathbf{r}(t)$ is given by

   $$\mathbf{r}'(t) = \mathbf{v}(t) = \lim_{\Delta t \to 0} \frac{\mathbf{r}(t + \Delta t) - \mathbf{r}(t)}{\Delta t}, \tag{3.13}$$

   provided this limit exists. Fortunately, this is exactly the same as you have done in single-variable calculus, only now you do it two or three times (2D or 3D respectively), and you differentiate with respect to the independent variable t instead of x.

2. **Differentiation: Informal Definition**

   If the vector valued function $\mathbf{r}(t) = \langle x(t), y(t), z(t) \rangle$, then the derivative of $\mathbf{r}(t)$ is given by

   $$\mathbf{r}'(t) = \mathbf{v}(t) = \langle x'(t), y'(t), z'(t) \rangle \tag{3.14}$$

   In words, the derivative of a vector-valued function is just *term by term* differentiation. The resulting vector is one that is parallel to the direction of motion on the curve described by $\mathbf{r}(t)$ as t increases.

3. **Position, Velocity, Speed, and Acceleration**

   $$\text{Position} = \mathbf{r}(t) = \langle x(t), y(t), z(t) \rangle, \tag{3.15}$$

   $$\text{Velocity} = \mathbf{v}(t) = \mathbf{r}'(t) = \langle x'(t), y'(t), z'(t) \rangle \tag{3.16}$$

   $$\text{Speed} = \|\mathbf{v}(t)\| \quad \text{is a non-negative scalar.} \tag{3.17}$$

   $$\text{Acceleration} = \mathbf{a}(t) = \mathbf{v}'(t) = \mathbf{r}''(t) = \langle x''(t), y''(t), z''(t) \rangle \tag{3.18}$$

Example in 2D: Given the position function

$$\mathbf{r}(t) = \langle\, 4\cos(t),\ 2\sin(t)\,\rangle, \quad t \in [0, 2\pi]$$

(a) Find $\mathbf{v}(t)$ and $\mathbf{a}(t)$

Answer: Find $\mathbf{v}(t)$ by differentiating $\mathbf{r}(t)$ term-by-term with respect to t

$$\mathbf{v}(t) = \langle -4\sin(t),\ 2\cos(t)\rangle$$

Differentiating one more time gives acceleration

$$\mathbf{a}(t) = \langle -4\cos(t),\ -2\sin(t)\rangle$$

(b) Find the velocity vector and speed at $t = \pi/3$.

Answer: To find the velocity velocity vector when $t = \pi/3$ we just plug it in;

$$\mathbf{v}(\pi/3) = \langle -4\sin(\pi/3),\ 2\cos(\pi/3)\rangle = \left\langle -2\sqrt{3},\ 1 \right\rangle$$

and the speed is $\|\mathbf{v}(\pi/3)\|$

$$\text{speed} = \sqrt{(-2\sqrt{3})^2 + 1^2} = \sqrt{13}$$

(c) Sketch the graph of $\mathbf{r}(t)$ for $t \in [0, 2\pi]$ along with $\mathbf{r}(\pi/3)$, $\mathbf{v}(\pi/3)$, and $\mathbf{v}(\pi/3)$ originating from the point $\mathbf{r}(\pi/3)$.

Answer: $\mathbf{r}(t)$ for $t \in [0, 2\pi]$ is the ellipse traced out in a counter-clockwise direction, $\mathbf{r}(\pi/3)$ and $\mathbf{v}(\pi/3)$ are vectors. And $\mathbf{v}(\pi/3)$ translated to originate at $\mathbf{r}(\pi/3)$ is the dashed vector - it gives the direction of motion at that specific time.

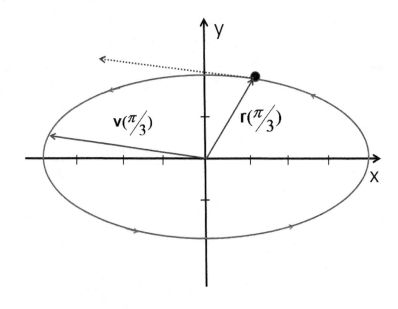

Example in 3D: Consider the helix defined by the vector-valued function:

$$\mathbf{r}(t) = \left\langle \frac{t}{\pi}, \quad 3\sin(2t), \ 4\cos(2t) \right\rangle \quad \text{for} \quad t \in [0, 4\pi]$$

pictured below (left):

Horizontal Helix

A Velocity Vector

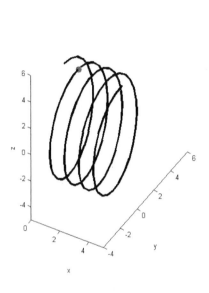 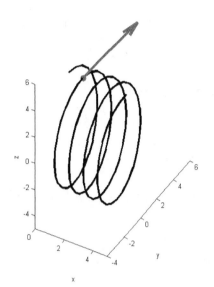

(a) Find $\mathbf{v}(t)$ and $\mathbf{a}(t)$

Answer: Differentiating term by term,

$$\mathbf{v}(t) = \left\langle \frac{1}{\pi}, \ 6\cos(2t), \ -8\sin(2t) \right\rangle \quad \text{and} \quad \mathbf{a}(t) = \langle \, 0, \ -12\sin(2t), \ -16\cos(2t) \, \rangle$$

(b) Find the velocity at the point $(1, 0, 4)$ denoted with a dot in the graph.

Answer: We really need t, not x, y, and z. However we can figure this out rather easily because if $x = 1$ and $x = t/\pi$, then $t = \pi$. So the velocity vector at this point is the velocity at $t = \pi$, and

$$\mathbf{v}(\pi) = \left\langle \frac{1}{\pi}, \ 6\cos(2\pi), \ -8\sin(2\pi) \right\rangle = \left\langle \frac{1}{\pi}, \ 6, \ 0 \right\rangle$$

(c) Sketch the velocity vector on the curve originating at $(1, 0, 4)$.

Answer: See graph above (right).

4. **Converting** $y = f(x)$ **to** $\mathbf{r}(t) = \langle x(t), y(t) \rangle$.

In the calculus of one variable you spent a great deal of time getting the slope of a tangent line to the graph of $y = f(x)$. You found the slope of this line to be $y' = f'(x)$. You can easily do the same by using vector-valued function

$$\mathbf{r}(t) = \langle t, f(t) \rangle$$

Example: Find the slope of the tangent line to the curve $y = x^2$ at the point (3,9).

- **One variable calculus:**

  You would consider the function $y = f(x)$ where $f(x) = x^2$.
  Then you would find the derivative of this function denoted $\frac{dy}{dx}$, $\frac{df}{dx}$, $y'(x)$, or $f'(x)$.
  $f'(x) = 2x$,
  and the slope of the tangent line at $x = 3$ would be $f'(3) = 6$.

- **Same Problem Using Vector Valued Functions:**
  Create the vector-valued function
  $$\mathbf{r}(t) = \langle t, t^2 \rangle$$
  then
  $$\mathbf{v}(t) = \langle 1, 2t \rangle$$
  and the velocity vector at $t = 3$ is given by
  $$\mathbf{v}(3) = \langle 1, 6 \rangle .$$
  The slope of this vector is $\frac{\text{rise}}{\text{run}} = \frac{6}{1} = 6$.

- **Summary:**
  – Graph:
  $$y = f(x) \quad \Longleftrightarrow \quad \mathbf{r}(t) = \langle\, t,\ f(t)\, \rangle$$
  – Slope:
  $$\text{slope} = f'(x) \quad \Longleftrightarrow \quad \mathbf{v}(t) = \langle\, 1,\ f'(t)\, \rangle$$

5. **A Projectile in Motion: 3D**

Previously we described the trajectory for a projectile in 3D given by

$$\mathbf{r}(t) = \left\langle v_o \cos(\theta) \cos(\phi)t, \quad v_o \sin(\theta) \cos(\phi)t, \quad h + v_o \sin(\phi)t - \frac{1}{2}gt^2 \right\rangle. \tag{3.19}$$

where h is the initial height (z-value), v_o is the initial velocity, ϕ is the angle of elevation, θ is the angle made with the positive x-axis, and g is the acceleration due to gravity. This equation can be differentiated with respect to t to get the velocity vector:

$$\mathbf{v}(t) = \langle v_o \cos(\theta) \cos(\phi), \quad v_o \sin(\theta) \cos(\phi), \quad v_o \sin(\phi) - gt \rangle. \tag{3.20}$$

and the acceleration vector is given by

$$\mathbf{a}(t) = \langle 0, \ 0, \ -g \rangle. \tag{3.21}$$

Example: Suppose a projectile is launched from the point (0,0,0). The angle of elevation is 30°, and the launcher is positioned to point 45° from the positive x-axis. The initial velocity is 80 feet/second. We found the trajectory for this problem in the last section:

$$\mathbf{r}(t) = \left\langle 20\sqrt{6}\, t, \quad 20\sqrt{6}\, t, \quad 40t - 16t^2 \right\rangle$$

as such, the velocity vector is given by:

$$\mathbf{v}(t) = \left\langle 20\sqrt{6}, \quad 20\sqrt{6}, \quad 40 - 32t \right\rangle$$

Notice: $\mathbf{v}(0) = \langle 20\sqrt{6}, \quad 20\sqrt{6}, \quad 40 \rangle$. And the $\|\mathbf{v}(0)\| = \sqrt{(20\sqrt{6})^2 + (20\sqrt{6})^2 + 40^2} = \sqrt{6400} = 80$ as prescribed in the problem.

This is a graph of the trajectory with a few velocity vectors superimposed at their associated points of origin. The velocity vector gives the direction of motion while the size of the velocity vector gives the speed.

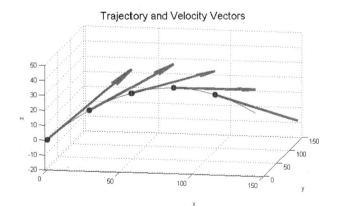

6. **A Bounce off the Ground:** Suppose a projectile hits the ground with an incoming velocity vector of $\mathbf{v}_0$. This projectile may then bounce off the ground and we want to know where it will go. We will call the velocity vector after the bounce $\mathbf{v}_1$. This is easily computed once we introduce the normal vector $\mathbf{n} = \langle 0, 0, 1 \rangle$. The bounce vector is found using the formula

$$\mathbf{v}_1 = \mathbf{v}_0 - 2 \, \mathrm{Proj}_{\mathbf{n}} \mathbf{v}_0 \tag{3.22}$$

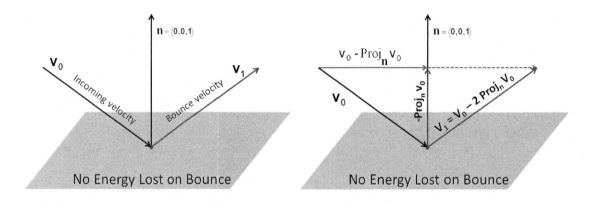

Currently, this bounce vector ($\mathbf{v}_1$) only changes the sign of the z component of the incoming velocity vector. This is because the normal vector to the *ground* is $\langle 0, 0, 1 \rangle$. Later, when we start dealing with different planes and surfaces, this will not be the case. The formula for $\mathbf{v}_1$ will remain valid but the normal vector will not be $\langle 0, 0, 1 \rangle$. Furthermore, it doesn't matter what choice of $\mathbf{n}$ you use, as long as $\mathbf{n}$ is normal to the plane.

Damping: If there is energy lost on the bounce, then the bounce vector will have a smaller magnitude than the incoming vector. This can be modeled with a damping coefficient applied to equation (3.22) as

$$\mathbf{v}_1 = D \left(2 \, \mathrm{Proj}_{\mathbf{n}} \mathbf{v}_0 - \mathbf{v}_0 \right), \tag{3.23}$$

for $D \in (0, 1]$. If $D = 1$, there is no damping and no energy lost on the bounce. Otherwise,

$$\| \mathbf{v}_1 \| = D \, \| \mathbf{v}_0 \|.$$

Chapter 3.2 Problem Set

Numbers with an asterisk[*] have solutions in the back of the book.
A review of **differentiation rules** can be found in Appendix B on page 173

1.[*] Consider the ellipse with x-radius $= 2$ and y-radius $= 8$ traced out counter-clockwise by the vector-valued function $\mathbf{r}(t) = \langle\, 2\cos(t),\, 8\sin(t)\rangle$, for $t \in [0, 2\pi]$.

   (a) Find the velocity function: $\mathbf{v}(t)$.

   (b) Find the velocity vector at the point $P(2, 0)$.

   (c) Find the velocity vector at the point $P(0, -8)$.

   (d) Find the velocity vector at the point $P(-\sqrt{2},\, 4\sqrt{2})$.

   (e) Sketch the ellipse, place the above points on the ellipse, and sketch the velocity vectors originating at the point on the ellipse.

2. Consider the ellipse with x-radius $= 2$ and y-radius $= 8$ traced out clockwise by the vector-valued function $\mathbf{r}(t) = \langle\, 2\cos(t),\, -8\sin(t)\rangle$, for $t \in [0, 2\pi]$.

   (a) Determine the velocity vector-valued function.

   (b) Find the velocity vector at the point $P(2, 0)$.

   (c) Find the velocity vector at the point $P(0, -8)$.

   (d) Find the velocity vector at the point $P(-\sqrt{2},\, 4\sqrt{2})$.

   (e) Sketch the ellipse, place the above points on the ellipse, and sketch the velocity vectors originating at the point on the ellipse.

3.[*] Consider the 3-D helix described by $\mathbf{r}(t) = \langle\cos(t), \sin(t), t\rangle$ for $t \in [0, 4\pi]$

   (a) Find $\mathbf{v}(t)$ and $\mathbf{a}(t)$.

   (b) Comment on the acceleration in the z-direction.

   (c) Use software to sketch the Helix with the velocity vectors at $t = \pi/2$, 2π, and $7\pi/2$.

4. Consider the helix described by $\mathbf{r}(t) = \langle\, 4\sin(t),\quad 4\cos(t),\quad 2\pi - t\,\rangle$ for $t \in [0, 4\pi]$

   (a) Find the general velocity vector-valued function: $\mathbf{v}(t)$.

   (b) Find the velocity vector at the point $(0,4,0)$. This point is indicated by the dot on the curve.

   (c) Find the acceleration vector at the point $(0,4,0)$.

   (d) Sketch the velocity and acceleration vectors (from parts (b) and (c)) on the curve originating from the point $(0,4,0)$.

5.* Consider the vector-valued function defined by $\mathbf{r}(t) = \langle t\cos(t), \sin(4t), 3t^2 \rangle$

    (a) Find $\mathbf{v}(t)$

        You might look up the product rule if you don't remember it.

    (b) Find the initial velocity and speed.

    (c) Find the acceleration vector: $\mathbf{a}(t) = \mathbf{r}''(t)$.

6.* Consider the vector-valued function given by

$$\mathbf{r}(t) = \left\langle\ 2t,\ t^2 + 1,\ \frac{1}{2}t^3\ \right\rangle$$

Find the velocity vector at the point $(4,5,4)$.

7. Consider the vector-valued function given by

$$\mathbf{r}(t) = \left\langle\ t\sin(t),\ e^{2t},\ 3t\ \right\rangle$$

Find the velocity vector at the point $(0,\ e^{2\pi},\ 3\pi)$.

8.* **Projectile in 3D:** Consider the projectile that is launched from the point $(0,0,60)$. The angle of elevation is 30°, and the launcher is positioned to point 45° from the positive x-axis. The initial velocity is 100 feet/second.

    (a) Determine the velocity vector when the ball hits the ground.

    (b) Determine the speed at which the ball is traveling when it hits the ground.

    (c) Determine the velocity vector coming off of the bounce after hitting the ground assuming no energy is lost on the bounce.

9. **Projectile in 3D:** Consider the projectile that is launched from the point $(0,0,10)$. The angle of elevation is 60°, and the launcher is positioned to point 70° from the positive x-axis. The initial velocity is 100 feet/second.

    (a) Determine the velocity vector when the ball hits the ground.

    (b) Determine the speed at which the ball is traveling when it hits the ground.

    (c) Determine the velocity vector coming off of the bounce after hitting the ground assuming no energy is lost on the bounce.

3.3 Euler's Method

When dealing with animations of projectiles through space. We will usually only know the current position and the direction in which it is heading. As such, it is impossible to know the full trajectory of the object at all times. So we just go step-by-step. The object is at a current position, it intends on going in a certain direction. But, it might hit something. At this time, we must determine where it will be at the next time step. The way we deal with this *one-step-at-a-time* approach is through a method developed by a guy named Leonard Euler. His last name is pronounced *Oiler*.

Here is one way of describing it mathematically. If

$$\mathbf{r}'(t) = \mathbf{v}(t) = \lim_{\Delta t \to 0} \frac{\mathbf{r}(t + \Delta t) - \mathbf{r}(t)}{\Delta t},$$

then if Δt is small we can say that

$$\mathbf{v}(t) \approx \frac{\mathbf{r}(t + \Delta t) - \mathbf{r}(t)}{\Delta t},$$

or

$$\mathbf{r}(t + \Delta t) \approx \mathbf{r}(t) + \Delta t \, \mathbf{v}(t). \tag{3.24}$$

If this makes sense to you, then moving points through space is really a simple task. What the above approximation say is this: *if you know the current position of a point ($\mathbf{r}(t)$) and the velocity vector of motion ($\mathbf{v}(t)$), then you can approximate its position as t increases by Δt.* The important part is that the approximation is only valid if Δt is small.

There is some notational issues to resolve here. First, there is the true position vector denoted $\mathbf{r}(t)$. Now, we need to give the approximation a different name. Let's call it $\tilde{\mathbf{r}}(t)$. This notation is a necessary part of the approximation game because we don't want to imply that we know the exact value of $\mathbf{r}(t)$. Assuming we know our original point at $\mathbf{r}(0)$, the approximation sequence looks like this

$$
\begin{aligned}
\tilde{\mathbf{r}}(0) &= \mathbf{r}(0) \quad \text{(known)}. \\
\tilde{\mathbf{r}}(\Delta t) &\approx \tilde{\mathbf{r}}(0) + \Delta t \, \mathbf{v}(0) \\
\tilde{\mathbf{r}}(2\Delta t) &\approx \tilde{\mathbf{r}}(\Delta t) + \Delta t \, \mathbf{v}(\Delta t) \\
\tilde{\mathbf{r}}(3\Delta t) &\approx \tilde{\mathbf{r}}(2\Delta t) + \Delta t \, \mathbf{v}(2\,\Delta t) \\
&\vdots \\
\tilde{\mathbf{r}}(n\Delta t) &\approx \tilde{\mathbf{r}}((n-1)\,\Delta t) + \Delta t \, \mathbf{v}((n-1)\,\Delta t)
\end{aligned}
$$

Now we can continue this process. There are some propagated approximation errors and round-off errors to be expected. However, if you keep Δt small, these errors will be minimized.

Example in 2D: Suppose a ball is kicked from the ground at an initial angle of 30° with an initial velocity of 80 feet per second. Neglecting the effects of wind or air resistance, depict the ball's approximate trajectory using Euler's method with a time step of $\Delta t = 0.5$ seconds. Note: We know the exact trajectory in this case which is useful for comparing the approximate trajectory.

Answer: We did this in Chapter 2.5.2 and determined the the ball's trajectory was described by

$$
\begin{aligned}
\mathbf{r}(t) &= \left\langle [v_o \cos(\theta)]t, \quad h + [v_o \sin(\theta)]t - \frac{1}{2}gt^2 \right\rangle \\
&= \left\langle 40\sqrt{3}\, t, \quad 40t - 16t^2 \right\rangle \qquad \text{for} \quad t \in [0, 2.5]
\end{aligned}
$$

and therefore

$$
\begin{aligned}
\mathbf{v}(t) &= \left\langle v_o \cos(\theta), \quad v_o \sin(\theta) - gt \right\rangle \\
&= \left\langle 40\sqrt{3}, \quad 40 - 32t \right\rangle
\end{aligned}
$$

Proceeding through the approximation process with $\Delta t = 0.5$ produces

$$
\begin{aligned}
\tilde{\mathbf{r}}(0) &= (0,0) \\
\tilde{\mathbf{r}}(.5) &\approx \mathbf{r}(0) + 0.5\,\mathbf{v}(0) = (34.6, 20) \\
\tilde{\mathbf{r}}(1) &\approx \tilde{\mathbf{r}}(.5) + 0.5\,\mathbf{v}(.5) = (69.3, 32) \\
\tilde{\mathbf{r}}(1.5) &\approx \tilde{\mathbf{r}}(1) + 0.5\,\mathbf{v}(1) = (103.9, 36) \\
\tilde{\mathbf{r}}(2.0) &\approx \tilde{\mathbf{r}}(1.5) + 0.5\,\mathbf{v}(1.5) = (138.6, 32) \\
\tilde{\mathbf{r}}(2.5) &\approx \tilde{\mathbf{r}}(2.0) + 0.5\,\mathbf{v}(2.0) = (173.2, 20)
\end{aligned}
$$

Below is a depiction of this approximation (in red), with the true trajectory and points (in black) at the same values of t. Notice: Very Bad Approximation!

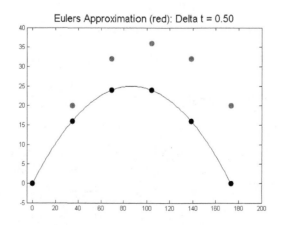

Eulers Approximation (red): Delta t = 0.50

Euler's method becomes more accurate as the time-step (Δt) gets small

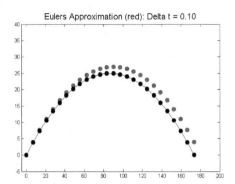
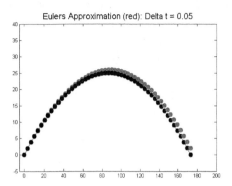

Below is the code used to generate these approximations.

```
%% This is Euler2D.m in Chapter 3
clf; clc; clear; % clears console, figure, and all variables respectively

%% Initial Values
Ro = [0,0];     % this is the initial position.
vo = 80; thetadegrees = 30; theta = thetadegrees*pi/180;
tend = 2.5; deltaT = 0.05; tsteps = tend/deltaT;

%% Plot True Trajectory
tTrue = linspace(0,2.5,100);
xTrue = vo*cos(theta)*tTrue; yTrue = vo*sin(theta)*tTrue - 16*tTrue.^2;
plot(xTrue,yTrue,'k-');  hold on; % plot the true trajectory
plot(Ro(1), Ro(2),'k.','markersize',30);  % plot the initial point.
axis([-5,200,-5,40]);

%%  Plot Euler's Approximation
tildeRo = Ro; t = 0;
for i = 1:tsteps
   v = [vo*cos(theta),  vo*sin(theta) - 32*t];      %% current velocity
   tildeR1 = tildeRo + deltaT*v;                    %% next Euler point
   plot(tildeR1(1),tildeR1(2), 'r.', 'markersize',30)  %% plot it.
   t = t + deltaT;                                  %% advance time
   R1 = [vo*cos(theta)*t, vo*sin(theta)*t - 16*t^2];  %% True point
   plot(R1(1),R1(2),'k.','markersize',30)           %% Plot it.
   tildeRo = tildeR1;                               %% Update Euler point
end
text = sprintf('Eulers Approximation (red): Delta t = %1.2f',deltaT);
title(text,'fontsize',16)
```

What about velocity? You should notice from the previous development (and code) that we still need to know the velocity function at all times. This might be a problem. However, we can use Euler's Method (again) to approximate velocity. Since acceleration ($\mathbf{a}$) is the derivative of velocity ($\mathbf{v}$),

$$\mathbf{a}(t) = \lim_{\Delta t \to 0} \frac{\mathbf{v}(t + \Delta t) - \mathbf{v}(t)}{\Delta t},$$

then if Δt is small we can say that

$$\mathbf{a}(t) \approx \frac{\mathbf{v}(t + \Delta t) - \mathbf{v}(t)}{\Delta t}, \qquad \text{or} \qquad \mathbf{v}(t + \Delta t) \approx \mathbf{v}(t) + \Delta t\, \mathbf{a}(t).$$

The nice thing here is that if acceleration is constant, this approximation is actually an equality and

$$\mathbf{v}(t + \Delta t) = \mathbf{v}(t) + \Delta t\, \mathbf{a} \qquad \text{(provided } \mathbf{a} \text{ is constant)} \tag{3.25}$$

Here is the code that implements this process. It has been simplified from the previous code. Notice, there is no need for any position or velocity function beyond time zero.

```matlab
1    %% This is Euler2D_R_and_V.m in Chapter 3
2    % This is a simplified version of Euler2D.
3    % It uses Euler's Method to approximate position(R) and velocity (V).
4  - clf; clc; clear; % clears console, figure, and variables
5    %% Initial Values
6  - vo = 80;                % Initial Velocity
7  - thetadegrees = 30;      % Initial Angle
8  - h = 0;                  % Initial Height
9  - g = 32;                 % Gravity Constant
10 - tend = 2.5;             % Ending Time
11 - deltaT = 0.1;           % Step Size
12   %% Some calculated terms
13 - theta = thetadegrees*pi/180;            % theta in Radians
14 - R = [0,h];                              % Initial Position.
15 - V = [vo*cos(theta), vo*sin(theta)];     % Initial Velocity Vector.
16 - a = [0,-g];                             % Constant Acceleration Vector
17 - tsteps = tend/deltaT;                   % Number of Time Steps
18 - plot(R(1), R(2),'k.','markersize',30);  % plot the initial point.
19 - hold on; axis([-5,200,-5,40]);
20   %% Plot the positions
21 - for i = 1:tsteps
22 -     R = R + deltaT*V                     % Next Position
23 -     plot(R(1),R(2),'b.', 'markersize',30)  % Plot It.
24 -     V = V+deltaT*a;                      % Next Velocity Vector.
25 - end
26 - text = sprintf('Eulers Approximation (blue): Delta t = %1.2f',deltaT);
27 - title(text,'fontsize',16)
```

Chapter 3.3 Problem Set

Problems with an asterisk[*] have solutions in the back of the book.

1. Consider the projectile launched with an initial velocity of 80 ft/sec, at an angle of $30°$ from an initial height of 10 feet. Assume no air resistance and a gravity constant of 32 ft/(sec)^2.

   (a)[*] Using the exact solution, determine where the ball hits the ground.

   (b)[*] Use Euler's Approximation to determine where the ball hits the ground using $\Delta t = 0.10$ seconds. In this case you won't know what the final time is. Just set $\Delta t = 0.10$ and continue to advance time until $\tilde{y} \leq 0$. When this happens, check $\tilde{x}$. That's the approximation to where the ball lands. The graph of the trajectory should look like that in the figure.

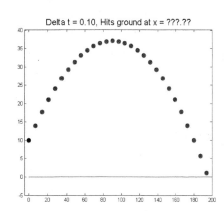

   (c) Use Euler's Approximation to determine where the ball hits the ground using $\Delta t = 0.05$ seconds.

   (d) Use Euler's Approximation to determine where the ball hits the ground using $\Delta t = 0.01$ seconds.

   (e)[*] At what value of Δt does the approximate landing position come within 0.1 feet of the actual landing position?

3.4   Bouncing Around in 2D

If you are happy enough with the Euler approximation we can stop worrying about where the object will be for all times and just let time go. This is especially important if you want to bounce around. However, there are some preliminary issues to resolve.

Notation:

$R = (x_o, y_o)$	Current Position (Point)
$\mathbf{v}$	Current Velocity Vector
$\mathbf{V} = \Delta t\, \mathbf{v}$	Change in Position Vector: $\langle \Delta x, \Delta y \rangle$
$R_1 = (x_1, y_1)$	Next Position (Point): $R_1 = R + \mathbf{V}$
$\mathbf{v}_1$	Next Velocity Vector
$\mathbf{V}_1 = \Delta t\, \mathbf{v}_1$	Next Change in Position Vector

Constant Acceleration: If acceleration vector is constant, we don't need a velocity function for all time. We can use Euler's method to get $\mathbf{v}_1$ from $\mathbf{v}$ by

$$\mathbf{v}_1 = \mathbf{v} + \Delta t\, \mathbf{a} \qquad \text{where} \qquad \mathbf{a} = \langle 0, -g \rangle$$

Bounce Point P:

When bouncing around, it is unlikely the ball will hit the ground at exactly $y = 0$. More than likely, R_1 will be below ground. When this happens, we want to determine where the ball actually hits $y = 0$. The parametric equations for line from R to R_1 are given by $R + s\mathbf{V}$ or

$$x = x_o + s\,\Delta x \qquad \text{and} \qquad y = y_o + s\,\Delta y$$

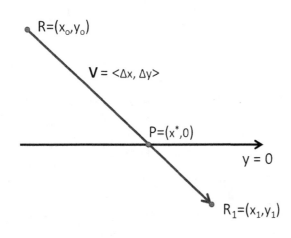

Denote P by $(x^*, 0)$ and find x^*

Find s so that $y_o + s\,\Delta y = 0$

to get $s = -\dfrac{y_o}{\Delta y}$

so $x^* = x_o - \dfrac{y_o}{\Delta y}\Delta x$

This could be a problem if $\Delta y = 0$.
But the ball can't go from above $y = 0$ to below $y = 0$ if $\Delta y = 0$.
So this shouldn't happen.

Bounce Vector $\mathbf{V}_1$:

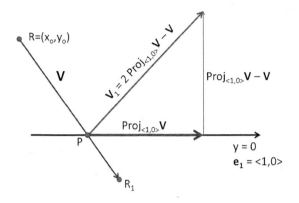

If $\mathbf{V}$ takes the ball below $y = 0$, we want to bounce from P in the appropriate direction. With a *perfect bounce* (no loss of energy), the bounce vector ($\mathbf{V}_1$) will have the same magnitude ($\mathbf{V}$). In this case, the bounce vector $\mathbf{V}_1$ is found by

$$\mathbf{V}_1 = 2 \operatorname{Proj}_{\langle 1,0 \rangle} \mathbf{V} - \mathbf{V} \qquad (3.26)$$

Note: We just calculated the change in position vector($\mathbf{V}_1$). The new velocity vector is given by

$$\mathbf{v}_1 = \frac{1}{\Delta t} \mathbf{V}_1$$

Damping: If there is energy lost on the bounce, then the bounce vector will have a smaller magnitude than the incoming vector. This can be modeled with a damping coefficient applied to equation (3.26) as

$$\mathbf{V}_1 = D \left(2 \operatorname{Proj}_{\langle 1,0 \rangle} \mathbf{V} - \mathbf{V} \right) \qquad (3.27)$$

for $D \in (0, 1]$. If $D = 1$, there is no damping and no energy lost on the bounce. Otherwise,

$$||\mathbf{V}_1|| = D \, ||\mathbf{V}||.$$

Let Time Roll: Here is a bouncing ball animation with no damping ($D = 1$).

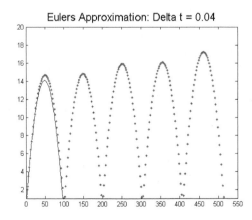

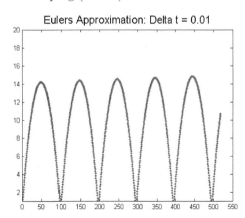

The code is on the next page.

MATLAB® code: Euler2DBounce.m

```
C:\_dropbox\Dropbox\_My Books\MV3D-Book\Chapter-3\Chapter 3 MATLAB Examples\Euler2DBounce.m

File  Edit  Text  Go  Cell  Tools  Debug  Desktop  Window  Help

Stack: Base    fx

- 1.0  +  ÷ 1.1  ×

1       %% This is Euler2DBounce.m
2       % Performs a bouncing ball simulation.
3   -   clf; clc; clear;
4
5       %% Initial Values
6   -   vo = 60; thetadegrees = 30; h=0; g = 32;
7   -   t_end = 10; delta_t = .04; t_steps = t_end/delta_t;
8   -   R=[0,0];    %/ initial position.
9   -   theta = thetadegrees*pi/180;
10  -   accel = [0,-g];   %/ the constant acceleration vector.
11  -   D = 1;    %/ D = damping on the bounce (between 0 and 1)
12
13      %% Initial graph up to first bounce.
14  -   Initialtend = (vo*sin(theta) + sqrt((vo*sin(theta))^2 + 2*g*h))/g;
15  -   t = linspace(0,Initialtend,50);
16  -   xtraj = R(1) + (vo * cos(theta))*t;
17  -   ytraj = R(2) + vo *sin(theta)*t - (g/2)*t.^2;
18  -   plot(xtraj,ytraj,'k-'); hold on; plot(R(1),R(2),'r.');
19  -   axis([0,550,1,20]);
20  -   title('click to start','fontsize',16);
21  -   waitforbuttonpress % waits for a click on the graph.
22  -   title('running','fontsize',16);
23
24      %% Animation Loop
25  -   v = vo*[cos(theta), sin(theta)];    % initial velocity vector
26  - ┌ for i = 1:1:t_steps
27  - │   V = delta_t * v;             % Current Position Change
28  - │   R1 = R + V;                  % Next Position
29  - │   v1 = v + delta_t*accel;  % Next Velocity Vector (no bounce)
30  - │   if R1(2)<0                          % Collision Detection: Is y1 < 0?
31  - │     disp('bounce')                    % Display 'bounce' to console
32  - │     V1 = D*(2*ProjUV(V,[1,0]) - V);   % Next Change in Position Vector
33  - │     R1 = [R(1) - R(2)* v(1)/v(2), 0];  % Intersection Point
34  - │     v1 = V1/delta_t;                  % Next Velocity Vector
35  - │   end
36  - │   pause(.005);
37  - │   plot(R1(1),R1(2), 'r.'); hold on; %pause(.01)  %% plot the new point.
38  - │   R = R1; v = v1;   % Reset R and V to the updated values.
39  - └ end
40  -   text = sprintf('Eulers Approximation: Delta t = %1.2f',delta_t);
41  -   title(text,'fontsize',16)

                                        script              Ln 4    Col 1   OVR
```

Bouncing off other things: In the previous example we bounced a ball off of the $y = 0$ axis. Here we look at finding the bounce point and bounce vector when a ball bounces off some other line. Suppose $R(x_o, y_o)$ represents the original point of the ball and the change in position vector ($\mathbf{V}$) has it landing in the other side of a wall at R_1. The wall is defined by an original point $W(x_w, y_w)$ and a terminal point W_1. The wall vector is denoted $\mathbf{w} = \overrightarrow{WW_1}$.

Bounce Point P: We want to find P

The line from R to R_1 is $R + s\,\mathbf{V}$
$$x = x_o + s\,v_1$$
$$y = y_o + s\,v_2$$

The line from W to W_1 is $W + r\,\mathbf{w}$
$$x = x_w + r\,w_1$$
$$y = y_w + r\,w_2$$

Goal: Find s and t so that
$$x_o + s\,v_1 = x_w + r\,w_1$$
$$y_o + s\,v_2 = y_w + r\,w_2$$

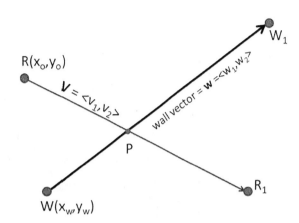

$$\begin{array}{ccc}
x_o + s\,v_1 = x_w + r\,w_1 \\
y_o + s\,v_2 = y_w + r\,w_2
\end{array} \quad \sim \quad
\begin{array}{ccc}
-r\,w_1 + s\,v_1 = x_w - x_o \\
-r\,w_2 + s\,v_2 = y_w - y_o
\end{array} \quad \rightarrow \quad
\begin{bmatrix} -w_1 & v_1 \\ -w_2 & v_2 \end{bmatrix}
\begin{bmatrix} r \\ s \end{bmatrix} =
\begin{bmatrix} x_w - x_o \\ y_w - y_o \end{bmatrix}$$

Notice, the determinant of the matrix is $-w_1 v_2 + w_2 v_2$ which is only zero if $\mathbf{w}$ is parallel to $\mathbf{v}$. In this case, there should be no intersection and no intersection point. Solving this matrix equation gets us s and t, either of which can be used to get the bounce point by

$$P = R + s\,\mathbf{V} \qquad \text{or} \qquad P = W + r\,\mathbf{w}$$

Bounce Vector $\mathbf{V}_1$:

The bounce vector is found by the exact same procedure used to find the bounce vector off the ground. The only difference is that the ground-vector $\langle 1, 0 \rangle$ is replaced with the wall-vector $\mathbf{w}$.

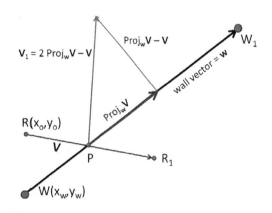

$$\mathbf{V}_1 = 2\,\text{Proj}_{\mathbf{w}}\mathbf{V} - \mathbf{V} \qquad (3.28)$$

and

$$\mathbf{v}_1 = \frac{1}{\Delta t}\mathbf{V}_1$$

MATLAB® code: Euler_2D_Bounce_Wall.m

```matlab
%% This is Euler_2D_Bounce_Wall.m
% Performs a bouncing ball simulation with a non-horizontal wall
clf; clc; clear;
%% Initial Values
vo = 85; thetadegrees = 50; h=0; g = 32;
t_end = 7; delta_t = .05; t_steps = t_end/delta_t;
R=[0,h];   %/ initial position.
theta = thetadegrees*pi/180;
accel = [0,-g];   %/ the constant acceleration vector.
D = .8;   %/ D = damping on the bounce (between 0 and 1)
%% Wall
W=[160,0]; W1=[200,80]; w=(W1-W); slopeW = w(2)/w(1);
%% Plot first Point and  Wall
plot(R(1),R(2),'r.'); hold on;
plot([W(1),W1(1)],[W(2),W1(2)],'k-','linewidth',4);
hold on; axis equal; axis([0,200,0,80]);
title('click to start','fontsize',16);
waitforbuttonpress % waits for a click on the graph.
title('Euler Bounce with Wall','fontsize',16);
%% Animation Loop
v = vo*[cos(theta), sin(theta)];   % initial velocity vector
for i = 1:1:t_steps
   V = delta_t*v;
   R1 = R + V;        % Next Position
   v1 = v + delta_t*accel;   % Next Velocity Vector
   if R1(2)<0                          % Detect ground hit
       disp('hit ground');
       V1 = D*(2*ProjUV(V,[1,0]) - V);     % New V1
       R1 = [R(1) - R(2)* V(1)/V(2), 0];   % New R1
       v1 = V1/delta_t;                    % New v1
   end
   if R1(1) >= W(1) & R1(1) <= W1(1) & R1(2) <= W(2)+slopeW*(R1(1)-W(1))
       disp('hit wall')                    % detect wall hit
       V1 = D*(2*ProjUV(V,w) - V);         % New V1
       rs=[-w(1),V(1);-w(2),V(2)]\[W(1)- R(1); W(2) - R(2)];
       R1 = R + rs(2)*V;                   % New R1
       v1 = V1/delta_t;                    % New v1
   end
   pause(.005);
   plot(R1(1),R1(2), 'r.','markersize',20);   %% plot the new point.
   R = R1; v = v1;   % Reset R and v.
end
```

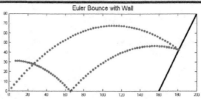
Euler Bounce with Wall

Chapter 3.4 Problem Set

Problems with an asterisk[*] have solutions in the back of the book.

1. (**MATLAB**®): Edit the MATLAB® file `Euler2Dbounce.m` to perform a bouncing simulation with the following requirements:

   (a) The ball starts at (0,20).

   (b) The ball is launched with an initial velocity of 60 feet per second.

   (c) The angle of elevation is -30°.

   (d) The simulation runs for 10 seconds.

   (e) The time step is 0.02 seconds.

   Your final graph should look like the the one below.

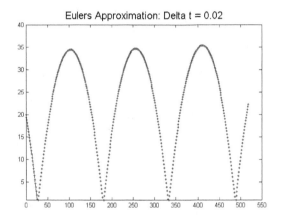

2. (**MATLAB**®): Edit the MATLAB® file `Euler2Dbounce.m` to perform a bouncing simulation (with damping) that results in the following bouncing trajectory over the course of 10 seconds. You should be able to match all the bounce points and bounce heights. Let $\Delta t = 0.02$.

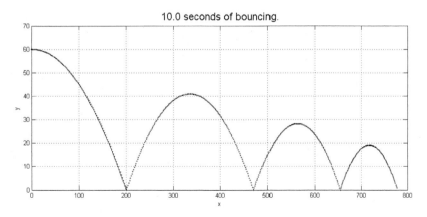

3.* (**MATLAB**®): Edit the MATLAB® file `Euler_2D_bounce_Wall.m` to perform a bouncing simulation that results in the following bouncing trajectory over the course of 9 seconds.

Preliminary Information: $v_o = 80$, $\theta = 20^o$, $D = 0.8$, $\Delta t = 0.05$, and the vertices of the triangle are (100,0), (160,40), and (160,0).

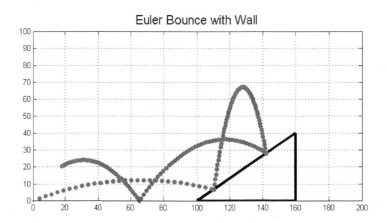

4. (**MATLAB**®): Edit the MATLAB® file `Euler_2D_bounce_Wall.m` to perform a bouncing simulation that results in the following bouncing trajectory over the course of 9 seconds.

Preliminary Information: $v_o = 90$, $\theta = 27^o$, $D = 0.8$, $\Delta t = 0.05$, and the vertices of the triangle are (60,0), (100,40), and (140,0).

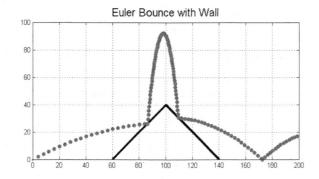

Chapter 4

Multi-Variable Functions and Surfaces

A surface in 3D is created by any equation of the general form:

$$F(x, y, z) = 0 \tag{4.1}$$

Here, $F(x, y, z)$ is a **multi-variable function** and the surface is defined **implicitly**. Usually, but not always, the same surface can be expressed in one of these three **explicit** forms:

$$z = f(x, y), \qquad y = g(x, z), \quad \text{or} \quad x = h(y, z). \tag{4.2}$$

In these cases, f, g, and h are multi-variable functions with two variables instead of three. We will start with explicit functions of the first form in (4.2).

4.1 Surfaces: $z = f(x, y)$

Here we consider multi-variable functions of the form

$$z = f(x, y) \tag{4.3}$$

The function here, $f(x, y)$, is the multi-variable function. There are two independent variables, x and y, and one dependent variable; z.

A familiar example: a plane

We have already seen one example of a surface defined implicitly in 3-space.

$$\text{plane:} \quad ax + by + cz - d = 0$$

Provided $c \neq 0$, we can define this surface explicitly as

$$\text{plane:} \quad z = \frac{ax + by - d}{c} = \frac{a}{c}\, x + \frac{b}{c}\, y - \frac{d}{c} = f(x, y) \tag{4.4}$$

If $c = 0$ we will have to choose one of the other explicit forms from (4.2). Notice, this looks a lot like the equation for a line in 2D. Here, $-d/c$ is z-intercept. The *slope* is defined in terms of the coefficients of x and y. We will resolve the issue of slope later in this chapter.

Example: Paraboloid

Consider the surface created by the multi-variable function:

$$z = x^2 + y^2 + 2 \tag{4.5}$$

To sketch something like this by hand it is best to start by sketching **traces** in various planes.

1. The **trace** in the xz-plane is found by letting $y = 0$.

$$z = x^2 + 2$$

   which is just a parabola in the xz-plane.

2. The **trace** in the yz-plane is found by letting $x = 0$.

$$z = y^2 + 2$$

   which is another parabola in the yz-plane.

3. The **trace** in the xy-plane is found by letting $z = 0$.

$$0 = x^2 + y^2 + 2 \quad \text{or} \quad x^2 + y^2 = -2$$

   and this has no solutions. As such, there is no *trace* in the xy-plane.

4. Let's try some traces at different values of z. These are called **level curves**.

   (a) $z = 2 \quad \rightarrow \quad x^2 + y^2 = 0$. This is just the point $(x, y) = (0, 0)$.

   (b) $z = 3 \quad \rightarrow \quad x^2 + y^2 = 1$. This is the circle centered at $(0,0)$ with radius 1.

   (c) $z = 6 \quad \rightarrow \quad x^2 + y^2 = 4$. This is the circle centered at $(0,0)$ with radius 2.

   (d) $z = 11 \quad \rightarrow \quad x^2 + y^2 = 9$. This is the circle centered at $(0,0)$ with radius 3.

   When you piece all of the traces and level curves together you should get the picture of the surface:

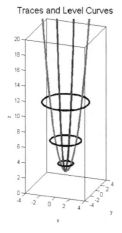
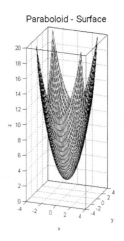

The code used to create these graphs is on the next page

MATLAB® Code: `PlottingParaboloidTraces.m`

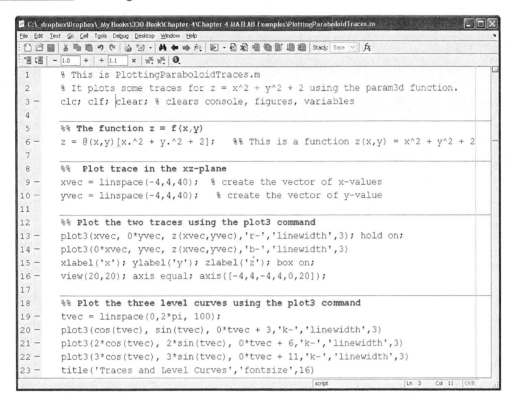

```
1       % This is PlottingParaboloidTraces.m
2       % It plots some traces for z = x^2 + y^2 + 2 using the param3d function.
3 —     clc; clf; clear; % clears console, figures, variables
4
5       %% The function z = f(x,y)
6 —     z = @(x,y)[x.^2 + y.^2 + 2];   %% This is a function z(x,y) = x^2 + y^2 + 2
7
8       %%  Plot trace in the xz-plane
9 —     xvec = linspace(-4,4,40);  % create the vector of x-values
10 —    yvec = linspace(-4,4,40);   % create the vector of y-value
11
12      %% Plot the two traces using the plot3 command
13 —    plot3(xvec, 0*yvec, z(xvec,yvec),'r-','linewidth',3); hold on;
14 —    plot3(0*xvec, yvec, z(xvec,yvec),'b-','linewidth',3)
15 —    xlabel('x'); ylabel('y'); zlabel('z'); box on;
16 —    view(20,20); axis equal; axis([-4,4,-4,4,0,20]);
17
18      %% Plot the three level curves using the plot3 command
19 —    tvec = linspace(0,2*pi, 100);
20 —    plot3(cos(tvec), sin(tvec), 0*tvec + 3,'k-','linewidth',3)
21 —    plot3(2*cos(tvec), 2*sin(tvec), 0*tvec + 6,'k-','linewidth',3)
22 —    plot3(3*cos(tvec), 3*sin(tvec), 0*tvec + 11,'k-','linewidth',3)
23 —    title('Traces and Level Curves','fontsize',16)
```

MATLAB® Code: `PlottingParaboloid.m`

```
1       % This is PlottingParaboloid.m
2       % It plots the paraboloid z = x^2 + y^2 + 2 using the surf command.
3 —     clc; clf; clear; % clears console, figures, variables
4
5       %% The function z = f(x,y)
6 —     zfunction = @(x,y)[x.^2 + y.^2 + 2];   %% This is a function z(x,y) = x^2 + y^2 + 2
7
8       %% Plot the surface using the surf command
9 —     xvec = linspace(-3,3,40);  % create the vector of x-values
10 —    yvec = linspace(-3,3,40);   % create the vector of y-value
11 —    [x y] = meshgrid(xvec,yvec);  % create a full array of x & y values
12 —    z = zfunction(x,y);  % creates the full array of z-values
13 —    surf(x, y, z,'FaceColor', 'yellow');  % Plots the surface
14 —    title('Paraboloid - Surface','fontsize',16)
15 —    xlabel('x'); ylabel('y'); zlabel('z'); box on;
16 —    view(20,20); axis equal; axis([-4,4,-4,4,0,20]);
```

Chapter 4.1 Problem Set

Numbers with an asterisk[*] have solutions in the back of the book.

1.[*] Consider the surface defined by

$$z = \cos\left(\sqrt{x^2 + y^2}\right) \quad \text{for} \quad x \in [-2\pi, 2\pi] \quad \text{and} \quad y \in [-2\pi, 2\pi]$$

(a) Sketch the trace of this surface in the xz-plane.

(b) Sketch the trace of this curve in the yz-plane.

(c) Sketch these traces in 3-Space.

(d) Sketch the level curves for the following values of z.

  i. $z = 0$

  ii. $z = -1$

  iii. $z = 1$

(e) Plot the surface using software

2. Consider the surface defined by

$$z = 4\, e^{-(x^2 + y^2)} \quad \text{for} \quad x \in [-2, 2] \quad \text{and} \quad y \in [-2, 2]$$

(a) Sketch the trace in the xz-plane.

(b) Sketch the trace in the yz-plane.

(c) Sketch these traces in 3-Space.

(d) Describe the level curves for the following values of z.

  i. $z = 4$

  ii. $z = 2$

  iii. $z = 1$

(e) Plot the surface using software

3.[*] Consider the surface defined by

$$z = f(x, y) = \frac{3}{1 + x^2 + y^2}$$

(a) Define and sketch the traces in the xz and yz planes.

(b) Use the traces to help plot the surface in 3-space.

4. Consider the surface defined by

$$z = f(x, y) = -4x^2 - y^2$$

(a) Define and sketch the traces in the xz and yz planes.

(b) Use the traces to help plot the surface in 3-space.

5.* Consider the plane defined by the equation $3x + 2y - 4z = 6$.

(a) Express this plane in the form $z = f(x, y)$.

(b) Express this plane in the form $F(x, y, z) = 0$.

6. Consider the sphere with radius 5 and centered at (2,1,-2) defined by the equation

$$(x - 2)^2 + (y - 1)^2 + (z + 2)^2 = 25.$$

(a) Express this sphere in the form $z = f(x, y)$.

(b) Anything upsetting about your answer to (a)?

(c) Express this sphere in the form $F(x, y, z) = 0$.

4.2 Partial Derivatives, Gradients, and Normal Vectors

When working with multi-variable functions, there is no longer a single derivative of the function. Instead, there are two or more **partial derivatives**. These can be used to find slopes of tangent lines to a surface in any direction instead of just the positive x-direction found in single-variable calculus. The partial derivatives also allow us to find gradients and normal vectors to surfaces which are nice to have when you start bouncing around in 3D. For now we will consider the only directions that are needed.

Partial Derivatives, Formal Definition

Given a multi-variable function of the form $z = f(x, y)$, the *partial derivative of f with respect to x*, denoted $\dfrac{\partial f}{\partial x}$ or f_x, is defined by

$$\frac{\partial f}{\partial x} = f_x(x, y) = \lim_{\Delta x \to 0} \frac{f(x + \Delta x, y) - f(x, y)}{\Delta x} \tag{4.6}$$

and likewise, the partial derivative of f with respect to y, denoted $\dfrac{\partial f}{\partial y}$ or f_y, is defined by

$$\frac{\partial f}{\partial y} = f_y(x, y) = \lim_{\Delta y \to 0} \frac{f(x, y + \Delta y) - f(x, y)}{\Delta y}. \tag{4.7}$$

Geometrically speaking, f_x is the slope (dz/dx) of the line parallel to the x-axis that is tangent to the surface $z = f(x, y)$. Likewise, f_y is the slope (dz/dy) of the line parallel to the y-axis that is tangent to the surface $z = f(x, y)$. These are both specific examples of *directional* derivatives. However, they turn out to be the only ones you really need.

Partial Derivatives, Informal Definition

When finding the partial derivative of a function with respect to a certain variable, you just differentiate with respect to that variable considering all other variables constant.

- **Example 1:** Consider the paraboloid defined by $z = f(x, y) = x^2 + y^2 + 2$.
  The partial derivatives are
  $$f_x(x, y) = 2x \quad \text{and} \quad f_y(x, y) = 2y$$

- **Example 2:** Consider the surface defined by $z = f(x, y) = 3x^2 y^3$.
  The partial derivatives are
  $$f_x(x, y) = 6xy^3 \quad \text{and} \quad f_y(x, y) = 9x^2y^2$$

- **Example 3(harder):** Consider the surface defined by $z = f(x, y) = \cos\left(\sqrt{x^2 + y^2}\right)$.
  The partial derivatives are
  $$f_x(x, y) = \frac{-x \sin\left(\sqrt{x^2 + y^2}\right)}{\sqrt{x^2 + y^2}} \quad \text{and} \quad f_y(x, y) = \frac{-y \sin\left(\sqrt{x^2 + y^2}\right)}{\sqrt{x^2 + y^2}}$$

The Gradient Vector: The gradient of a function $f(x, y)$ is denoted ∇f.

$$\nabla f = \langle\, f_x,\ f_y\, \rangle \tag{4.8}$$

- **Example 1:** If $f(x, y) = x^2 + y^2 + 2$ then $\nabla f = \langle\, 2x,\ 2y\, \rangle$

- **Example 2:** If $f(x, y) = 3x^2\, y^3$. then $\nabla f = \langle\, 6xy^3,\ 9x^2y^2\, \rangle$

- **Example 3:** If $f(x, y) = \cos(\sqrt{x^2 + y^2})$ then $\nabla f = \left\langle\, \dfrac{-x \sin(\sqrt{x^2 + y^2})}{\sqrt{x^2 + y^2}},\ \dfrac{-y \sin(\sqrt{x^2 + y^2})}{\sqrt{x^2 + y^2}}\, \right\rangle$

A practical implication: The gradient of a function $z = f(x, y)$ gives the direction (in the xy-plane) that leads to the greatest increase in z for a unit step-size.

- **Example:** If you are sitting on the surface $z = x^2 + y^2 + 2$ at the point (2,-2,10), what is the direction to move in the xy-plane that leads to the greatest increase?

  Answer: $\nabla f(2, -2) = \langle f_x(2, -2),\ f_y(2, -2) \rangle = \langle\, 4,\ -4\, \rangle$ depicted below.

MATLAB® code: `PlottingParaboloidAndGradient.m`

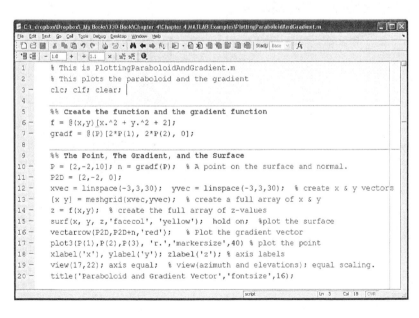
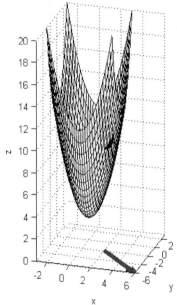

Paraboloid and Gradient Vector

The General Form of the Gradient and Normal Vectors

Suppose you have a surface defined by $F(x, y, z) = 0$, the gradient of F is

$$\nabla F = \langle\, F_x,\ F_y,\ F_z \,\rangle. \tag{4.9}$$

and $\pm \nabla F$ produces a vector that is <u>normal to the surface</u> defined by $F(x, y, z) = 0$.

<u>Practical Usage:</u> If you have a surface defined by $z = f(x, y)$, this surface can be defined by $f(x, y) - z = 0$ or $z - f(x, y) = 0$. Using these expressions for $F(x, y, z)$, the normal vectors to the surface are

$$\mathbf{n}_1 = \langle f_x,\ f_y,\ -1 \rangle \quad \text{and} \quad \mathbf{n}_2 = \langle -f_x,\ -f_y,\ 1 \rangle \tag{4.10}$$

- **Example:** Consider the surface defined by $z = x^2 + y^2 + 2$.
  Find the normal vector to the surface at the point $(2, -2, 10)$ that is pointing down.

  Answer: We choose the $\mathbf{n}_1$ normal from equations (4.10) because it has the negative z component.

$$\mathbf{n}_1 = \langle f_x,\ f_y,\ -1 \rangle = \langle\, 2x,\ 2y,\ -1 \,\rangle$$

  Evaluating this at the point (2,-2,0) gives $\mathbf{n}_1 = \langle 4,\ -4,\ -1 \rangle$. The surface and this normal are depicted in the graph from the following code.

MATLAB® code: `PlottingParaboloidAndNormal.m`

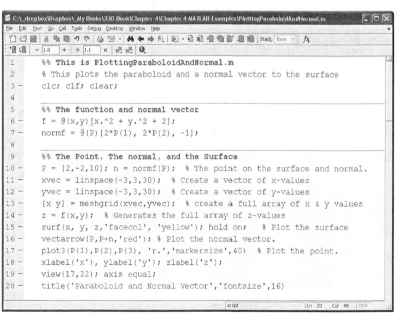

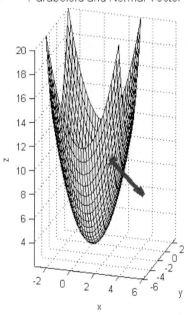

Paraboloid and Normal Vector

Chapter 4.2 Problem Set

Numbers with an asterisk* have solutions in the back of the book.

1.* Use MATLAB® to plot the surface

$$z = \cos\left(\sqrt{x^2 + y^2}\right) \quad \text{for} \quad x \in [-2\pi, 2\pi] \quad \text{and} \quad y \in [-2\pi, 2\pi]$$

and plot the normal vector to the surface at the point $(1, 0, \cos(1))$ that points upward. You should get a graph like the one below.

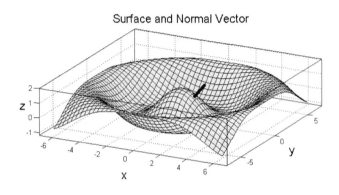

2. Consider the surface defined by

$$z = f(x, y) = 4\, e^{-(x^2 + y^2)} \quad \text{for} \quad x \in [-2, 2] \quad \text{and} \quad y \in [-2, 2]$$

(a) Find f_x

(b) Find f_y

(c) Find the **unit** normal vector to the surface at the point $(1, 0, f(1, 0))$ depicted below.

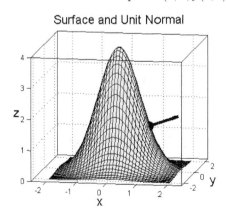

3.[*] Consider the surface defined by

$$z = f(x,y) = \frac{3}{1+x^2+y^2} \quad = \quad 3\left(1+x^2+y^2\right)^{-1}$$

(a) Find f_x

(b) Find f_y

(c) Find the **unit** normal vector to the surface at the point $(-1, 1, 1)$ depicted below.

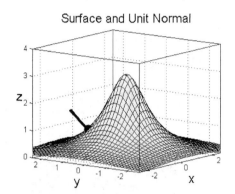

4. Consider the surface defined by

$$z = f(x,y) = -4x^2 - y^2$$

(a) Find f_x

(b) Find f_y

(c) Find the **unit** normal vector to the surface at the point $(1, 1, -5)$ depicted below.

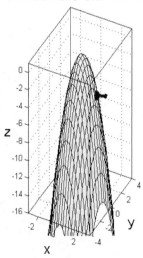

5. Consider the plane defined by

$$\text{plane:} \quad 3x + 2y - 4z = 6$$

Find two **unit** normal vectors at the point (2,0,0) via two different methods.

(a) Express the plane as $z = f(x, y)$ and then $\mathbf{n} = \pm \langle f_x, f_y, -1 \rangle$.

(b) Express the plane as $F(x, y, z) = 0$ and then $\mathbf{n} = \pm \langle F_x, F_y, F_z \rangle$.

6.* Consider the sphere with radius 5 and centered at (2,1,-2) defined by the equation

$$(x - 2)^2 + (y - 1)^2 + (z + 2)^2 = 25.$$

Find a normal vector to the surface of the sphere at the point (2,4,-6) which points away from the center via the following two different methods.

(a) Express the part of the sphere with point (2,4,-6) as $z = f(x, y)$, find $\mathbf{n} = \pm \langle f_x, f_y, -1 \rangle$, and determine which one ($\pm$) points away from the center.

(b) Express the plane as $F(x, y, z) = 0$ and then $\mathbf{n} = \pm \langle F_x, F_y, F_z \rangle$.

7. Find the partial derivatives f_x and f_y for the following functions.

(a)* $f(x, y) = xy + x^2 + y^2$

(b) $f(x, y) = \cos(x^2 + y^2)$

(c)* $f(x, y) = xy \cos(2x)$

(d) $f(x, y) = ye^{2xy}$

8. Find the gradient of the given function.

(a)* $F(x, y, z) = 3x^2 - 2y - 3\sin(z) - 12$

(b) $F(x, y, z) = 3x^2yz^2$

9.* If the surface $2z^2 = 4x^2 - y^2$ is defined by $F(x, y, z) = 0$, find $F(x, y, z)$.

10. Consider the surface defined by the equation $x^2 - y^2 - 7z^3 = 0$. Find a normal vector to the surface at the point (4,3,1).

4.3   Bouncing Around in 3D

In this chapter we will bounce objects around in 3-space. We will bounce them off of surfaces that are not necessarily planes. The bounce vectors will be based on the incoming trajectory with respect to the normal vector at the point of contact. With this ability and Euler's Method for moving around in real-time, we can then bounce around in space until something happens .. or not.

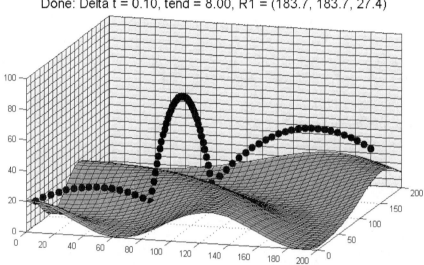

Done: Delta t = 0.10, tend = 8.00, R1 = (183.7, 183.7, 27.4)

Important Stuff:

- You move around via Euler's method. (let $\mathbf{r}_n$ be the current location, $\mathbf{v}_n$ be the current velocity vector, Δt be the time step, and $\mathbf{r}_{n+1}$ be the next position):

$$\mathbf{r}_{n+1} = \mathbf{r}_n + \Delta t\, \mathbf{v}_n$$

If acceleration is constant (gravity), there is no air resistance, and no external forces, then

$$\mathbf{v}_n = \mathbf{v}_{n-1} + \Delta t\, \langle 0, 0, -g \rangle \quad \text{and}$$

$$\mathbf{r}_{n+1} = \mathbf{r}_n + \Delta t\, (\mathbf{v}_{n-1} + \Delta t\, \langle 0, 0, -g \rangle)$$

where g is the acceleration due to gravity (32 feet/sec^2, or 9.8 m/sec^2).

- If you hit something with unit normal vector $\mathbf{n}$, and damping term D:

$$\mathbf{r}_{n+1} = \mathbf{r}_n + \Delta t\, (\mathbf{v}_n - 2\mathrm{Proj}_{\mathbf{n}}\mathbf{v}_n)\, D$$

- Be very careful about leaving the playing area. You might go away and never come back. This can happen if the velocity gets too great or the time step is too large.

A Bounce in 3D

Suppose an object hits a surface with an incoming velocity vector of $\mathbf{v}_0$ at a point with a normal vector $\mathbf{n}$ (found using the gradient of the function) and we want it to bounce off of the surface in a appropriate manner. The bounce vector, denoted $\mathbf{v}_1$ is found using the formula

$$\mathbf{v}_1 = \mathbf{v}_0 - 2\,\mathrm{Proj}_{\mathbf{n}}\mathbf{v}_0 \qquad (4.11)$$

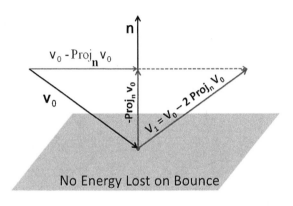

If $\mathbf{v}_0$ hits the surface perfectly
$\mathbf{v}_1 = \mathbf{v}_0 - 2\,\mathrm{Proj}_{\mathbf{n}}\mathbf{v}_0$

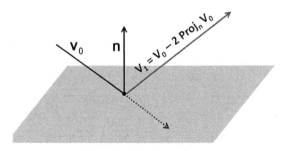

Even if
$\mathbf{v}_0$ goes through the surface
$\mathbf{v}_1 = \mathbf{v}_0 - 2\,\mathrm{Proj}_{\mathbf{n}}\mathbf{v}_0$

Finding the actual point of contact with the surface is tricky!

Equation (4.11) remains valid regardless of your choice for $\mathbf{n}$ so long as it is indeed normal to the surface.

Damping: If there is energy lost on the bounce, then the bounce vector will have a smaller magnitude than the incoming vector. This can be modeled with a damping coefficient applied to equation (4.11) as

$$\mathbf{v}_1 = D\left(2\,\mathrm{Proj}_{\mathbf{n}}\mathbf{v}_0 - \mathbf{v}_0\right), \qquad (4.12)$$

for $D \in (0,1]$. If $D = 1$, there is no damping and no energy lost on the bounce. Otherwise,

$$\|\mathbf{v}_1\| = D\,\|\mathbf{v}_0\|.$$

MATLAB® code: BounceAround.m

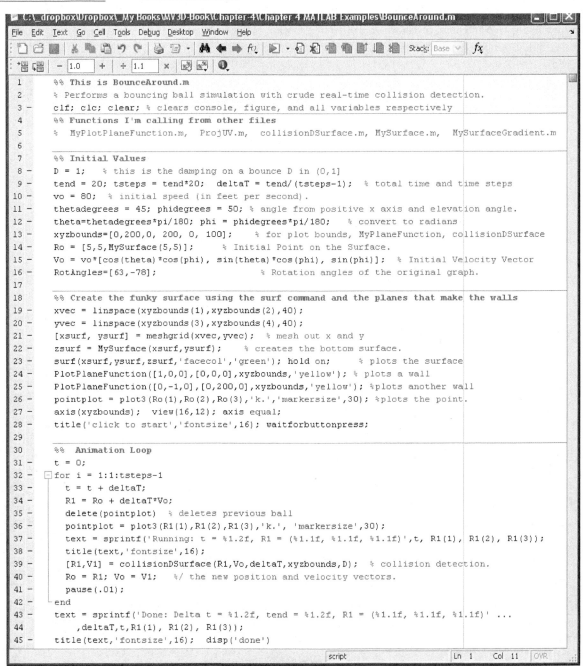

```
     1     %% This is BounceAround.m
     2     % Performs a bouncing ball simulation with crude real-time collision detection.
     3 −   clf; clc; clear; % clears console, figure, and all variables respectively
     4     %% Functions I'm calling from other files
     5     %  MyPlotPlaneFunction.m,  ProjUV.m,  collisionDSurface.m, MySurface.m,  MySurfaceGradient.m
     6
     7     %% Initial Values
     8 −   D = 1;   % this is the damping on a bounce D in (0,1]
     9 −   tend = 20; tsteps = tend*20;  deltaT = tend/(tsteps-1); % total time and time steps
    10 −   vo = 80;  % initial speed (in feet per second).
    11 −   thetadegrees = 45; phidegrees = 50; % angle from positive x axis and elevation angle.
    12 −   theta=thetadegrees*pi/180; phi = phidegrees*pi/180;   % convert to radians
    13 −   xyzbounds=[0,200,0, 200, 0, 100];  % for plot bounds, MyPlaneFunction, collisionDSurface
    14 −   Ro = [5,5,MySurface(5,5)];      % Initial Point on the Surface.
    15 −   Vo = vo*[cos(theta)*cos(phi), sin(theta)*cos(phi), sin(phi)];  % Initial Velocity Vector
    16 −   RotAngles=[63,-78];               % Rotation angles of the original graph.
    17
    18     %% Create the funky surface using the surf command and the planes that make the walls
    19 −   xvec = linspace(xyzbounds(1),xyzbounds(2),40);
    20 −   yvec = linspace(xyzbounds(3),xyzbounds(4),40);
    21 −   [xsurf, ysurf] = meshgrid(xvec,yvec);  % mesh out x and y
    22 −   zsurf = MySurface(xsurf,ysurf);     % creates the bottom surface.
    23 −   surf(xsurf,ysurf,zsurf,'facecol','green'); hold on;    % plots the surface
    24 −   PlotPlaneFunction([1,0,0],[0,0,0],xyzbounds,'yellow'); % plots a wall
    25 −   PlotPlaneFunction([0,-1,0],[0,200,0],xyzbounds,'yellow'); %plots another wall
    26 −   pointplot = plot3(Ro(1),Ro(2),Ro(3),'k.','markersize',30); %plots the point.
    27 −   axis(xyzbounds);  view(16,12); axis equal;
    28 −   title('click to start','fontsize',16); waitforbuttonpress;
    29
    30     %%  Animation Loop
    31 −   t = 0;
    32 −   for i = 1:1:tsteps-1
    33 −       t = t + deltaT;
    34 −       R1 = Ro + deltaT*Vo;
    35 −       delete(pointplot)  % deletes previous ball
    36 −       pointplot = plot3(R1(1),R1(2),R1(3),'k.', 'markersize',30);
    37 −       text = sprintf('Running: t = %1.2f, R1 = (%1.1f, %1.1f, %1.1f)',t, R1(1), R1(2), R1(3));
    38 −       title(text,'fontsize',16);
    39 −       [R1,V1] = collisionDSurface(R1,Vo,deltaT,xyzbounds,D);  % collision detection.
    40 −       Ro = R1; Vo = V1;   %/ the new position and velocity vectors.
    41 −       pause(.01);
    42 −   end
    43 −   text = sprintf('Done: Delta t = %1.2f, tend = %1.2f, R1 = (%1.1f, %1.1f, %1.1f)' ...
    44         ,deltaT,t,R1(1), R1(2), R1(3));
    45 −   title(text,'fontsize',16);  disp('done')
```

MATLAB® code: MySurface.m

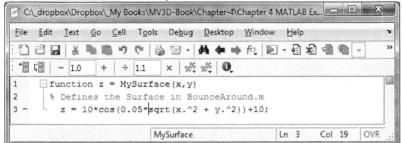

```matlab
1   function z = MySurface(x,y)
2     % Defines the Surface in BounceAround.m
3       z = 10*cos(0.05*sqrt(x.^2 + y.^2))+10;
```

MATLAB® code: MySurfaceGradient.m

```matlab
1   function [R1,V1] = collisionDSurface(R1,Vo,deltaT,xyzbounds,D);
2     % The collision detection function which finds the new velocity vector.
3       x = R1(1);  y=R1(2);  z=R1(3);
4       xmin = xyzbounds(1); ymin = xyzbounds(3); zmin = MySurface(x,y);
5       xmax = xyzbounds(2); ymax = xyzbounds(4); zmax = xyzbounds(6);
6       if x > xmin & x < xmax & y > ymin & y < ymax & z > zmin & z < zmax
7           V1 = Vo - [0,0,32*deltaT];
8       else
9         if x <= xmin
10            n = [1,0,0]; x = xmin;  % could use n = [-1,0,0]
11        elseif x>= xmax
12            n = [-1,0,0]; x = xmax; % could use n = [1,0,0]
13        elseif y <= ymin
14            n = [0,1,0]; y = 0;     % could use n = [0,-1,0]
15        elseif y>= ymax
16            n = [0,-1,0]; y = ymax; % could use n = [0,1,0]
17        elseif z >= zmax
18            n = [0,0,-1]; z = zmax; % could use n = [0,0,1]
19        else n = MySurfaceGradient(x,y,z);  z = zmin;
20        end
21        V1 = D*(Vo - 2*ProjUV(Vo,n)); % new velocity vector
22        R1 = [x,y,z];
23      end
```

MATLAB® code: collisionDSurface.m

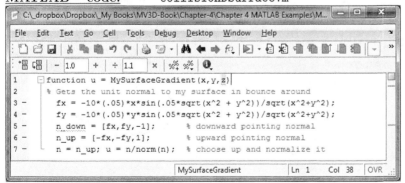

```matlab
1   function u = MySurfaceGradient(x,y,z)
2     % Gets the unit normal to my surface in bounce around
3       fx = -10*(.05)*x*sin(.05*sqrt(x^2 + y^2))/sqrt(x^2+y^2);
4       fy = -10*(.05)*y*sin(.05*sqrt(x^2 + y^2))/sqrt(x^2+y^2);
5       n_down = [fx,fy,-1];     % downward pointing normal
6       n_up = [-fx,-fy,1];      % upward pointing normal
7       n = n_up; u = n/norm(n); % choose up and normalize it
```

Chapter 4.3 Problem Set

Numbers with an asterisk[*] have solutions in the back of the book.

1.[*] Consider the surface defined by
$$z = f(x, y) = \cos\left(\sqrt{x^2 + y^2}\right).$$
Suppose a ball hits this surface at the point $(1, 0, \cos(1))$ with an incoming velocity vector of $\mathbf{v}_o = \langle 0, 0, -3 \rangle$. Find the bounce vector $\mathbf{v}_1$ with no damping ($D = 1$). The graph to the right depicts this bounce.

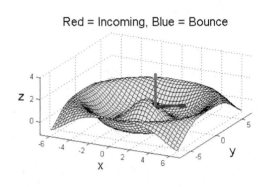

2. Consider the surface defined by
$$z = f(x, y) = 4\, e^{-(x^2 + y^2)}.$$
Suppose a ball hits this surface at the point $(1, 0, f(1, 0))$ with an incoming velocity vector of $\mathbf{v}_o = \langle -1, 0, -1 \rangle$. Find the bounce vector $\mathbf{v}_1$ with no damping ($D = 1$). The graph to the right depicts this bounce.

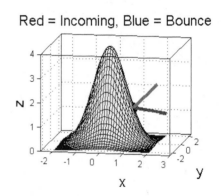

3.[*] Consider the surface defined by
$$z = f(x, y) = \frac{3}{1 + x^2 + y^2}.$$
Suppose a ball hits this surface at the point $(-1, 1, 1)$ with an incoming velocity vector of $\mathbf{v}_o = \langle 0, -1, -1 \rangle$. Find the bounce vector $\mathbf{v}_1$ with no damping ($D = 1$). The graph to the right depicts this bounce.

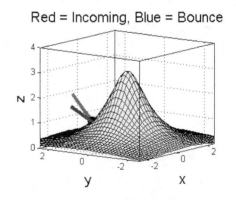

4. Consider the surface defined by
$z = f(x, y) = -4x^2 - y^2$.
Suppose a ball hits this surface at the point
$(1, 1, -5)$ with an incoming velocity vector of
$\mathbf{v}_o = \langle -2, 0, -2 \rangle$. Find the bounce vector $\mathbf{v}_1$
with no damping ($D = 1$). The graph to the
right depicts this bounce.

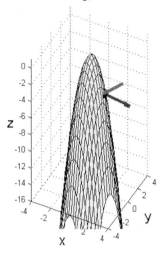

Red = Incoming, Blue = Bounce

5.[*] Suppose a ball hits the plane defined by $2x + 2y - z = 12$ at the point $(4, 3, 2)$ with an incoming velocity
of $\mathbf{v}_0 = \langle 2, 3, 6 \rangle$. Find the bounce vector $\mathbf{v}_1$ with no damping ($D = 1$).

6. Suppose a ball hits the plane defined by $x - 2y + 3z = 2$ at the point $(1, 1, 1)$ with an incoming velocity
of $\mathbf{v}_0 = \langle 1, -2, 2 \rangle$. Find the bounce vector $\mathbf{v}_1$ if 20% of the energy is lost after the bounce ($D = 0.80$).

7. (MATLAB®) Write a program similar to the
one presented in this section only change the surface from $f(x, y) = \cos\left(\sqrt{x^2 + y^2}\right)$ to one of
your choosing. Have the projectile *bounce around*
for $t \in [0, 15]$ with a time step of no larger than
0.05 seconds. You can do this with minimal
editing to `BounceAround.m`, but you will have
to change the functions in `MySurface.m` and the
derivatives in `MySurfaceGradient.m` (below).

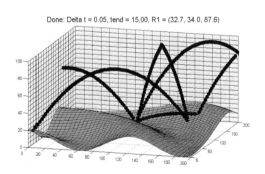

Done: Delta t = 0.05, tend = 15.00, R1 = (32.7, 34.0, 87.6)

Appendix A

Trigonometry Review

Here we go through some trigonometry review. We start off briefly with some *triangle trig*, then move onto *unit-circle trig*, and then to trig as periodic functions of a continuous variable. We end with how to create circles and ellipses and a brief description of the Tangent function.

Contents

A.1   Triangle Trig

Consider the right triangle below. We will focus on three trigonometric functions. These are cosine (cos), sine (sin), and tangent (tan). They are functions defined in terms of an angle θ (*theta*).

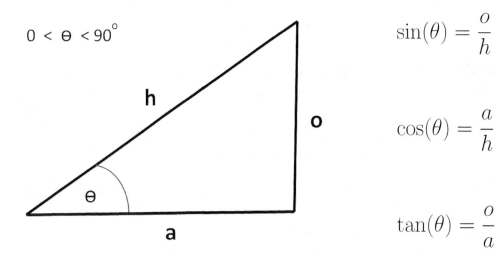

1. There are quite a few things you can do with this.

   - If you know two of the side lengths, you can utilize Pythagorean's theorem ($a^2 + o^2 = h^2$) to get the third side length and hence all of the trig functions of all of the angles. Through inverse trig functions you can get both of the unknown angles as well.

   - If you know θ and one side length, you can, through various identities and inverse trig functions determine the other two side lengths, all of the trig functions of that angle, and the other angle.

   - Once you include the law of sines and/or the law of cosines you can start to play with non-right triangles as well.

2. But, there is a lot you can not do.

   - Notice, with this limited view of the trigonometric functions, the angle must be between 0 and 90°.

   - Non-right triangles are very difficult to handle. If, by chance, you recall the law of cosines, you'll remember that it was not a pleasant formula.

   - You would not immediately recognize that the trig functions are actually periodic. And that is very important.

A.2 Unit-Circle Trig

Consider the circle centered at (0,0) in the cartesian plane with radius equal to one. Now we define our trig functions in terms of the angle traced out by the ray moving counter-clockwise around the circle.

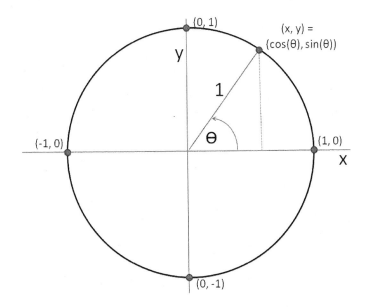

For every point (x,y) on the unit circle:

$$\cos(\theta) = x$$

$$\sin(\theta) = y$$

$$\tan(\theta) = \frac{y}{x}$$

- Notice: These match the triangle trig functions when $0 < \theta < 90^{o}$. (because $h = 1$)

- We can use any angle we want, even negative angles.

- It is immediately obvious what $cos(\theta)$ and $\sin(\theta)$ are for $\theta = 0, 90, 180, 270, 360, \ldots$.

- It is obvious that sin and cos functions repeat themselves after every full rotation. In other words, **these functions are periodic**.

- **Radians:**. Instead of measuring θ in degrees we now measure it with respect to the arc-length traced out by the unit-circle to the point (x, y). This type of angle measurement is called radians. One full revolution is $360^{o} = 2\pi$ radians. A half a revolution $180^{o} = \pi$ radians. A quarter revolution $90^{o} = \pi/2$ radians. Almost all calculators and software calculate trig functions assuming the argument is in radians.

- **Converting between Degrees and Radians**: If r is radians and d is degrees then

$$d = \frac{180}{\pi} r \quad \text{and} \quad r = \frac{\pi}{180} d$$

- If the radius is r instead of one then triangle trig gives us:

$$\cos(\theta) = \frac{x}{r} \qquad \text{and} \qquad x = r\cos(\theta) \tag{A.1}$$

$$\sin(\theta) = \frac{y}{r} \qquad \text{and} \qquad y = r\sin(\theta) \tag{A.2}$$

A.3   Trig as a collection of periodic functions

Here we look at cosine and sine as periodic functions of a continuous variable. We will save tangent for later. Consider the unit circle as the angle (now denoted by t in **radians**) goes around the circle in a counterclockwise direction. Track $x = \cos(t)$ and $y = \sin(t)$ to plot these functions.

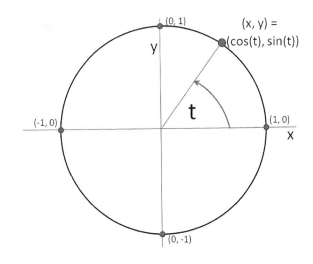

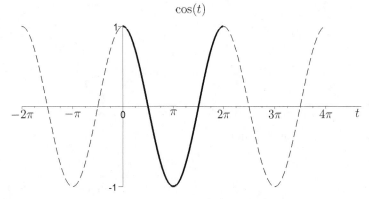

$\cos(t)$

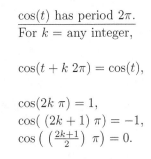

$\cos(t)$ has period 2π.
For $k =$ any integer,

$\cos(t + k\,2\pi) = \cos(t)$,

$\cos(2k\,\pi) = 1$,
$\cos(\,(2k+1)\,\pi) = -1$,
$\cos\left(\left(\frac{2k+1}{2}\right)\pi\right) = 0$.

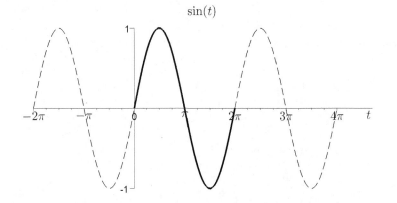

$\sin(t)$

$\sin(t)$ has period 2π.
For $k =$ any integer,

$\sin(t + k\,2\pi) = \sin(t)$,

$\sin(k\,\pi) = 0$,
$\sin\left(\left(\frac{4k+1}{2}\right)\pi\right) = 1$.
$\sin\left(\left(\frac{4k-1}{2}\right)\pi\right) = -1$.

A.4 Translations and Transformations of Trig Functions

<u>Horizontal and Vertical Translations:</u> $y = \cos(x - \phi) + B$ and $y = \sin(x - \phi) + B$

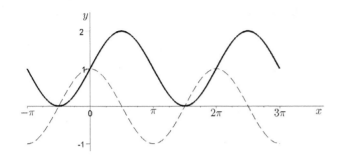

Dashed: $y = \cos(x)$.

Solid: $y = \cos(x - \pi/2) + 1$

Horizontal shift by $\pi/2$

Vertical shift by 1.

<u>Amplitude Changes:</u> $y = A \cos(x)$ and $y = A \sin(x)$, $A =$ Amplitude.

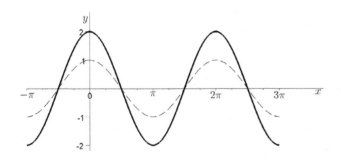

Dashed: $y = \cos(x)$.

Solid: $y = \mathbf{2}\cos(x)$

Vertical Stretch by 2.

Amplitude increases.

<u>Period (Frequency) Changes:</u> $y = \cos(\omega x)$ and $y = \sin(\omega x)$, Period $= \dfrac{2\pi}{\omega}$.

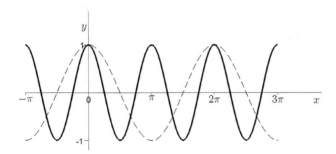

Dashed: $y = \cos(x)$.

Solid: $y = \cos(\mathbf{2}x)$

Period $= (2\pi/\mathbf{2}) = \pi$

Period decreases and Frequency increases.

A.5   Circles and Ellipses

If you recall, getting the graph of a circle in terms of $y = f(x)$ was very tricky. Defining the graph of an ellipse was even trickier. These curves are much easier to create when you define them as a set of trigonometric **parametric** equations. In a parametric curve, the values of x and y are both determined in terms of another variable (parameter) usually denoted t or θ.

An ellipse with center (x_o, y_o), x-radius of r_x, and y-radius of r_y is defined by

$$x(t) = x_o + r_x \cos(t), \quad y = y_o + r_y \sin(t), \quad t \in [0, 2\pi] \qquad (A.3)$$

To make partial ellipses and circles let the parameter range over an appropriate subset.

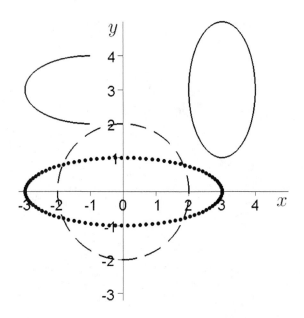

Dashed (circle)	Dotted (ellipse)	Solid (ellipse)	Solid (half-ellipse)
$x(t) = 2\cos(t)$	$x(t) = 3\cos(t)$	$x(t) = 3 + \cos(t)$	$x(t) = -1 + 2\cos(t)$
$y(t) = 2\sin(t)$	$y(t) = \sin(t)$	$y(t) = 3 + 2\sin(t)$	$y(t) = 3 + \sin(t)$
$t \in [0, 2\pi]$	$t \in [0, 2\pi]$	$t \in [0, 2\pi]$	$t \in [\pi/2, 3\pi/2]$

A.6 The Tangent Function

The tangent (tan) function is defined in terms of cosine and sine functions by

$$\tan(x) = \frac{\sin(x)}{\cos(x)} \tag{A.4}$$

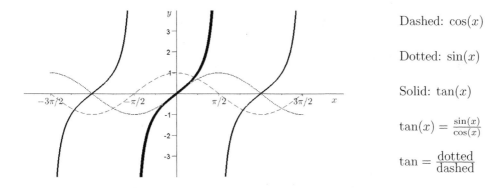

Dashed: $\cos(x)$

Dotted: $\sin(x)$

Solid: $\tan(x)$

$\tan(x) = \frac{\sin(x)}{\cos(x)}$

$\tan = \frac{\text{dotted}}{\text{dashed}}$

- Notes about the tangent function:

  - **Period:** Unlike sine and cosine, tangent has a period of π (not 2π).
  - **Undefined:** $tan(x)$ is undefined at $\frac{2k+1}{2}\pi$ for all integers k and the graph of $\tan(x)$ has vertical asymptotes at these locations.

- The **arctangent** function is the inverse of the tangent functions (sometimes denoted $\tan^{-1}$).

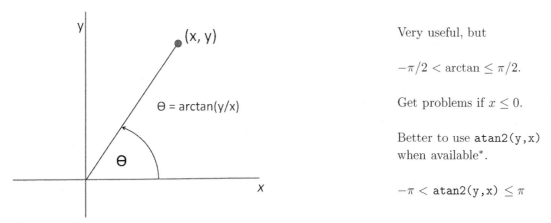

Very useful, but

$-\pi/2 < \arctan \leq \pi/2$.

Get problems if $x \leq 0$.

Better to use `atan2(y,x)` when available*.

$-\pi < $ `atan2(y,x)` $\leq \pi$

* Most calculators and software contain an `atan2` function which resolves all of the issues of using the arctan function when $x \leq 0$.

A.7   Trigonometry Review - Problem Set

1. Find the requested information:

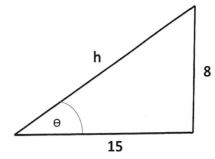

$h =$

$\sin(\theta) =$

$\cos(\theta) =$

$\tan(\theta) =$

$\theta =$

2. Suppose θ takes you 2/3 of the way around the circle centered at (0,0) with radius 8. Find the angle θ (in degrees and radians) and the point (x, y) on the circle.

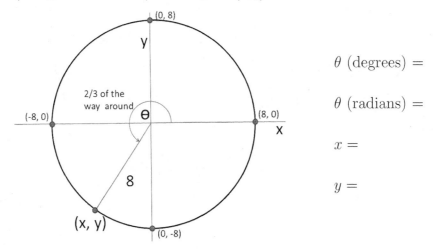

θ (degrees) $=$

θ (radians) $=$

$x =$

$y =$

3. Consider $y = A\cos(\omega t) + B$. Find A, ω, and B that produces an oscillating periodic function with period $= 3$, that oscillates between 4 and 8 on the y-axis. Plot this function for $t \in [-3, 6]$.

4. Find the parametric equations for the ellipse centered at (2,-4) pictured below. Make sure the curve is traced in the counter-clockwise direction as the parameter t increases.

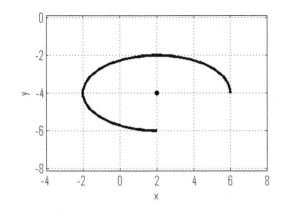

$$x(t) =$$

$$y(t) =$$

$$t \in$$

5. Sketch the graph of the ellipse defined by the parametric equations:

$$x = 4 + 5\cos(t)$$

$$y = -2 + 2\sin(t)$$

$$t \in [0, 2\pi]$$

6. Find θ in radians and degrees.

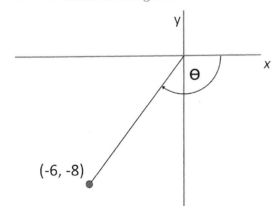

$$\theta \text{ (radians)} =$$

$$\theta \text{ (degrees)} =$$

Appendix B

Review of Differentiation Rules

This appendix contains a list of the basic differentiation rules you should have seen in Calculus I.

Notation: If u is a differentiable function of x then the derivative of u with respect to x is denoted by

$$\frac{du}{dx} = \frac{d}{dx}u = u'$$

General Single-Variable Differentiation Rules:

Assume u and v are differentiable functions of x, and c is a constant.

- $\dfrac{d}{dx}c = 0$

- $\dfrac{d}{dx}(cu) = cu'$

- $\dfrac{d}{dx}(u + v) = u' + v'$

- Chain Rule: $\dfrac{d}{dx}u(v(x)) = \dfrac{du}{dv}\dfrac{dv}{dx} = \dfrac{du}{dv}\,v'$

- Product Rule: $\dfrac{d}{dx}[\,u\,v\,] = u\,v' + v\,u'$

- Quotient Rule: $\dfrac{d}{dx}\left[\dfrac{u}{v}\right] = \dfrac{vu' - uv'}{v^2}$

Polynomials and the Power Rule

Assume u is a differentiable functions of x and n is any real number not equal to zero.

- $\dfrac{d}{dx} x^n = n\, x^{n-1}$ provided $n \neq 0$.

- $\dfrac{d}{dx}\left[\, u^n \,\right] = n\, u^{n-1}\, u'$ provided $n \neq 0$

Trigonometric Functions

Assume u is a differentiable function of x.

- $\dfrac{d}{dx}\left[\, \sin u \,\right] = (\cos u)\, u'$

- $\dfrac{d}{dx}\left[\, \cos u \,\right] = -(\sin u)\, u'$

- $\dfrac{d}{dx}\left[\, \tan u \,\right] = (\sec^2 u)\, u'$

- $\dfrac{d}{dx}\left[\, \sec u \,\right] = (\sec u\ \tan u)\, u'$

- $\dfrac{d}{dx}\left[\, \csc u \,\right] = -(\csc u\ \cot u)\, u'$

- $\dfrac{d}{dx}\left[\, \cot u \,\right] = -(\csc^2 u)\, u'$

Exponentials and Logarithms

Assume u is a differentiable function of x.

- $\dfrac{d}{dx}\left[\, e^{ax} \,\right] = ae^{ax}$

- $\dfrac{d}{dx}\left[\, e^u \,\right] = e^u\, u'$

- $\dfrac{d}{dx}\left[\, \ln x \,\right] = \dfrac{1}{x}$ for $x > 0$

- $\dfrac{d}{dx}\left[\, \ln u \,\right] = \dfrac{1}{u}\, u'$ for $u > 0$

Appendix C

A Quick Guide to MATLAB®

In this course we will be using the software package MATLAB® . The most recent version can be purchased directly from the MATLAB® web site: http://www.mathworks.com/academia/student_version/index.html

MATLAB® is a high-level technical computing language and interactive environment for algorithm development, data visualization, data analysis, and numerical computation. We will use MATLAB® for it's ability to easily perform matrix and vector operations as well as it's exceptional ease of graphing and animating objects in 2 and 3 dimensions. This Quick Guide to MATLAB® is meant to demonstrate some of the more popular tasks that we will be performing with MATLAB® .

Contents

C.1   Running MATLAB®

When you first start MATLAB® the desktop will open. A great introduction to the desktop can be found at

$$\text{http://www.mathworks.com/help/techdoc/learn\_matlab/f1-28564.html}$$

The original desktop has too much going on. Remove all windows except the Command Window.

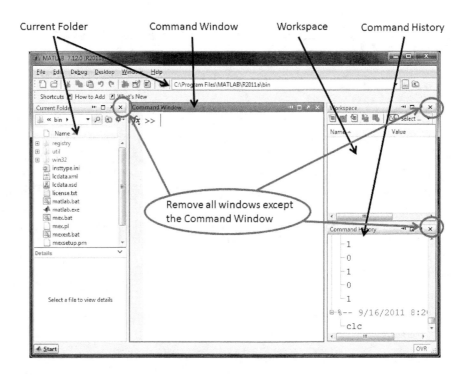

The Desktop Becomes

Type in the commands below. The first line x = 0:.1:6 creates an array of x values starting at zero and incrementing by 0.1 up to 6. Don't forget the semicolons.

Type in these commands exactly
and a figure window opens

"Dock" the Figure Window into the Desktop

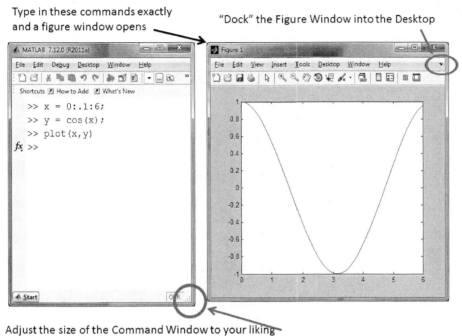

Adjust the size of the Command Window to your liking

The Desktop Becomes

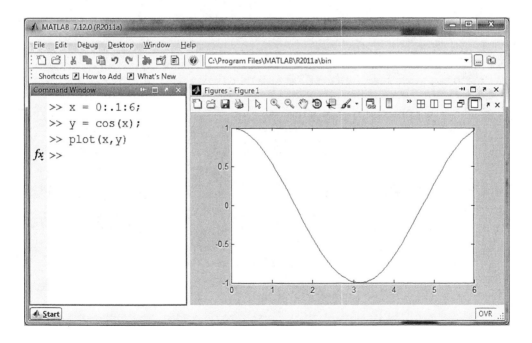

1) Click on Desktop and check the editor option.

2) An editor window will open. This is where we write code.

3) Close the Figure window, for now.

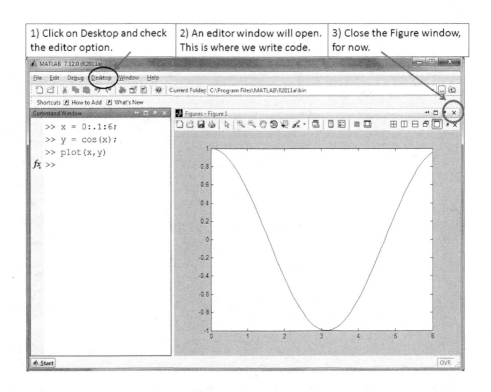

Create a new ".m" script file by clicking here.

Later, we will open ".m" script files by clicking here.

Clear the Command Window by typing and entering "clc"

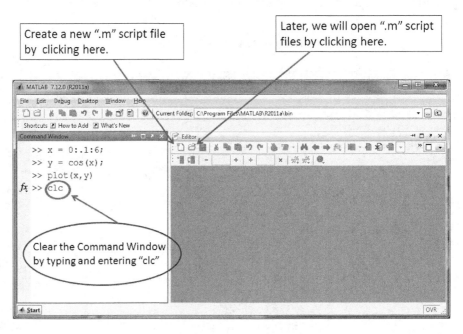

1) Give this file a title with %% preceding it.
2) Give it some commands to execute later.
3) The disp command prints to the Command Window.
4) Save it as Example_1.m to a folder you can find later.
5) Hit the green arrow to run it.

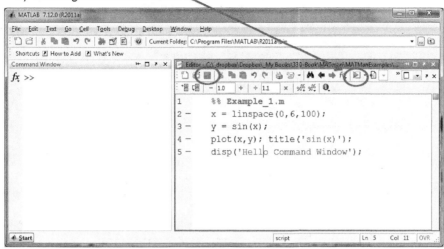

This file is probably not saved in the current folder where MATLAB is run
You can either change the current folder to that containing the file or
you can add a path to the folder containing the file.
I usually just Change Folder

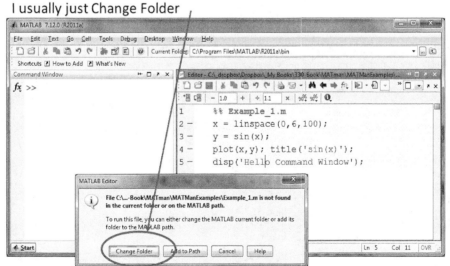

The file is then executed line-by-line.

A Figure window opens with the graph.

Your message is displayed in the Command Window

Now, "Dock" the Figure Window

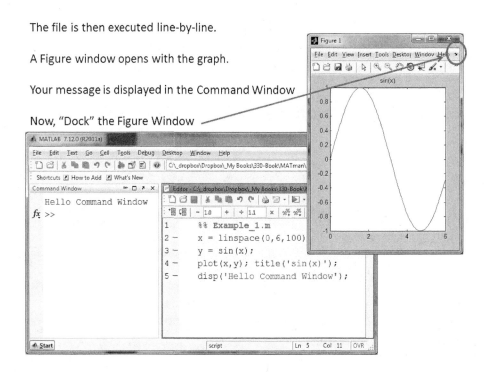

The figure is now docked but it is tabbed with the Editor.   I don't like this

Grab the figure window by the blue bar

Drag into the bottom of the Command Window

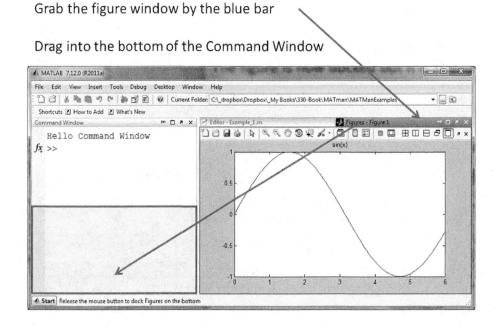

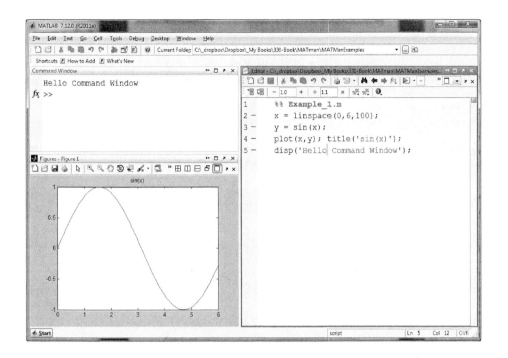

- Resize and move things around to your liking.

- The next time you open MATLAB® it will remember how you like it.

- Play around with the code. Hit the green arrow to run it.

- Save it just like any other file. It must have a .m extension.

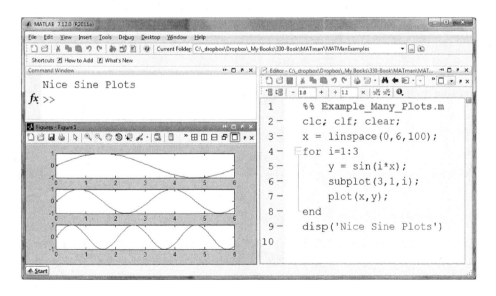

C.2   Creating your own functions

Often we will want to create functions that take input and return output. These *functions* can be nested within a program or saved in a separate file called a function file.

- ## Function Files (best - most versatile)

  Here, we create a file that acts as a function. These are nice because your function can be composed of many parts, it can return numerous variables, or none at all. A function file can be used to create graphs with various features described by the input variables.

  Important Stuff:

  1. The function file must be in your working directory or a path to it must be created.

  2. The first line must be `function [output variable(s)] = Function_Name(input variable(s))`

  3. The file must be named `Function_Name.m`.

  Usage:

  ```
  function [output variable(s)] = Function_Name(input variable(s))
          function operations;
          output variables;
          ⋮
          other stuff;
  ```

- ## Anonymous Functions (good - less versatile but easy)

  Here you create the function directly in the program - this is nice. The problem is the function must consist of only one line of code. Multi-part functions with a `for` loop (for example) can't be used. An anonymous function can return more than one variable (good).

  Usage:
  ```
  function_name = @(input variables)[function output variable(s)]
  ```

- ## Inline Functions (bad - least versatile)

  Again, you must complete your function in one line. Additionally this type of function can only return one variable but it can accept numerous input variables.

  Usage:
  ```
  function_name = inline('operation', 'input variable 1', 'input variable 2')
  ```

Function Files: Here, we create a file that acts as a function. We can call this function from the command window (as below) or from another program file.

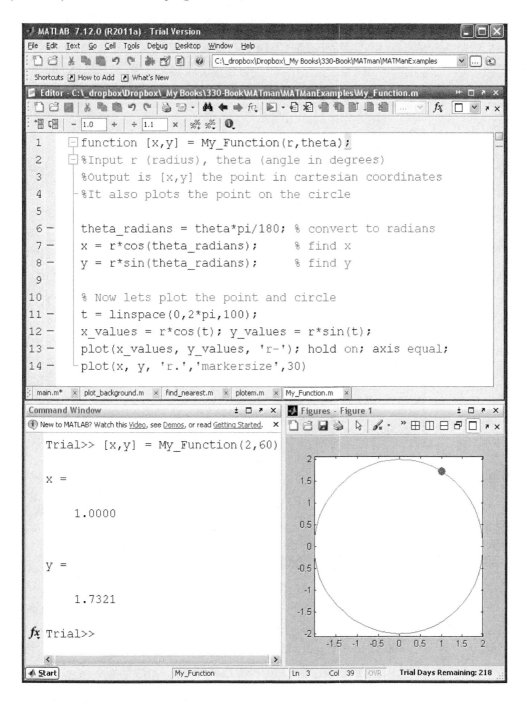

Anonymous Function: Versatile and Easy

MATLAB® Notation	Math Notation	Description
f = @(x)[x.^2]	$f(x) = x^2$	One input (x), One output (f)
area = @(l,w)[l * w]	$\text{area}(l, w) = lw$	Two inputs (l,w), One output (area)
F = @(r,t)[r*cos(t), r*sin(t)]	$\mathbf{F}(r, t) = [r\cos(t), r\sin(t)]$	Two inputs (r,t), Two outputs (x,y)

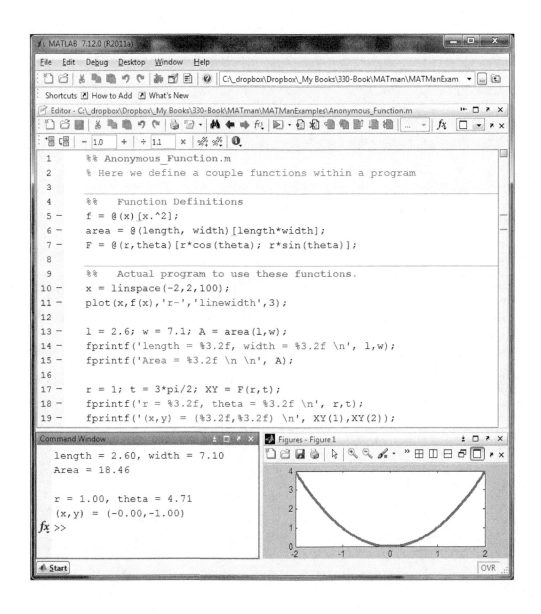

<u>**Inline Functions:**</u> **Bad** - mainly because you can only return one variable.

MATLAB® Inline Function Notation	Math Notation
f = inline('x.^2')	$f(x) = x^2$
area = inline('length * width', 'length','width')	$area(l, w) = lw$

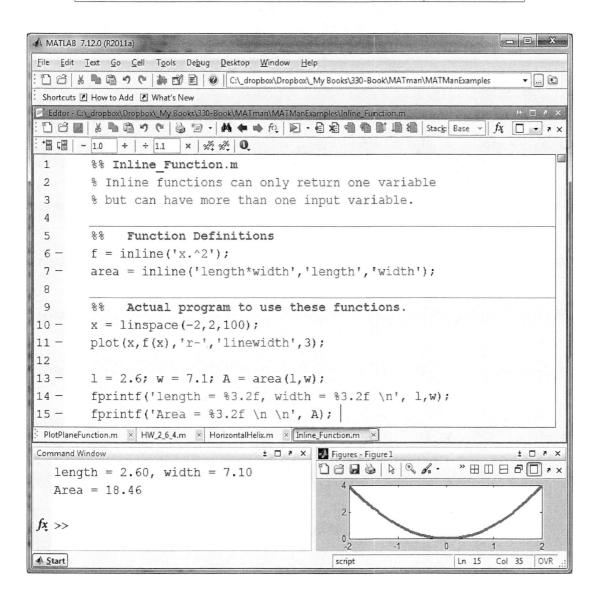

C.3   Graphing with MATLAB®

Here you find some examples of the built in graphing capabilities of MATLAB® . I'll demonstrate some simple ones and others with bells and whistles. For more details check the help browser (click on `help` or ? in the toolbar) and search. The internet is well populated with MATLAB® help. I can usually find what I need faster by typing my question in any internet search engine.

Plotting y = f(x)

```
x = linspace(0,4,100);
y = cos(x);
plot(x,y, optional list of specifications)
```

Parametric Curves in 2D: x = f(t) and y = g(t)

```
t = linspace(0,2 * pi, 100);
x = cos(t);
y = sin(t);
plot(x,y, optional list of specifications)
```

Animations

```
for i = 1:n,
   ballplot = plot(x,y,..)
   update x and y
   delete(ballplot)
   pause(.01)
end
```

Plotting 3D Surfaces: z = f(x,y)

```
x1 = linspace(a, b, n);
y1 = linspace(c, d, m);
[x2, y2]= meshgrid(x1,y1)
z = f(x2,y2);
surf(x2, y2, z, optional list of specifications)
```

Parametric Curves in 3D: x = f(t), y = g(t), z = h(t)

```
t = linspace(a,b,n);
x = f(t);
y = g(t);
z = h(t);
plot3(x,y,z, optional list of specifications)
```

```
1        %% Example_Plot.m
2 —      clc; clf; % clears the console (clc) and figures (clf)
3
4        %% Make the x and y vectors
5 —      x =  linspace(0,2*pi,100); % create a vector of x-values
6        % this vector starts at 0, ends at 2*pi, and has 100 terms
7 —      y1 = cos(x);      % define a vector of y-values called y1
8 —      y2 = sin(x);      % define a vector of y-values called y2
9
10       %% Start Plotting
11 —     subplot(1,2,1) % Create the first in a 1x2 array of plots
12          % subplot is used to create different graphs in one figure
13 —     plot(x,y1);    % minimum requirements
14 —     hold on;       % Don't erase the graph
15 —     plot(x,y2,'r','linewidth',3);  % 'r' = red and thicker
16 —     title('blue=cos(x), red=sin(x)')
17
18 —     subplot(1,2,2) % Create the second in 1x2 array of plots
19 —     plot(x,y1,'b.');  % 'b.' = green dots.
20 —     hold on;
21 —     plot(x,y2,'ko','markerface','r');  % black (k) circles
22 —     plot([pi],[sin(pi)],'g.','markersize',30);
23 —     title('Green dot at (pi,sin(pi))','fontsize',16)
24 —     xlabel('x label here','fontsize',16)
25 —     ylabel('y label here','fontsize',16)
26 —     axis([0,2*pi,-1.1,1.1]); % bounds [xmin, xmax, ymin, ymax]
```

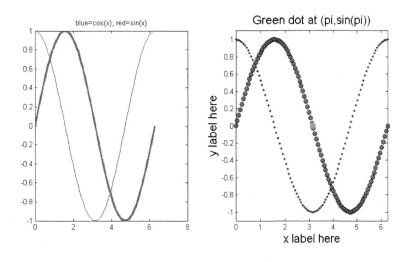

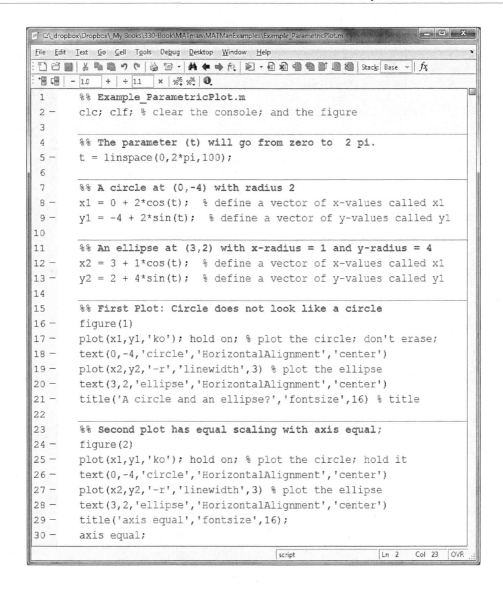

```
1        %% Example_ParametricPlot.m
2   —    clc; clf; % clear the console; and the figure
3
4        %% The parameter (t) will go from zero to  2 pi.
5   —    t = linspace(0,2*pi,100);
6
7        %% A circle at (0,-4) with radius 2
8   —    x1 = 0 + 2*cos(t);  % define a vector of x-values called x1
9   —    y1 = -4 + 2*sin(t);  % define a vector of y-values called y1
10
11       %% An ellipse at (3,2) with x-radius = 1 and y-radius = 4
12  —    x2 = 3 + 1*cos(t);  % define a vector of x-values called x1
13  —    y2 = 2 + 4*sin(t);  % define a vector of y-values called y1
14
15       %% First Plot: Circle does not look like a circle
16  —    figure(1)
17  —    plot(x1,y1,'ko'); hold on; % plot the circle; don't erase;
18  —    text(0,-4,'circle','HorizontalAlignment','center')
19  —    plot(x2,y2,'-r','linewidth',3) % plot the ellipse
20  —    text(3,2,'ellipse','HorizontalAlignment','center')
21  —    title('A circle and an ellipse?','fontsize',16) % title
22
23       %% Second plot has equal scaling with axis equal;
24  —    figure(2)
25  —    plot(x1,y1,'ko'); hold on; % plot the circle; hold it
26  —    text(0,-4,'circle','HorizontalAlignment','center')
27  —    plot(x2,y2,'-r','linewidth',3) % plot the ellipse
28  —    text(3,2,'ellipse','HorizontalAlignment','center')
29  —    title('axis equal','fontsize',16);
30  —    axis equal;
```

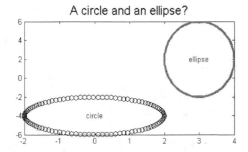

A circle and an ellipse?

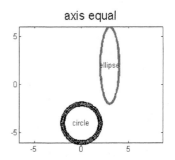

axis equal

```
                C:\_dropbox\Dropbox\_My Books\330-Book\MATman\MATManExamples\Bouncing_Ball_Animation.m

 File   Edit   Text   Go   Cell   Tools   Debug   Desktop   Window   Help

                                                                           Stack: Base ▾   fx

    1      %%    This is Bouncing_Ball_Animation.m
    2  -   clc; clf; clear; % clears console, figure, and all variables
    3
    4      %% The path the ball will follow:
    5  -   path = @(x)[20*exp(-.1*x) .* abs(sin(.5*x))];
    6
    7      %% Initial Set-Up
    8  -   n = 300;                    % number of frames.
    9  -   x = linspace(0,35,n); y = path(x);    % x and y values of the path.
   10
   11  -   t = linspace(0,2*pi,100);   % the parameter t.
   12  -   original_xball = 2*cos(t);  % the x-values of the ball graph.
   13  -   original_yball = 2*sin(t);  % the y-values of the ball graph.
   14
   15      %% Make original plot
   16  -   pathplot = plot(x,y,'-k'); hold on; % plot the path
   17  -   ballplot = plot(original_xball,original_yball,'-r');
   18  -   title('Bouncing Ball - Click to Start','fontsize',16);
   19  -   axis equal; axis([-2,37,-2,20]);
   20
   21      % Initiate animation
   22  -   waitforbuttonpress;
   23  -   title('Bouncing Ball Animation','fontsize',16)
   24  -   delete(pathplot);
   25
   26      %% Aimation Starts Here
   27  -  ┌for i=1:n,          % begin for loop
   28  -   │  xball = original_xball+x(i);    % move ball x-values along path.
   29  -   │  yball = original_yball+y(i);    % move ball y-values along path.
   30  -   │  delete(ballplot);              % delete old ballplot
   31  -   │  ballplot = plot(xball, yball, '-r');  % make new ball plot
   32  -   │  pause(.01);                    % slows it down a little.
   33  -  └end                              % end the animation loop.

                                                script          Ln 20   Col 1    OVR
```

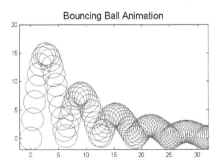

Bouncing Ball Animation

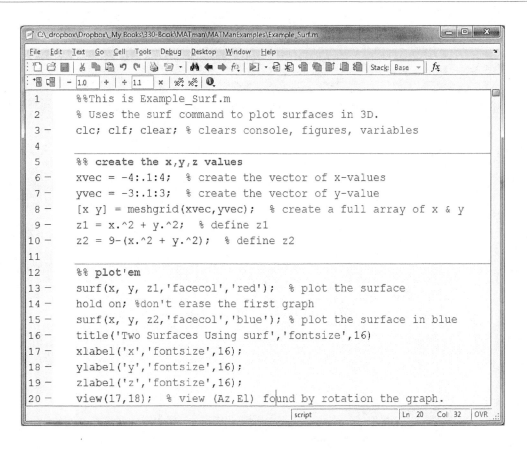

```
1        %%This is Example_Surf.m
2        % Uses the surf command to plot surfaces in 3D.
3 -      clc; clf; clear; % clears console, figures, variables
4
5        %% create the x,y,z values
6 -      xvec = -4:.1:4;   % create the vector of x-values
7 -      yvec = -3:.1:3;   % create the vector of y-value
8 -      [x y] = meshgrid(xvec,yvec);  % create a full array of x & y
9 -      z1 = x.^2 + y.^2;  % define z1
10 -     z2 = 9-(x.^2 + y.^2);  % define z2
11
12       %% plot'em
13 -     surf(x, y, z1,'facecol','red');  % plot the surface
14 -     hold on; %don't erase the first graph
15 -     surf(x, y, z2,'facecol','blue'); % plot the surface in blue
16 -     title('Two Surfaces Using surf','fontsize',16)
17 -     xlabel('x','fontsize',16);
18 -     ylabel('y','fontsize',16);
19 -     zlabel('z','fontsize',16);
20 -     view(17,18);  % view (Az,El) found by rotation the graph.
```

- Rotate the graph.

- Observe the Az and El numbers in the lower left

- use view(az,el) to replicate the desired viewing angle.

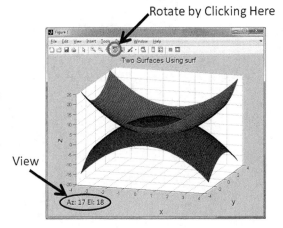

Rotate by Clicking Here

View

```
1   %% This is Example_Plot3.m. Plots curves, points, and a surface in 3D.
2 - clc; clf; clear;  % clear console, figure, and variables respectively
3
4   %% First, plot a parametric curve in 3D using the standard form of plot3.
5 - t = linspace(0,20,200);  % this is the parameter
6 - x = cos(t); % this defines the x-values on the curve.
7 - y = sin(t); % this defines the corresponding y-values
8 - z = t;  % and this defines the corresponding z-values.
9 - plot3(x,y,z,'r-','linewidth',3);   % simplest form of param3d.
10 - hold on;
11
12   %% Let's plot a couple points
13 - plot3(cos(0),sin(0),0,'g.','markersize',50);        % green dot
14 - plot3(cos(20),sin(20), 20 ,'b.','markersize',50);  % blue dot
15
16   %% How about a little surface in there
17 - x1 = linspace(-1,1,100); y1 = linspace(-1,1,100);
18 - [x2,y2]=meshgrid(x1,y1); z = -10*(x2.^2 + y2.^2);
19 - surf(x2,y2,z);
20 - view(20,22)   % found using the rotation button on the figure
21 - title('Sproing!','fontsize',20);
```

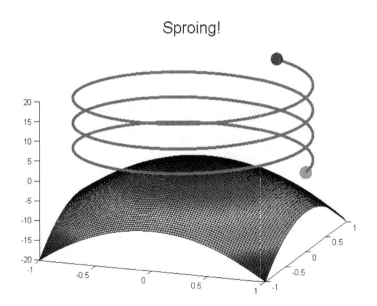

C.4   Input and Output to and from the Command Window or Graph

While a program is running there are many situations where you will want to get input from the Command Window or graph and display information to the command window or graph.

Input from the Command Window - `input`

Here I use the `input` command to get numbers or strings from the console while a program is running. The default value of input is a number.

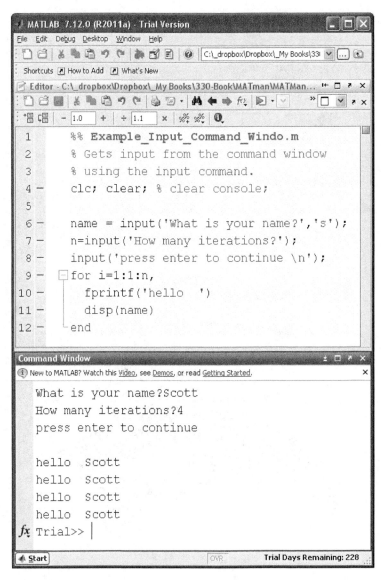

Input from a Graph - ginput

Here I use the `ginput` command to get a point from a mouse click on a graph.

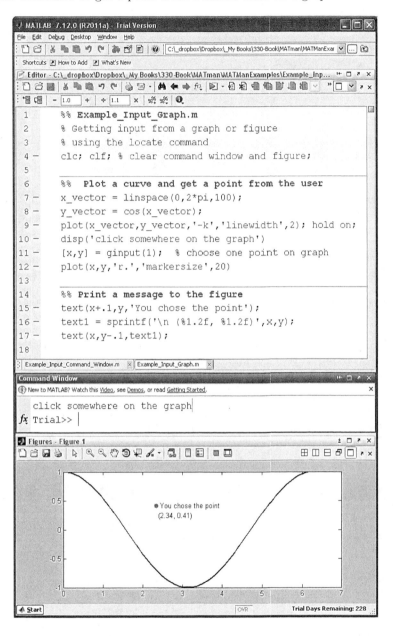

Output to the Command Window - disp, sprintf, fprintf

Here I display information to the console while the program is running.

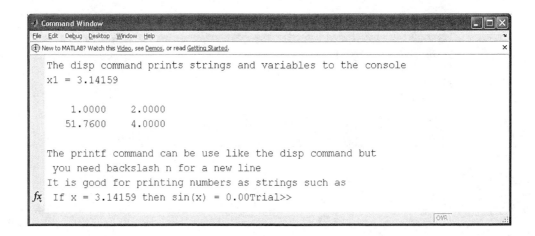

Output to a Graph - `text`, `sprintf`

Here I display text to a specific place on the graph using the **text** command.

```
%% This is Example_Output_Graph.m
% This demonstrates how you can send output to a graph.
clc; clf; clear; % clears console, figure, and variables.

%% we will plot y = sin(x) at 40 evenly located x-values
x_vector = linspace(0,2*pi,40);  % x = 0 to 2 pi with 40 points.
y_vector = sin(x_vector);
x1 = pi;   % an x-value

%% Plot some stuff with a message in the graph
plot(x_vector,y_vector,'linewidth',3); hold on;
plot([x1],[sin(x1)],'kd','markersize',20,'markerface','green')
    % Above: plot the point (x1,sin(x1)) with a green diamond.
 title('y = sin(x)', 'fontsize',16,'color','red');
 xlabel('x label','fontsize',16,'color','blue');
 ylabel('y label');
text_stuff = sprintf('This point is \n (%1.2f, %1.2f)',x1,sin(x1));
text(x1+.1,sin(x1)+.2,text_stuff,'fontsize',16);
```

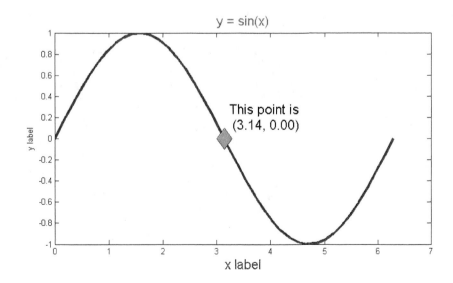

C.5   Assignment

Create a Face.

That's it, just create a face using the plotting commands introduced in this chapter.

- Minimum Requirements (C)

    - The face must have a mouth, nose, and two eyes.

    - The features must be distinguished by different plotting styles.

    - It must be significantly different from the one below.

    - It must contain at least 3 ellipses and 1 trig (sin or cos) function.

    - It must contain at least 1 polygon (like a triangle).

- Recommendations (B)

    - Additional facial features.

    - Prompt user for types of facial features.

- Additional Ideas (A)

    - Prompt user for facial feature location by clicking on the graph.

    - Animate the face.

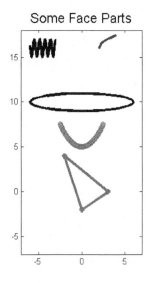
Some Face Parts

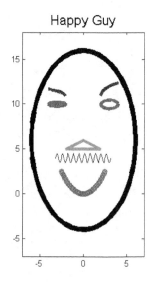
Happy Guy

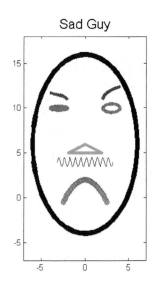
Sad Guy

Here is some code for various face parts. It first prompts the user for a frown or a smile.

```
C:\_dropbox\Dropbox\_My Books\330-Book\MATman\MATManExamples\Example_My_Face_Parts.m

File  Edit  Text  Go  Cell  Tools  Debug  Desktop  Window  Help

1       %% This is Example_My_Face_Parts.m
2   --  clf; clc; clear;
3   --  smile = input('input smile (1) or frown (0)');
4
5       %% Make a triangle and plot it
6   --  triangle_X = [-2,3,0,-2]; triangle_Y=[4,0,-2,4];
7   --  plot(triangle_X,triangle_Y,'-r*','linewidth',3);   hold on;
8
9       %% Make some hair, eyebrows, and plot them
10  --  hair_X=linspace(-6,-3,100); hair_Y=sin(10*hair_X) + 16;
11  --  plot(hair_X,hair_Y,'k','linewidth',3)
12  --  eyebrowX = linspace(2,4,10);
13  --  eyebrowY = 16+sqrt(eyebrowX-2);
14  --  plot(eyebrowX,eyebrowY,'linewidth',3);
15
16      %% Make a face (ellipse) and plot it
17  --  face_T = linspace(0,2*pi,50);
18  --  face_X = 6*cos(face_T); face_Y = 10 + sin(face_T);
19  --  plot(face_X,face_Y,'k','linewidth',3);
20
21      %% Make a smile (or frown) and plot it
22  --  mouth_X = linspace(-2.5,2.5,50);  %x-values for the mouth
23  --  mouth_Y = 0.4*mouth_X.^2 + 5;  % .^2 squares term by term.
24  --  if smile ~= 1,                 % The ~= means 'not equal to'
25  --    mouth_Y = -mouth_X.^2;          % Makes a downward parabola
26  --  end
27  --  plot(mouth_X,mouth_Y,'ro','markerface','green');
28
29      %% Some graphics directives
30  --  title('Some Face Parts','fontsize',16);
31  --  axis equal;   % Makes circles look like circles!
32  --  axis([-7,7,-7,18]);   % graph bounds [xmin,xmax,ymin,ymax]

                                    script        Ln 1    Col 35    OVR
```

Some Graphing Tricks:

- If you want to draw an ellipse (or circle for that matter). Do so in parametric form;

$$x(t) = x_o + r_x \cos t, \qquad y(t) = y_o + r_y \sin t, \qquad \text{for} \quad t \in [0, 2\pi].$$

  then just `plot(x,y)`. This ellipse has center at (x_o, y_o), x-radius of r_x, and y-radius of r_y.

- Suppose you graph $y = f(x)$, then

  - $y = f(x) + a$ moves the graph up a units.
  - $y = f(x - a)$ moves the graph to the right a units.
  - $y = -f(x)$ flips the graph around the x-axis.
  - $y = f(-x)$ flips the graph around the y-axis.
  - $y = a \cdot f(x)$ scales (makes it taller or shorter) the graph by a units.

Detailed Solutions to Worksheets

Chapter 1.1 Worksheet - Solutions

Use Gaussian elimination with back-substitution to determine if the system of equations is consistent (has at least one solution). If it is consistent, solve for the variables. If you get infinitely many solutions, give the **general solution** in terms of a parameter (t) and give one **particular solution**.

1.

$$
\begin{aligned}
x_1 - 3x_3 &= 8 \\
2x_1 + 2x_2 + 9x_3 &= 7 \\
x_2 + 5x_3 &= -2
\end{aligned}
$$

Expressing this system in augmented matrix form and performing Gaussian Elimination:

$$
\left[\begin{array}{ccc|c}
1 & 0 & -3 & 8 \\
2 & 2 & 9 & 7 \\
0 & 1 & 5 & -2
\end{array}\right]
\sim
\left[\begin{array}{ccc|c}
1 & 0 & -3 & 8 \\
0 & 2 & 15 & -9 \\
0 & 1 & 5 & -2
\end{array}\right]
\sim
\left[\begin{array}{ccc|c}
1 & 0 & -3 & 8 \\
0 & 1 & 5 & -2 \\
0 & 2 & 15 & -9
\end{array}\right]
$$

$$
\sim
\left[\begin{array}{ccc|c}
1 & 0 & -3 & 8 \\
0 & 1 & 5 & -2 \\
0 & 0 & 5 & -5
\end{array}\right]
\sim
\left[\begin{array}{ccc|c}
1 & 0 & -3 & 8 \\
0 & 1 & 5 & -2 \\
0 & 0 & 1 & -1
\end{array}\right]
$$

Equation 3: $x_3 = -1$.

Equation 2: $x_2 + 5x_3 = -2 \rightarrow x_2 + 5(-1) = -2 \rightarrow x_2 = 3$.

Equation 1: $x_1 - 3x_3 = 8 \rightarrow x_1 - 3(-1) = 8 \rightarrow x_1 = 5$.

The system is **consistent** with unique solution $(\mathbf{x_1, x_2, x_3}) = (\mathbf{5, 3, -1})$.

2.

$$
\begin{aligned}
x_2 - 4x_3 &= 8 \\
2x_1 - 3x_2 + 2x_3 &= 1 \\
5x_1 - 8x_2 + 7x_3 &= 1
\end{aligned}
$$

Expressing this system in augmented matrix form and performing Gaussian Elimination:

$$
\left[\begin{array}{ccc|c}
0 & 1 & -4 & 8 \\
2 & -3 & 2 & 1 \\
5 & -8 & 7 & 1
\end{array}\right]
\sim
\left[\begin{array}{ccc|c}
2 & -3 & 2 & 1 \\
0 & 1 & -4 & 8 \\
5 & -8 & 7 & 1
\end{array}\right]
\sim
\left[\begin{array}{ccc|c}
1 & -3/2 & 1 & 1/2 \\
0 & 1 & -4 & 8 \\
5 & -8 & 7 & 1
\end{array}\right]
$$

$$
\sim
\left[\begin{array}{ccc|c}
1 & -3/2 & 1 & 1/2 \\
0 & 1 & -4 & 8 \\
0 & -1/2 & 2 & -3/2
\end{array}\right]
\sim
\left[\begin{array}{ccc|c}
1 & -3/2 & 1 & 1/2 \\
0 & 1 & -4 & 8 \\
0 & -1 & 4 & -3
\end{array}\right]
\sim
\left[\begin{array}{ccc|c}
1 & -3/2 & 1 & 1/2 \\
0 & 1 & -4 & 8 \\
0 & 0 & 0 & 5
\end{array}\right]
$$

Equation 3: $0x_1 + 0x_2 + 0x_3 = 5$.

There are no solutions to this equation and hence no solution to the system of equations.

Therefore, the system is **inconsistent**.

3.

$$
\begin{aligned}
x_1 + 2x_2 + 6x_3 &= 10 \\
x_1 + 5x_3 &= 6 \\
2x_2 + x_3 &= 4
\end{aligned}
$$

Expressing this system in augmented matrix form and performing Gaussian Elimination:

$$\begin{bmatrix} 1 & 2 & 6 & | & 10 \\ 1 & 0 & 5 & | & 6 \\ 0 & 2 & 1 & | & 4 \end{bmatrix} \sim \begin{bmatrix} 1 & 2 & 6 & | & 10 \\ 0 & -2 & -1 & | & -4 \\ 0 & 2 & 1 & | & 4 \end{bmatrix} \sim \begin{bmatrix} 1 & 2 & 6 & | & 10 \\ 0 & -2 & -1 & | & -4 \\ 0 & 0 & 0 & | & 0 \end{bmatrix}$$

Equation 3 is useless. We will get infinitely many solutions so the system is **consistent and dependent**.

Option 1:
Let x_3 be the free variable.
Equation 2: $-2x_2 - x_3 = -4 \rightarrow x_2 = 2 - x_3/2$.
Equation 1: $x_1 + 2x_2 + 6x_3 = 10 \rightarrow x_1 = -2x_2 - 6x_3 + 10 = -2(2 - x_3/2) - 6x_3 + 10 = 6 - 5x_3$.
So, letting the free variable $x_3 = t$ we get the general solution:
$(\mathbf{x_1, x_2, x_3}) = (\mathbf{6 - 5t, 2 - t/2, t})$ for $-\infty < t < \infty$
and a particular solution is found by setting $t = 0$ for $(\mathbf{6, \ 2, \ 0})$.

Option 2:
Let x_2 be the free variable.
Equation 2: $-2x_2 - x_3 = -4 \rightarrow x_3 = 4 - 2x_2$.
Equation 1: $x_1 + 2x_2 + 6x_3 = 10 \rightarrow x_1 = -2x_2 - 6x_3 + 10 = -2x_2 - 6(4 - 2x_2) + 10 = 10x_2 - 14$.
So, letting the free variable $x_2 = s$, the general solution is
$(\mathbf{x_1, x_2, x_3}) = (\mathbf{10s - 14, s, 4 - 2s})$ for $-\infty < s < \infty$,
and a particular solution is found by setting $s = 0$ for $(\mathbf{-14, \ 0, \ 4})$.

Do these two options give the same solution set?
Yes. If we **let $\mathbf{t = 4 - 2s}$**, then x_3 from both sets match.
Furthermore, $x_2 = 2 - t/2 = 2 - (4 - 2s)/2 = s$ and x_2 from both sets match.
Finally, $x_1 = 6 - 5t = 6 - 5(4 - 2s) = -14 + 10s$ and x_1 from both sets match.
Both general solutions yield the same solution set. You could even start by letting x_1 be the free variable and get the same solution set. So choose whichever option is easiest.

Chapter 1.2 Worksheet - Solutions

1. (**MATLAB**®) Recall the following systems that you solved by hand in Section 1.1.

(a)

$$x_1 - 3x_3 = 8$$
$$2x_1 + 2x_2 + 9x_3 = 7$$
$$x_2 + 5x_3 = -2$$

(b)

$$x_2 - 4x_3 = 8$$
$$2x_1 - 3x_2 + 2x_3 = 1$$
$$5x_1 - 8x_2 + 7x_3 = 1$$

(c)

$$x_1 + 2x_2 + 6x_3 = 10$$
$$x_1 + 5x_3 = 6$$
$$2x_2 + x_3 = 4$$

You should have found that (a) had a unique solution $[x_1, x_2, x_3] = [5, 3, -1]$, (b) (inconsistent) had no solutions, and (c) (dependent) had infinitely many solutions of the form $[x_1, x_2, x_3] = [6 - 5t, 2 - \frac{t}{2}, t]$.

Assignment: Use MATLAB® to solve these three systems of equations. You should run into problems. You will get warnings for parts (b) and (c). In part (b) MATLAB® actually gives you a solution that is not a solution and in part (c) MATLAB® does not return a solution.

(**a**)
Here, you set A = [1 0 -3; 2 2 9; 0 1 5] and b = [8 7 -2].
Then you get the solution is x = A\b = [5 3 -1] with no error message.

(**b**)
Here, you set A = [0 1 -4; 2 -3 2; 5 -8 7] and b = [8 1 1].
When you enter the command A\b you get a message.

```
Warning:  Matrix is close to singular or badly scaled.
Results may be inaccurate.  RCOND = 3.416071e-018.
```

However, it gives you a solution $(1.0e + 016) * [-1.1259, -0.9007, -0.2252]$. These are huge numbers because they are being multiplied by $\approx 10^{16}$. If you check this answer it is not really a solution.

(**c**)
Here, you set A = [1 2 6; 1 0 5; 0 2 1] and b = [10 6 4].
When you enter the command A\b you get a message.

```
Warning:  Matrix is singular to working precision.
```

It gives you a solution [NaN, NaN, NaN]'. Here, NaN means not a number. This will stop a program from running, which is good.

Observation: MATLAB® will give you a unique solution with no error message if a unique solution exists. However, if you have either no solutions or infinitely many solutions, MATLAB® will give you an error about the matrix being close to singular. It might give you a solution that is not a solution at all. It could also stop the process and not return any answer. The message about a singular matrix will be discussed later. For now, it is sufficient to say, if your coefficient matrix is singular - you got problems. The nice thing is, it doesn't happen that often. But when it happens things can turn ugly.

Chapter 1.3 Worksheet - Solutions

1. (**MATLAB®**) Recall the systems you solved by hand in Section 1.1 and with MATLAB® in 1.2:

(a)

$$
\begin{aligned}
x_1 - 3x_3 &= 8 \\
2x_1 + 2x_2 + 9x_3 &= 7 \\
x_2 + 5x_3 &= -2
\end{aligned}
$$

(b)

$$
\begin{aligned}
x_2 - 4x_3 &= 8 \\
2x_1 - 3x_2 + 2x_3 &= 1 \\
5x_1 - 8x_2 + 7x_3 &= 1
\end{aligned}
$$

(c)

$$
\begin{aligned}
x_1 + 2x_2 + 6x_3 &= 10 \\
x_1 + 5x_3 &= 6 \\
2x_2 + x_3 &= 4
\end{aligned}
$$

You should have found that (a) had a unique solution $[x_1, x_2, x_3] = [5, 3, -1]$, (b) (inconsistent) had no solutions, and (c) (dependent) had infinitely many solutions of the form $[x_1, x_2, x_3] = [6 - 5t, 2 - \frac{t}{2}, t]$.

Assignment: Enter the coefficient matrices into MATLAB® , then find the determinants and inverses of these three matrices. You should run into problems.

For part (a), you should get a non-zero determinant and nice inverse matrix. For part (b), you should get something very close to zero for the determinant, and when you try to find its inverse you should get a warning and an inverse with crazy huge numbers. For part (c) you should get zero for the determinant and when you try to get its inverse you get a message that the matrix is singular and it returns a matrix of non-numbers.

(**a**) Here, you set A = [1 0 -3; 2 2 9; 0 1 5].
Then det(A) = -5 and inv(A) = $\begin{bmatrix} -0.2 & 0.6 & -1.2 \\ 3 & -1 & 3 \\ -0.4 & 0.2 & -0.4 \end{bmatrix}$. No error messages.

(**b**) Here, you set A = [0 1 -4; 2 -3 2; 5 -8 7]. Then det(A) = 2.2204e-15. This is close to zero (2.22×10^{-15}) but is not zero as it should be. Since, as far as the software knows, this is not zero, it will try to get the inverse. When you enter inv(A), you get the error message:

```
Warning :  matrix is close to singular or badly scaled.
Results may be inaccurate.   rcond = 3.416071e-018.
```

It then gives you an inverse with huge numbers.

(**c**) Here, you set A = [1 2 6; 1 0 5; 0 2 1]. Then det(A) = 0 as it should and when you enter inv(A) you get the message:

```
Warning:  Matrix is singular to working precision.
```

It then returns a matrix with all terms Inf (which stands for infinity) - not a number. In this case, MATLAB® was able to tell you that the matrix has no inverse.

Observation: Inside of a machine the determinant of a matrix might not always give the exact value. This is a problem because if the determinant is zero, there is no inverse. If it is not zero, there is an inverse. Fortunately, when there is a problem you will usually be alerted by some type of message stating that the matrix is close to singular. It is always a good idea to figure out what caused these warnings.

Chapter 2.6 Worksheet - Solutions

Way back when solving systems of equations we came across the 3 x 3 system:

$$\begin{aligned} x_2 - 4x_3 &= 8 \\ 2x_1 - 3x_2 + 2x_3 &= 1 \\ 5x_1 - 8x_2 + 7x_3 &= 1 \end{aligned}$$

and we determined that there were no solutions. Allowing each equation to represent the graph of a plane, you can see that the planes are not parallel. Graph the 3 planes in such a way that you can ascertain why there is no point of intersection.

The normal vectors are
$$\mathbf{n}_1 = \langle 0, 1, -4 \rangle, \quad \mathbf{n}_2 = \langle 2, -3, 2 \rangle, \quad \mathbf{n}_3 = \langle 5, -8, 7 \rangle.$$

Since the normal vectors are not parallel, the planes are not parallel. Getting one point from each plane:
$$P_1 = (0, 8, 0), \quad P_2 = (0, 0, \tfrac{1}{2}), \quad P_3 = (0, 0, \tfrac{1}{7}).$$

With the normal vectors and points we can use the `PlotPlaneFunction`. Below are the graphs of the planes. The second graph looks down the middle of the triangular cross-section of the first graph.

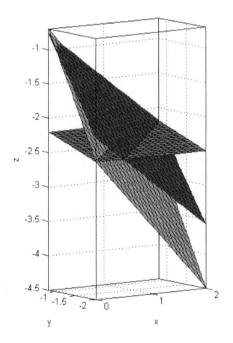 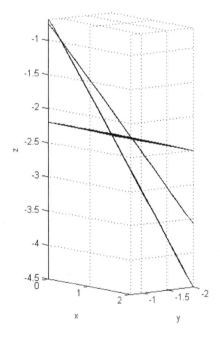

Detailed Solutions to Selected Problems

Chapter 1.1

2 (a)
$$\begin{matrix} x + 3y - z &=& 1 \\ y - z &=& 1 \\ 2x - y + 5z &=& 2 \end{matrix} \rightarrow \left[\begin{array}{ccc|c} 1 & 3 & -1 & 1 \\ 0 & 1 & -1 & 1 \\ 2 & -1 & 5 & 2 \end{array}\right] \sim \left[\begin{array}{ccc|c} 1 & 3 & -1 & 1 \\ 0 & 1 & -1 & 1 \\ 0 & -7 & 7 & 0 \end{array}\right] \sim \left[\begin{array}{ccc|c} 1 & 3 & -1 & 1 \\ 0 & 1 & -1 & 1 \\ 0 & 0 & 0 & 7 \end{array}\right]$$

The last row represents the equation $0x + 0y + 0z = 7$, which has no solutions. The system has no solutions and is therefore **inconsistent**.

(b)
$$\begin{matrix} x + 3y - z &=& 1 \\ y - z &=& 1 \\ 2x - y + 5z &=& -5 \end{matrix} \rightarrow \left[\begin{array}{ccc|c} 1 & 3 & -1 & 1 \\ 0 & 1 & -1 & 1 \\ 2 & -1 & 5 & -5 \end{array}\right] \sim \left[\begin{array}{ccc|c} 1 & 3 & -1 & 1 \\ 0 & 1 & -1 & 1 \\ 0 & -7 & 7 & -7 \end{array}\right] \sim \left[\begin{array}{ccc|c} 1 & 3 & -1 & 1 \\ 0 & 1 & -1 & 1 \\ 0 & 0 & 0 & 0 \end{array}\right]$$

The last row represents the equation $0x + 0y + 0z = 0$, which has infinitely many solutions. Let z be free. The second row represents the equation $y - z = 1$ so $y = z + 1$. The first row represents the equation $x + 3y - z = 1 \rightarrow x + 3(z + 1) - z = 1 \rightarrow x + 2z + 3 = 1 \rightarrow x = -2z - 2$. So, letting the free variable $z = t$, the **general solution looks like** $(x, y, z) = (-2t - 2, t + 1, t)$ **for** $-\infty < t < \infty$. One such solution can be obtained by letting $t = 0$, in which case a **particular solution** is $(-2, 1, 0)$, but there are infinitely many.

(c)
$$\begin{matrix} x - 3z &=& -5 \\ 2x + y + 2z &=& 7 \\ 3x + 2y + z &=& 7 \end{matrix}$$

$$\rightarrow \left[\begin{array}{ccc|c} 1 & 0 & -3 & -5 \\ 2 & 1 & 2 & 7 \\ 3 & 2 & 1 & 7 \end{array}\right] \sim \left[\begin{array}{ccc|c} 1 & 0 & -3 & -5 \\ 0 & 1 & 8 & 17 \\ 0 & 2 & 10 & 22 \end{array}\right] \sim \left[\begin{array}{ccc|c} 1 & 0 & -3 & -5 \\ 0 & 1 & 8 & 17 \\ 0 & 0 & -6 & -12 \end{array}\right] \sim \left[\begin{array}{ccc|c} 1 & 0 & -3 & -5 \\ 0 & 1 & 8 & 17 \\ 0 & 0 & 1 & 2 \end{array}\right]$$

The third row represents the equation $z = 2$. The second row represents the equation $y + 8z = 17 \rightarrow y + 8(2) = 17 \rightarrow y = 1$. The first equation represents the equation $x - 3z = -5 \rightarrow x - 3(2) = -5 \rightarrow x = 1$. Because there is a solution, the system is consistent. The system has the **unique solution** $(x, y, z) = (1, 1, 2)$.

$$\textbf{4 (a)} \quad \begin{matrix} x + 2y + 3z & = & 6 \\ 2y - z & = & 1 \\ x + 4y + 2z & = & 7 \end{matrix} \rightarrow \left[\begin{array}{ccc|c} 1 & 2 & 3 & 6 \\ 0 & 2 & -1 & 1 \\ 1 & 4 & 2 & 7 \end{array}\right] \sim \left[\begin{array}{ccc|c} 1 & 2 & 3 & 6 \\ 0 & 2 & -1 & 1 \\ 0 & 2 & -1 & 1 \end{array}\right] \sim \left[\begin{array}{ccc|c} 1 & 2 & 3 & 6 \\ 0 & 2 & -1 & 1 \\ 0 & 0 & 0 & 0 \end{array}\right]$$

The last row represents the equation $0x + 0y + 0z = 0$, which has infinitely many solutions.
If you let $z = t$ be a free parameter, the second row represents $2y - z = 1$ or $y = \frac{1}{2} + \frac{t}{2}$. Subbing both of these into equation 1: $x + 2y + 3z = 6 \rightarrow x + (1 + t) + 3t = 6 \rightarrow x = 5 - 4t$. So, the **general solution** is $\begin{bmatrix} x \\ y \\ z \end{bmatrix} = \begin{bmatrix} 5 - 4t \\ \frac{1}{2} + \frac{t}{2} \\ t \end{bmatrix}$. Letting $t = 0$, a **specific solution** is $\begin{bmatrix} 5 \\ 0.5 \\ 0 \end{bmatrix}$.

If you let $y = t$ be a free parameter, the second row represents $2y - z = 1$ or $z = 2t - 1$. Subbing both these into equation 1: $x + 2y + 3z = 6 \rightarrow x + 2t + 3(2t - 1) = 6 \rightarrow x = 9 - 8t$. So, the **general solution** is $\begin{bmatrix} x \\ y \\ z \end{bmatrix} = \begin{bmatrix} 9 - 8t \\ t \\ 2t - 1 \end{bmatrix}$. Letting $t = 0$, a **specific solution** is $\begin{bmatrix} 9 \\ 0 \\ -1 \end{bmatrix}$.

If you can use MATLAB®'s *least squares solution* for a **specific solution** $= [0, 1.125, 1.25]^T$.

$$\textbf{(b)} \quad \begin{matrix} x + 2y + 3z & = & 2 \\ 2y - z & = & -3 \\ x + 4y + 2z & = & -5 \end{matrix} \rightarrow \left[\begin{array}{ccc|c} 1 & 2 & 3 & 2 \\ 0 & 2 & -1 & -3 \\ 1 & 4 & 2 & 5 \end{array}\right] \sim \left[\begin{array}{ccc|c} 1 & 2 & 3 & 2 \\ 0 & 2 & -1 & -3 \\ 0 & 2 & -1 & 3 \end{array}\right] \sim \left[\begin{array}{ccc|c} 1 & 2 & 3 & 2 \\ 0 & 2 & -1 & -3 \\ 0 & 0 & 0 & 6 \end{array}\right]$$

The last row represents the equation $0x + 0y + 0z = 6$. **No Solutions!**

$$\textbf{(c)} \quad \begin{matrix} x + 2y + 3z & = & -8 \\ 2y - z & = & 10 \\ x + 4y + z & = & 6 \end{matrix}$$

$$\rightarrow \left[\begin{array}{ccc|c} 1 & 2 & 3 & -8 \\ 0 & 2 & -1 & 10 \\ 1 & 4 & 1 & 6 \end{array}\right] \sim \left[\begin{array}{ccc|c} 1 & 2 & 3 & -8 \\ 0 & 2 & -1 & 10 \\ 0 & 2 & -2 & 14 \end{array}\right] \sim \left[\begin{array}{ccc|c} 1 & 2 & 3 & -8 \\ 0 & 2 & -1 & 10 \\ 0 & 0 & -1 & 4 \end{array}\right] \sim \left[\begin{array}{ccc|c} 1 & 2 & 3 & -8 \\ 0 & 2 & -1 & 10 \\ 0 & 0 & 1 & -4 \end{array}\right]$$

So, the last row says $z = -4$, the second row says $2y - z = 10 \rightarrow y = 3$, and the first row says $x + 2y + 3z = -8 \rightarrow x + 6 - 12 = -8 \rightarrow x = -2$. So, $(x, y, z) = (-2, 3, -4)$.

Chapter 1.2

1a Here, order doesn't matter because this is a dot product. $\mathbf{x} \cdot \mathbf{y} = \mathbf{y} \cdot \mathbf{x} = 1(4) + 2(5) + 3(6) = \textbf{32}$.

1b In this case x is a 1x3 matrix and y is a 3x1 matrix so xy is going to be a 1x1 matrix which is just a scalar: $1(4) + 2(5) + 3(6) = \textbf{32}$

1c In this case y is 3x1 matrix and x is a 1x3 matrix. The result of yx is going to be a 3x3 matrix. It is probably not what you want but it does work.

$$\begin{bmatrix} 4 \\ 5 \\ 6 \end{bmatrix} [1\ 2\ 3] = \begin{bmatrix} 4(1) & 4(2) & 4(3) \\ 5(1) & 5(2) & 5(3) \\ 6(1) & 6(2) & 6(3) \end{bmatrix} = \begin{bmatrix} 4 & 8 & 12 \\ 5 & 10 & 15 \\ 6 & 12 & 18 \end{bmatrix}$$

3a $M^T = \begin{bmatrix} 1 & 0 & 0 \\ 0 & 2 & 0 \\ 0 & 0 & 5 \end{bmatrix} \quad N^T = \begin{bmatrix} -1 & 10 & 0 \\ 3 & 1 & 2 \\ -2 & 1 & 3 \end{bmatrix}$

3b These solutions were found using software.

$$MN = \begin{bmatrix} -1 & 3 & -2 \\ 20 & 2 & 2 \\ 0 & 10 & 15 \end{bmatrix} \quad NM = \begin{bmatrix} -1 & 6 & -10 \\ 10 & 2 & 5 \\ 0 & 4 & 15 \end{bmatrix} \qquad \text{Note: } MN \neq NM.$$

3c $Mx = \begin{bmatrix} 1 \\ 0 \\ -5 \end{bmatrix}$

3d $x \cdot y = -6 + 0 - 1 = \mathbf{-7}$

3e $3\begin{bmatrix} 1 \\ 0 \\ -1 \end{bmatrix} - 2\begin{bmatrix} -6 \\ 10 \\ 1 \end{bmatrix} = \begin{bmatrix} 3 \\ 0 \\ -3 \end{bmatrix} + \begin{bmatrix} 12 \\ -20 \\ -2 \end{bmatrix} = \begin{bmatrix} 15 \\ -20 \\ -5 \end{bmatrix}$

4a $AB = \begin{bmatrix} 1 & 2 & 0 \\ 0 & 4 & -2 \\ 1 & 0 & 3 \end{bmatrix}\begin{bmatrix} 3 & 2 & -1 \\ 0 & 1 & 0 \\ -1 & 2 & 3 \end{bmatrix} =$

$$\begin{bmatrix} 1(3)+2(0)+0(-1) & 1(2)+2(1)+0(2) & 1(-1)+2(0)+0(3) \\ 0(3)+4(0)-2(-1) & 0(2)+4(1)-2(2) & 0(-1)+4(0)-2(3) \\ 1(3)+0(0)+3(-1) & 1(2)+0(1)+3(2) & 1(-1)+0(0)+3(3) \end{bmatrix} = \begin{bmatrix} 3 & 4 & -1 \\ 2 & 0 & -6 \\ 0 & 8 & 8 \end{bmatrix}$$

4b $AC = \begin{bmatrix} 1 & 2 & 0 \\ 0 & 4 & -2 \\ 1 & 0 & 3 \end{bmatrix}\begin{bmatrix} 3 & 0 & 0 \\ 0 & 2 & 0 \\ 0 & 0 & 4 \end{bmatrix} = \begin{bmatrix} 3 & 4 & 0 \\ 0 & 8 & -8 \\ 3 & 0 & 12 \end{bmatrix}$

Column 1 was multiplied by 3, Column 2 was multiplied by 2, and Column 3 was multiplied by 4.

$$CA = \begin{bmatrix} 3 & 0 & 0 \\ 0 & 2 & 0 \\ 0 & 0 & 4 \end{bmatrix}\begin{bmatrix} 1 & 2 & 0 \\ 0 & 4 & -2 \\ 1 & 0 & 3 \end{bmatrix} = \begin{bmatrix} 3 & 6 & 0 \\ 0 & 8 & -4 \\ 4 & 0 & 12 \end{bmatrix}$$

Row 1 was multiplied by 3, Row 2 was multiplied by 2, and Row 3 was multiplied by 4.

4c $Ax = \begin{bmatrix} 1 & 2 & 0 \\ 0 & 4 & -2 \\ 1 & 0 & 3 \end{bmatrix}\begin{bmatrix} 2 \\ -3 \\ 0 \end{bmatrix} = \begin{bmatrix} 1(2)+2(-3)+0(0) \\ 0(2)+4(-3)-2(0) \\ 1(2)+0(-3)+3(0) \end{bmatrix} = \begin{bmatrix} -4 \\ -12 \\ 2 \end{bmatrix}$

$$Bx = \begin{bmatrix} 3 & 2 & -1 \\ 0 & 1 & 0 \\ -1 & 2 & 3 \end{bmatrix} \begin{bmatrix} 2 \\ -3 \\ 0 \end{bmatrix} = \begin{bmatrix} 3(2) + 2(-3) - 1(0) \\ 0(2) + 1(-3) + 0(0) \\ -1(2) + 2(-3) + 3(0) \end{bmatrix} = \begin{bmatrix} 0 \\ -3 \\ -8 \end{bmatrix}$$

$$Cx = \begin{bmatrix} 3 & 0 & 0 \\ 0 & 2 & 0 \\ 0 & 0 & 4 \end{bmatrix} \begin{bmatrix} 2 \\ -3 \\ 0 \end{bmatrix} = \begin{bmatrix} 3(2) + 0(-3) + 0(0) \\ 0(2) + 2(-3) + 0(0) \\ 0(2) + 0(-3) + 4(0) \end{bmatrix} = \begin{bmatrix} 6 \\ -6 \\ 0 \end{bmatrix}$$

When x is multiplied by C on the left, the first term is multiplied by 3, the second term by 2, and the third term by 4.

5b The error message is `Inconsistent multiplication`.

6 (a)
$$\begin{array}{rcl} x - 3z &=& -5 \\ 2x + y + 2z &=& 7 \\ 3x + 2y + z &=& 7 \end{array} \quad \text{Let } A = \begin{bmatrix} 1 & 0 & -3 \\ 2 & 1 & 2 \\ 3 & 2 & 1 \end{bmatrix} \text{ and } \mathbf{b} = \begin{bmatrix} -5 \\ 7 \\ 7 \end{bmatrix}.$$
Then $\mathbf{x} = A \setminus \mathbf{b} = [1, 1, 2]^T$.
And the solution is $\boxed{x = 1,\ y = 1,\ \text{and } z = 2}$.

(b)
$$\begin{array}{rcl} x_1 + x_2 + 2x_3 &=& 8 \\ -x_1 - 2x_2 + 3x_3 &=& 1 \\ 3x_1 - 7x_2 + 4x_3 &=& 10 \end{array} \quad \text{Let } A = \begin{bmatrix} 1 & 1 & 2 \\ -1 & -2 & 3 \\ 3 & -7 & 4 \end{bmatrix} \text{ and } \mathbf{b} = \begin{bmatrix} 8 \\ 1 \\ 10 \end{bmatrix}.$$
Then $\mathbf{x} = A \setminus \mathbf{b} = [3, 1, 2]^T$.
And the solution is $\boxed{x_1 = 3,\ x_2 = 1,\ \text{and } x_3 = 2}$.

Chapter 1.3

1b Determinant: Performing a cofactor expansion of B along the first row we get
$$\begin{vmatrix} 1 & 0 & -2 \\ -3 & 1 & 4 \\ 2 & -3 & 4 \end{vmatrix} = (-1)^{(1+1)}(1) \begin{vmatrix} 1 & 4 \\ -3 & 4 \end{vmatrix} + (-1)^{(1+2)}(0) \begin{vmatrix} who \\ cares \end{vmatrix} + (-1)^{(1+3)}(-2) \begin{vmatrix} -3 & 1 \\ 2 & -3 \end{vmatrix}$$
$$= (1)(4 + 12) - 2(9 - 2) = 16 - 14 = \mathbf{2}.$$

Inverse: Setting up the augmented matrix:
$$[B|I_3] = \left[\begin{array}{ccc|ccc} 1 & 0 & -2 & 1 & 0 & 0 \\ -3 & 1 & 4 & 0 & 1 & 0 \\ 2 & -3 & 4 & 0 & 0 & 1 \end{array} \right] \sim \left[\begin{array}{ccc|ccc} 1 & 0 & -2 & 1 & 0 & 0 \\ 0 & 1 & -2 & 3 & 1 & 0 \\ 0 & -3 & 8 & -2 & 0 & 1 \end{array} \right]$$

$$\sim \left[\begin{array}{ccc|ccc} 1 & 0 & -2 & 1 & 0 & 0 \\ 0 & 1 & -2 & 3 & 1 & 0 \\ 0 & 0 & 2 & 7 & 3 & 1 \end{array} \right] \sim \left[\begin{array}{ccc|ccc} 1 & 0 & -2 & 1 & 0 & 0 \\ 0 & 1 & -2 & 3 & 1 & 0 \\ 0 & 0 & 1 & \frac{7}{2} & \frac{3}{2} & \frac{1}{2} \end{array} \right]$$

$$\sim \begin{bmatrix} 1 & 0 & 0 & | & 8 & 3 & 1 \\ 0 & 1 & 0 & | & 10 & 4 & 1 \\ 0 & 0 & 1 & | & \frac{7}{2} & \frac{3}{2} & \frac{1}{2} \end{bmatrix} = [I_3 | B^{-1}] \quad \text{so} \quad B^{-1} = \begin{bmatrix} 8 & 3 & 1 \\ 10 & 4 & 1 \\ \frac{7}{2} & \frac{3}{2} & \frac{1}{2} \end{bmatrix}$$

3a Let `A = [0, 1, 2; 1, 0, 3; 4, -3, 8]`,
then `b1 = [3, 1, 0]'`, `b2 = [1,1,1]'`, and `b3 = [0,0,0]'`.
Then solving each equation by `inv(A)*b1`, `inv(A)*b2`, and `inv(A)*b3` you get:

$$x_1 = \begin{bmatrix} -6.5 \\ -2 \\ 2.5 \end{bmatrix}, \quad x_2 = \begin{bmatrix} 1 \\ 1 \\ 0 \end{bmatrix}, \quad x_3 = \begin{bmatrix} 0 \\ 0 \\ 0 \end{bmatrix}.$$

3b Let `A = [0, 1, 2; 1, 0, 3; 4, -3, 8]`,
then `x1 = A\b1`, `x2 = A\b2`, `x3 = A\b3` you get:

$$x_1 = \begin{bmatrix} -6.5 \\ -2 \\ 2.5 \end{bmatrix}, \quad x_2 = \begin{bmatrix} 1 \\ 1 \\ 0 \end{bmatrix}, \quad x_3 = \begin{bmatrix} 0 \\ 0 \\ 0 \end{bmatrix}.$$

4 Any square matrices (with inverses) can be used to demonstrate the following inverse theorems in MATLAB® :

- `inv(A*B) = inv(A) * inv(B)`

- `inv(inv(A)) = A`

- `inv(A') = (inv(A))'`

- `inv(k*A) = 1/K * inv(A)`

Any square matrices can be used to demonstrate the following determinant theorems in MATLAB® :

- If A is a triangular matrix (upper or lower) then `det(A) = A(1,1) * A(2,2) ... * A(n,n)`.

- `det(A') = det(A)`

- `det(A*B) = det(A) * det(B)`

- `det(inv(A)) = 1/det(A)` provided `det(A)` $\neq$ `0`

Chapter 1.4

1 The left side of the equals sign is
$$a_1 \begin{bmatrix} 1 \\ 0 \\ 2 \end{bmatrix} + a_2 \begin{bmatrix} -2 \\ 1 \\ -3 \end{bmatrix} + a_3 \begin{bmatrix} 2 \\ 5 \\ 0 \end{bmatrix} = \begin{bmatrix} a_1 \\ 0 \\ 2a_1 \end{bmatrix} + \begin{bmatrix} -2a_2 \\ a_2 \\ -3a_2 \end{bmatrix} + \begin{bmatrix} 2a_3 \\ 5a_3 \\ 0 \end{bmatrix} = \begin{bmatrix} a_1 - 2a_2 + 2a_3 \\ a_2 + 5a_3 \\ 2a_1 - 3a_2 \end{bmatrix}$$
The right side of the equals sign is

$$\begin{bmatrix} 1 & -2 & 2 \\ 0 & 1 & 5 \\ 2 & -3 & 0 \end{bmatrix} \begin{bmatrix} a_1 \\ a_2 \\ a_3 \end{bmatrix} = \begin{bmatrix} a_1 - 2a_2 + 2a_3 \\ a_2 + 5a_3 \\ 2a_1 - 3a_2 \end{bmatrix}$$

These are indeed equal.

2a Here we must solve the system $Ma = x$ where $M = \begin{bmatrix} 1 & 2 \\ 4 & 7 \end{bmatrix}$, $a = \begin{bmatrix} a_1 \\ a_2 \end{bmatrix}$, and $x = \begin{bmatrix} -2 \\ 3 \end{bmatrix}$.

Using the formula for the inverse of a $2x2$ matrix or letting MATLAB® do you it. You get

$$M^{-1} = \begin{bmatrix} -7 & 2 \\ 4 & -1 \end{bmatrix} \quad \text{and} \quad \begin{bmatrix} a_1 \\ a_2 \end{bmatrix} = M^{-1}x = \begin{bmatrix} -7 & 2 \\ 4 & -1 \end{bmatrix} \begin{bmatrix} -2 \\ 3 \end{bmatrix} = \begin{bmatrix} 20 \\ -11 \end{bmatrix}$$

Or, you can use the MATLAB® command `a = M\x` and get the same answer.
Either way, $a_1 = 20$, **and** $a_2 = -11$.

3a Here we must solve the system $Ma = x$ where

$$M = \begin{bmatrix} 1 & 0 & -2 \\ -3 & 1 & 4 \\ 2 & -3 & 4 \end{bmatrix}, a = \begin{bmatrix} a_1 \\ a_2 \\ a_3 \end{bmatrix}, \text{ and } x = \begin{bmatrix} 1 \\ 1 \\ 1 \end{bmatrix}.$$

Calculating the inverse of M or letting MATLAB® do you it. You get

$$M^{-1} = \begin{bmatrix} 8 & 3 & 1 \\ 10 & 4 & 1 \\ 3.5 & 1.5 & 0.5 \end{bmatrix} \quad \text{and} \quad \begin{bmatrix} a_1 \\ a_2 \\ a_3 \end{bmatrix} = M^{-1}x = \begin{bmatrix} 8 & 3 & 1 \\ 10 & 4 & 1 \\ 3.5 & 1.5 & 0.5 \end{bmatrix} \begin{bmatrix} 1 \\ 1 \\ 1 \end{bmatrix} = \begin{bmatrix} 12 \\ 15 \\ 5.5 \end{bmatrix}$$

Or, you can use the MATLAB® command `a = M\x` and get the same answer.
Either way, $a_1 = 12$, $a_2 = 15$, **and** $a_3 = 5.5$.

Chapter 1.5

1a Create the matrix M:

$$M = \begin{bmatrix} \vdots & \vdots & \vdots \\ v_1 & v_2 & v_3 \\ \vdots & \vdots & \vdots \end{bmatrix} = \begin{bmatrix} 1 & 0 & 2 \\ 2 & 1 & 5 \\ 3 & 5 & 11 \end{bmatrix} \text{ and } \det(M) = 1(11 - 25) - 0(\text{who cares}) + 2(10 - 3) = 0.$$

Here we use the **Super Theorem (V2)** and conclude that since $\det(M) = 0$, the vectors **are not linearly independent** and **do not form a basis** for $\mathbb{R}^3$.

Now, can we find a nonzero linear combination of these vectors that result in the zero vector? To do this we need to find set up the equation: $Ma = 0$ and solve for a. Putting this equation in augmented matrix form:

$$\begin{bmatrix} 1 & 0 & 2 & | & 0 \\ 2 & 1 & 5 & | & 0 \\ 3 & 5 & 11 & | & 0 \end{bmatrix} \sim \begin{bmatrix} 1 & 0 & 2 & | & 0 \\ 0 & 1 & 1 & | & 0 \\ 0 & 5 & 5 & | & 0 \end{bmatrix} \sim \begin{bmatrix} 1 & 0 & 2 & | & 0 \\ 0 & 1 & 1 & | & 0 \\ 0 & 0 & 0 & | & 0 \end{bmatrix}$$

The last equation is useless and gives us a free variable a_3. The second equation says $a_2 + a_3 = 0$ or $a_2 = -a_3$. The first equations says that $a_1 + 2a_3 = 0$ or $a_2 = -2a_3$. Letting a_3 be the free parameter t we get $[a_1, a_2, a_3] = [-2t, -t, t]$ for $-\infty < t < \infty$. Letting t be any number other than zero can get a non-zero solution. For example, if we let $t = 1$, the solution becomes $a = [a_1, a_2, a_3] = [-2, -1, 1]$. So notice, $-2u_1 - u_2 + u_3 = [0, 0, 0]$ and we have a non-zero linear combination of the vectors which produces the zero vector.

1c We know that that there are not enough vectors to form a basis for $\mathbb{R}^3$. Can we prove that they are linearly independent? We need to determine if there is a non-zero linear combination of these vectors that result in the zero vector. That is we must solve the system:

$$a_1 v_1 + a_2 v_2 = \mathbf{0} \quad \rightarrow \quad \begin{bmatrix} 1 & 0 \\ 2 & 1 \\ 3 & 5 \end{bmatrix} \begin{bmatrix} a_1 \\ a_2 \end{bmatrix} = \begin{bmatrix} 0 \\ 0 \\ 0 \end{bmatrix}$$

Expressing this system in augmented matrix form:

$$\begin{bmatrix} 1 & 0 & 0 \\ 2 & 1 & 0 \\ 3 & 5 & 0 \end{bmatrix} \sim \begin{bmatrix} 1 & 0 & 0 \\ 0 & 1 & 0 \\ 0 & 5 & 0 \end{bmatrix}$$

The last equation states that $5a_2 = 0$, so $a_2 = 0$. The first equation states that $a_1 = 0$. As such, the only solution is $[a_1, a_2] = [0, 0]$ and the vectors are linearly independent.

2a Use these vectors as the columns in the matrix V:

$$V = \begin{bmatrix} 1 & 1 & 3 \\ -1 & 0 & -4 \\ 2 & 5 & 3 \end{bmatrix} \quad \text{and } \det(V) = 1(0 + 20) - 1(-3 + 8) + 3(-5 - 0) = 0$$

By the **Super Theorem (V2)** since determinant of V is 0 the columns are not linearly independent and do not form a basis for $\mathbb{R}^3$.

Chapter 1.6

1a Let $V = \begin{bmatrix} 1 & 2 & 0 \\ 2 & 3 & 0 \\ 1 & 0 & 2 \end{bmatrix}$ (the matrix with the new basis as column vectors).

Then the transition matrix is $T = V^{-1} = \begin{bmatrix} -3 & 2 & 0 \\ 2 & -1 & 0 \\ 1.5 & -1 & 0.5 \end{bmatrix}$ (using MATLAB®). The new point is

$$TP = \begin{bmatrix} -3 & 2 & 0 \\ 2 & -1 & 0 \\ 1.5 & -1 & 0.5 \end{bmatrix} \begin{bmatrix} 2 \\ 0 \\ 3 \end{bmatrix} = \begin{bmatrix} -6 \\ 4 \\ 4.5 \end{bmatrix}.$$ So, with respect to the new basis, $P = (-6, 4, 4.5)$.

2a Consider the radius vector $r = [3, 2]$ given with respect to the standard basis. If we choose a new basis consisting of $v_1 = [3, 0]^T$ and $v_2 = [0, 2]^T$ the radius vector is $1v_1 + 1v_2$. So, with respect to this new basis (called Ellipse Space), the radius vector is simply $r_{new} = [1, 1]$. In other words, our ellipse has been transformed into a unit circle. Now we want to transform the point $p = [1.8, 1.8]$ into Ellipse Space. So, the transition matrix is given by

$$T = V^{-1} = \begin{bmatrix} 3 & 0 \\ 0 & 2 \end{bmatrix}^{-1} = \begin{bmatrix} \frac{1}{3} & 0 \\ 0 & \frac{1}{2} \end{bmatrix}$$

So we multiply p on the left by T to get p_{new}:

$$p_{new} = Tp = \begin{bmatrix} \frac{1}{3} & 0 \\ 0 & \frac{1}{2} \end{bmatrix} \begin{bmatrix} 1.8 \\ 1.8 \end{bmatrix} = \begin{bmatrix} 0.6 \\ 0.9 \end{bmatrix}$$

So, now we just check to see if p_{new} is within the unit circle. So look at $x_{new}^2 + y_{new}^2 = (0.6)^2 + (0.9)^2 = 1.17$. Since this value is greater than 1, we conclude that p_{new} is outside of the transformed ellipse and so **the point p is outside of the ellipse**.

3a Consider the radius vector $r = [1, 2, 3]$ given with respect to the standard basis. If we choose a new basis consisting of $v_1 = [1, 0, 0]^T$, $v_2 = [0, 2, 0]^T$, and $v_3 = [0, 0, 3]^T$ the radius vector is $1v_1 + 1v_2 + 1v_3$. So, with respect to this new basis (called Ellipsoid Space), the radius vector is simply $r_{new} = [1, 1, 1]$. In other words, our ellipsoid has been transformed into a unit sphere. Now we want to transform the point $p = [0.5, 1.5, 2.0]$ into Ellipsoid Space. So, the transition matrix is given by

$$T = V^{-1} = \begin{bmatrix} 1 & 0 & 0 \\ 0 & 2 & 0 \\ 0 & 0 & 3 \end{bmatrix}^{-1} = \begin{bmatrix} 1 & 0 & 0 \\ 0 & \frac{1}{2} & 0 \\ 0 & 0 & \frac{1}{3} \end{bmatrix}$$

So we multiply p on the left by T to get p_{new}:

$$p_{new} = Tp = \begin{bmatrix} 1 & 0 & 0 \\ 0 & \frac{1}{2} & 0 \\ 0 & 0 & \frac{1}{3} \end{bmatrix} \begin{bmatrix} 0.5 \\ 1.5 \\ 2.0 \end{bmatrix} = \begin{bmatrix} 0.5 \\ 0.75 \\ 0.67 \end{bmatrix}$$

So, now we just check to see if p_{new} is within the unit sphere. Look at $x_{new}^2 + y_{new}^2 + z_{new}^2 = (0.5)^2 + (0.75)^2 + (0.67)^2 \approx 1.12$. Since this value is greater than 1, we conclude that p_{new} is outside the unit sphere and so **the original point p is outside of the ellipsoid**.

4 The original line has slope $= \frac{5}{7}$ and y-intercept $= 4$. The transition matrix is given by

$$T = V^{-1} = \begin{bmatrix} 3 & 0 \\ 0 & 2 \end{bmatrix}^{-1} = \begin{bmatrix} \frac{1}{3} & 0 \\ 0 & \frac{1}{2} \end{bmatrix}$$

Now, let's translate a couple points on the line, say $p = [0, 4]$ and $q = [7, 9]$. Translating these into *Ellipse Space*:

$$p_{new} = Tp = \begin{bmatrix} \frac{1}{3} & 0 \\ 0 & \frac{1}{2} \end{bmatrix} \begin{bmatrix} 0 \\ 4 \end{bmatrix} = \begin{bmatrix} 0 \\ 2 \end{bmatrix} \quad \text{and} \quad q_{new} = Tq = \begin{bmatrix} \frac{1}{3} & 0 \\ 0 & \frac{1}{2} \end{bmatrix} \begin{bmatrix} 7 \\ 9 \end{bmatrix} = \begin{bmatrix} 7/3 \\ 9/2 \end{bmatrix}$$

So the transformed points in ellipse space are $(0,2)$ and $(7/3, 9/2)$. Since we have two points, we can get the equation for this line as $y_{new} = m_{new}x_{new} + b_{new}$ where

$$m_{new} = \frac{9/2 - 2}{7/3 - 0} = \frac{5/2}{7/3} = \frac{5 \cdot \frac{1}{2}}{7 \cdot \frac{1}{3}} \cdot = \frac{15}{14}$$

The original slope was $\frac{5}{7}$. After the transformation, ΔY is changed by a factor of $\frac{1}{2}$ and Δx is changed by a factor of $\frac{1}{3}$ as the transition matrix would suggest.

The new y-intercept is given by p_{new} which is 2. Notice the original y-intercept is changed by a factor of $\frac{1}{2}$ as the transition matrix would suggest.

The equation of the transformed line with respect to the new basis is

$$y_{new} = \frac{15}{14}\, x_{new} + 2.$$

The slope and intercept are modified in the transformation according the the transition matrix T.

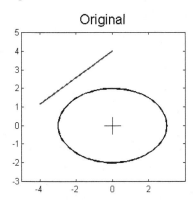
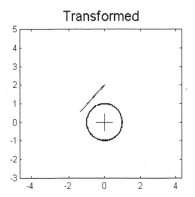

Chapter 1.7

1a The original point is denoted in vector form as $[0, 3]^T$. First, you have to add 1 unit to the x-value and 2 units to the y-value. Second, The rotation matrix is $R = \begin{bmatrix} \cos\theta & \sin\theta \\ -\sin\theta & \cos\theta \end{bmatrix}$ which rotates points in the clock-wise direction by θ radians. In this case, $\theta = -60^o$ which is $-60\frac{\pi}{180} = -\frac{\pi}{3}$ radians. The transformation looks like

$$\begin{bmatrix} x_{new} \\ y_{new} \end{bmatrix} = \begin{bmatrix} \cos\theta & \sin\theta \\ -\sin\theta & \cos\theta \end{bmatrix} \left(\begin{bmatrix} 0 \\ 3 \end{bmatrix} + \begin{bmatrix} 1 \\ 2 \end{bmatrix} \right) = \begin{bmatrix} \cos\theta & \sin\theta \\ -\sin\theta & \cos\theta \end{bmatrix} \begin{bmatrix} 1 \\ 5 \end{bmatrix} \approx \begin{bmatrix} -3.8 \\ 3.4 \end{bmatrix}$$

Which must be done in MATLAB® .

2a You know that the transformation goes like

$$\begin{bmatrix} 1 & 0 \\ 0 & -1 \end{bmatrix} \begin{bmatrix} \cos\theta & \sin\theta \\ -\sin\theta & \cos\theta \end{bmatrix} \begin{bmatrix} x \\ y \end{bmatrix} = \begin{bmatrix} -2 \\ 3 \end{bmatrix}$$

So, we must solve the equation above for $[x, y]^T$. There are many ways to do this but all of them require MATLAB® (using inverses or the \ command). You should get $[x, y]^T = [-0.23, \ -3.60]$. So, $(x, y) = (\mathbf{-0.23}, \mathbf{-3.60})$.

Chapter 2.1

1a $\mathbf{v} = \langle -3, -10 \rangle$

2a $\mathbf{u} = \langle -2, -5 \rangle$ and $\mathbf{v} = \langle -4, -1 \rangle$, not equivalent, not parallel.

2c $\mathbf{u} = \langle 3, -2 \rangle$ and $\mathbf{v} = \langle -6, 4 \rangle$, not equivalent but $\mathbf{v} = -2\,\mathbf{u}$ therefore parallel.

3a $\overrightarrow{PQ} = \langle 3, 6 \rangle$ and $\overrightarrow{PR} = \langle 2, 4 \rangle$. Notice, $\overrightarrow{PR} = \frac{2}{3}\overrightarrow{PQ}$ so these vectors are parallel and the points are collinear.

5a $\overrightarrow{PQ} = \langle 3, 4 \rangle$ and $\overrightarrow{PR} = \langle 8, w - 3 \rangle$. If $\overrightarrow{PR} = k\,\overrightarrow{PQ}$ then $3\,k = 8$ and $4\,k = w - 3$. Solving the first for k you get $k = 8/3$, then plugging this into the second you get $4\,\frac{8}{3} = w - 3$. Solving this for w you get $w = \frac{32}{3} + 3 = \frac{41}{3}$.

    A faster way: We need $\dfrac{8}{3} = \dfrac{w - 3}{4}$. You get the same answer.

6a $= \langle 0, -1 \rangle$

6b $= \langle 4, 7 \rangle$ Note: $\mathbf{v} - \mathbf{u} = \langle -4, -7 \rangle = -(\mathbf{u} - \mathbf{v})$.

6c $\|\mathbf{u}\| = \sqrt{2^2 + 3^2} = \sqrt{13}$ and $\|\mathbf{v}\| = \sqrt{(-2)^2 + (-4)^2} = \sqrt{20} = 2\sqrt{5}$.

6d $= \sqrt{0^2 + (-1)^2} = 1$.

6e It is true that $1 \le \sqrt{13} + 2\sqrt{5}$.

6f $= \langle -4, -6 \rangle + \langle -6, -12 \rangle = \langle -10, -18 \rangle$

7a $\mathbf{u} = \frac{1}{\|\mathbf{v}\|}\mathbf{v} = \frac{1}{5}\mathbf{v} = \langle \frac{3}{5}, -\frac{4}{5} \rangle$ Note: $\|\mathbf{u}\| = 1$ as it should.

9 From the previous problem, the unit vector in the direction of $\overrightarrow{PQ} = \mathbf{u} = \left\langle \frac{3}{\sqrt{73}}, \frac{8}{\sqrt{73}} \right\rangle$. So the vector of length 2 in this same direction is $2\mathbf{u} = \left\langle \frac{6}{\sqrt{73}}, \frac{16}{\sqrt{73}} \right\rangle \approx \langle 0.70, 1.87 \rangle$.

11a $= 2\,\mathbf{i} + 3\,\mathbf{j}$

11b $= \sqrt{3}\,\mathbf{i} - 7\,\mathbf{j}$

12 Since the vector must have length 3, we know that $\|\mathbf{u}\| = 3$, and $-120^o = -\frac{2\pi}{3}$.

    Expressed as a linear combination of $\mathbf{i}$ and $\mathbf{j}$

$$
\begin{aligned}
\mathbf{u} &= \|\mathbf{u}\|\,\cos\theta\,\mathbf{i} + \|\mathbf{u}\|\,\sin\theta\,\mathbf{j} \\
&= 3\,\cos\left(-\frac{2\pi}{3}\right)\mathbf{i} + 3\,\sin\left(-\frac{2\pi}{3}\right)\mathbf{j} \\
&= 3\,\frac{-1}{2}\,\mathbf{i} + 3\,\frac{-\sqrt{3}}{2}\,\mathbf{j} \\
&= \frac{-3}{2}\mathbf{i} - \frac{3\sqrt{3}}{2}\,\mathbf{j}
\end{aligned}
$$

Expressed in component form $\mathbf{u} = \left\langle \frac{-3}{2}, \frac{-3\sqrt{3}}{2} \right\rangle \approx \langle -1.5, -2.6 \rangle$.

Chapter 2.2

1a $x^2 + (y+4)^2 + (z-7)^2 = 16$

1c If this this sphere is to be tangent to the xz-plane, and the center is 3 units from the xz-plane then the radius must be 3.

$$(x+2)^2 + (x-3)^2 + (x-4)^2 = 9$$

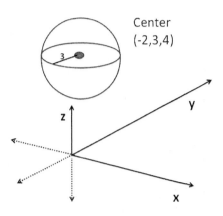

2a $\mathbf{v} = \langle -3, -10, 10 \rangle$

3a $\mathbf{u} \langle -2, -5, 2 \rangle$ and $\mathbf{v} = \langle -4, -1, 0 \rangle$, not equivalent, not parallel.

3c $\mathbf{u} = \langle 3, -2, 3 \rangle$ and $\mathbf{v} = \langle -6, 4, -6 \rangle$. Notice $\mathbf{v} = -2\mathbf{u}$ so the vectors are parallel but not equivalent.

4a $\overrightarrow{PQ} = \langle 3, 6, 9 \rangle$ and $\overrightarrow{PR} = \langle 2, 4, 6 \rangle$.
Notice: $\overrightarrow{PR} = \frac{2}{3} \overrightarrow{PQ}$ making the vectors parallel and the **points are collinear**.

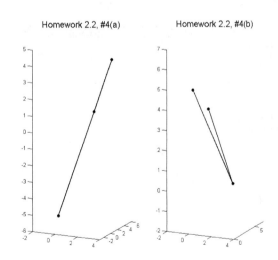

5a $\overrightarrow{PQ} = \langle 3, 4, -4 \rangle$ and $\overrightarrow{PR} = \langle x + 1, y - 3, 3 \rangle$. In order for these to be parallel we need

$$\frac{x+1}{3} = \frac{y-3}{4} = \frac{-3}{4}$$

Solving $\frac{x+1}{3} = \frac{-3}{4} \rightarrow x + 1 = \frac{-9}{4} \rightarrow x = \frac{-9}{4} - 1 = \frac{-13}{4}$

Solving $\frac{y-3}{4} = \frac{-3}{4} \rightarrow y - 3 = -3 \rightarrow y = 0$

So the answers are $\mathbf{x} = \frac{-13}{4}$ and $\mathbf{y} = \mathbf{0}$.

6a $= \langle 0, -1, -5 \rangle$

6b $= \langle 4, 7, -5 \rangle$

6c $\|\mathbf{u}\| = \sqrt{2^2 + 3^2 + (-5)^2} = \sqrt{38}$.

$\|\mathbf{v}\| = \sqrt{(-2)^2 + (-4)^2 + 0^2} = \sqrt{20} = 2\sqrt{5}$.

6d $= \| \langle 0, -1, -5 \rangle \| = \sqrt{0^2 + (-1)^2 + (-5)^2} = \sqrt{26}$.

6e It is true that $\sqrt{26} \leq 2\sqrt{5} + \sqrt{26}$ or approximately $5.1 \leq 9.6$.

6f $= \langle -4, -6, 10 \rangle + \langle -6, -12, 0 \rangle = \langle -10, -18, 10 \rangle$

6g $\dfrac{\mathbf{v}}{\|\mathbf{v}\|} = \dfrac{1}{\sqrt{20}} \langle -2, -4, 0 \rangle = \dfrac{1}{2\sqrt{5}} \langle -2, -4, 0 \rangle = \dfrac{1}{\sqrt{5}} \langle -1, -2, 0 \rangle$.

8 This is just a follow-up to the last problem, and similar problems in the previous section. We already have the unit vector in the desired direction as $\mathbf{u} = \frac{1}{2\sqrt{38}} \langle 4, 10, 6 \rangle$ from the last problem. Let, $\mathbf{v} = 2\mathbf{u}$, and add this to H in vector form $\langle 0, 0, 2 \rangle$. So, $\frac{2}{2\sqrt{38}} \langle 4, 10, 6 \rangle + \langle 0, 0, 2 \rangle \approx \langle 0.65, 1.62, 2.97 \rangle$ and the point $T = (0.65, 1.62, 2.97)$.

10 Here I use the plotting function file `vectarrow.m`.

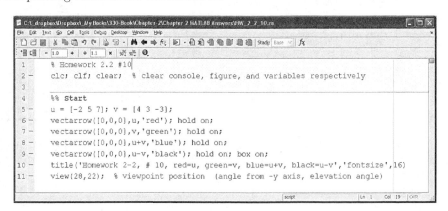

Chapter 2.3

1a $\mathbf{u} \cdot \mathbf{v} = -6 \qquad \mathbf{u} \cdot \mathbf{u} = 25 \qquad ||\mathbf{u}||^2 = 25 \qquad 2(\mathbf{u} \cdot \mathbf{v}) \, \mathbf{v} = \langle -24, 36 \rangle.$

2a $\mathbf{u} \cdot \mathbf{v} = ||\mathbf{u}|| \, ||\mathbf{v}|| \, \cos(\theta) = 24 \cos(\frac{7}{36}\pi) \approx 19.66.$

3a $\cos(\theta) = \frac{\mathbf{u} \cdot \mathbf{v}}{||\mathbf{u}|| \, ||\mathbf{v}||} = 0$ therefore $\theta = \frac{\pi}{2} = 90°$

4a $\cos(\theta) = \frac{\mathbf{u} \cdot \mathbf{v}}{||\mathbf{u}|| \, ||\mathbf{v}||} = \frac{4}{4\sqrt{2}} == \frac{1}{\sqrt{2}} = \frac{\sqrt{2}}{2}.$ Neither, the angle between them is acute because $\cos(\theta) > 0.$

4c $\cos(\theta) = \frac{\mathbf{u} \cdot \mathbf{v}}{||\mathbf{u}|| \, ||\mathbf{v}||} = \frac{-6}{\sqrt{14}\sqrt{3}} = \frac{-6}{\sqrt{42}}.$ Neither, the angle between them is obtuse because $\cos(\theta) < 0.$

5a We need $\mathbf{u} \cdot \mathbf{v} = 0$, and $\mathbf{u} \cdot \mathbf{v} = 3 - 4 + w$. Setting this equal to zero we get $-1 + w = 0$ or $w = 1$.

6a $\text{Proj}_{\mathbf{v}}\mathbf{u} = \left(\frac{\mathbf{u} \cdot \mathbf{v}}{||\mathbf{v}||^2} \right) \mathbf{v} = \left(\frac{4}{2} \right) \langle 1, 1 \rangle = \langle 2, 2 \rangle$

6c $\text{Proj}_{\mathbf{v}}\mathbf{u} = \left(\frac{\mathbf{u} \cdot \mathbf{v}}{||\mathbf{v}||^2} \right) \mathbf{v} = \left(\frac{-6}{3} \right) \langle -1, 1, -1 \rangle = \langle 2, -2, 2 \rangle$

8a Well-defined because the sum of two vectors is a vector and then this can be dotted with another vector of the same length.

8b Not defined because $\mathbf{u} \cdot \mathbf{v}$ is a scalar and you can't add a scalar to a vector.

8c Well-defined: $(\mathbf{u} \cdot \mathbf{v})$ is a scalar and you can multiply this by the vector $\mathbf{w}$.

8d Not defined because $(\mathbf{u} \cdot \mathbf{v})$ is a scalar and you can't have a dot product between a scalar and a vector.

8e Well defined: $||\mathbf{u}||$ is a scalar and you can multiply this by the vector $\mathbf{v} + \mathbf{w}$.

9 Below is the code and graph for this problem. The angle between the vectors (as solved using the `acos` function is $\theta = 49.6°.$

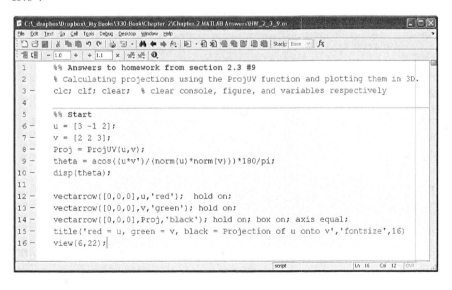

red = u, green = v, black = Projection of u onto v

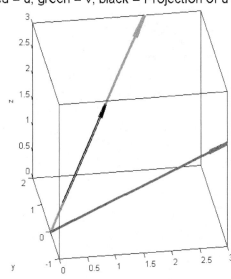

11a Using, $\text{Proj}_{\mathbf{v}}\mathbf{u} = \left(\dfrac{\mathbf{u}\cdot\mathbf{v}}{||\mathbf{v}||^2}\right)\mathbf{v}$.

$\text{Proj}_{(-\mathbf{v})}\mathbf{u} = \left(\dfrac{\mathbf{u}\cdot(-\mathbf{v})}{||-\mathbf{v}||^2}\right)(-\mathbf{v}) = -\left(\dfrac{\mathbf{u}\cdot\mathbf{v}}{||\mathbf{v}||^2}\right)(-\mathbf{v}) = \left(\dfrac{(\mathbf{u}\cdot\mathbf{v})}{||\mathbf{v}||^2}\right)(\mathbf{v}) = \text{Proj}_{\mathbf{v}}\mathbf{u}$

12 Your sequence might look somewhat different.

- Let $\mathbf{u} = \overrightarrow{PQ} \neq \mathbf{0}$ because P and Q are distinct.

- Let $\mathbf{v} = \overrightarrow{PR}$.

- if $||\mathbf{v}|| = 0$, then R is on the line (it is actually P).

- else if $\frac{\mathbf{u}\cdot\mathbf{v}}{||\mathbf{u}||\,||\mathbf{v}||} = \pm 1$, then R is on the line.

- else R is not on the line.

Chapter 2.4

1a $\mathbf{v}\times\mathbf{u} = -\mathbf{u}\times\mathbf{v} = -\mathbf{w}$.

1b $-\mathbf{u}\times\mathbf{v} = -(\mathbf{u}\times\mathbf{v}) = -\mathbf{w}$.

1c $||2\,\mathbf{u}\times 2\,\mathbf{v}|| = 4||\mathbf{u}\times\mathbf{v}|| = 4||\mathbf{w}||$.

1d Since $\mathbf{u}\times\mathbf{v}$ is orthogonal to both $\mathbf{u}$ and $\mathbf{v}$ then $\mathbf{w}$ is orthogonal to $\mathbf{u}$ which implies the dot product $\mathbf{w}\cdot\mathbf{u} = 0$.

2a Any multiple of $\mathbf{u} \times \mathbf{v}$ or $\mathbf{v} \times \mathbf{u}$ will be orthogonal to both $\mathbf{u}$ and $\mathbf{v}$.

$$
\begin{aligned}
\mathbf{u} \times \mathbf{v} &= \langle (u_2 v_3 - u_3 v_2), \, -(u_1 v_3 - u_3 v_1), \, (u_1 v_2 - u_2 v_1) \rangle \\
&= \langle ((-1)(0) - (1)(3)), \, -((1)(0) - (1)(-2)), \, ((1)(3) - (-1)(-2)) \rangle = \langle -3, -2, 1 \rangle
\end{aligned}
$$

. or, using the matrix determinant method:

$$
\mathbf{u} \times \mathbf{v} = \begin{vmatrix} \mathbf{i} & \mathbf{j} & \mathbf{k} \\ 1 & -1 & 1 \\ -2 & 3 & 0 \end{vmatrix} = -3\mathbf{i} - 2\mathbf{j} + 1\mathbf{k} = \langle -3, -2, 1 \rangle \,.
$$

Normalizing this to have length one, a unit vector is $\dfrac{1}{\sqrt{14}} \langle -3, -2, 1 \rangle$. So the two unit vectors orthogonal to both $\mathbf{u}$ and $\mathbf{v}$ are $\dfrac{\pm 1}{\sqrt{14}} \langle -3, -2, 1 \rangle \approx \langle -0.8018, \, -0.5345, \, 0.2673 \rangle$

Chapter 2.5

1b Let the direction vector be $\overrightarrow{PQ} = \langle -3, -3, 0 \rangle$. Now you can use either point to get

$$
x = 2 - 3t, \quad y = 3 - 3t, \quad z = 4 \quad \text{for} \quad t \in (-\infty, \infty)
$$

or

$$
x = -1 - 3s, \quad y = -3s, \quad z = 4 \quad \text{for} \quad s \in (-\infty, \infty)
$$

If you let $t = 1 + s$ you'll see the equations are the same.

1d If the line is perpendicular to $\mathbf{u}$ and $\mathbf{v}$, it must be parallel to $\mathbf{u} \times \mathbf{v}$ and

$$
\mathbf{u} \times \mathbf{v} = \begin{vmatrix} \mathbf{i} & \mathbf{j} & \mathbf{k} \\ 1 & -1 & 1 \\ -2 & 3 & 0 \end{vmatrix} = -3\mathbf{i} - 2\mathbf{j} + 1\mathbf{k} = \langle -3, -2, 1 \rangle \,.
$$

and the parametric equations for the line are

$$
x = 2 - 3t, \quad y = 3 - 2t, \quad z = 4 + t, \quad \text{for} \quad t \in (-\infty, \infty)
$$

2a You need to determine if there are values for t and s where (x, y, z) are the same for both lines. So we need to solve these three equations for the two unknown values of s and t.

$$
\begin{aligned}
4t + 2 &= 2s + 2 \\
3 &= 2s + 3 \\
-t + 1 &= s + 1
\end{aligned}
\quad \sim \quad
\begin{aligned}
4t - 2s &= 0 \\
-2s &= 0 \\
-t - s &= 0
\end{aligned}
\quad \sim \quad
\begin{bmatrix} 4 & -2 \\ 0 & -2 \\ -1 & -1 \end{bmatrix} \begin{bmatrix} t \\ s \end{bmatrix} = \begin{bmatrix} 0 \\ 0 \\ 0 \end{bmatrix}
$$

Expressing these equations in augmented matrix form, you can use Gaussian Elimination to solve for the variables (or have software do it for you but be careful of the *no solution* problems that can occur).

$$\left[\begin{array}{cc|c} 4 & -2 & 0 \\ 0 & -2 & 0 \\ -1 & -1 & 0 \end{array}\right] \sim \left[\begin{array}{cc|c} -1 & -1 & 0 \\ 0 & -2 & 0 \\ 4 & -2 & 0 \end{array}\right] \sim \left[\begin{array}{cc|c} 1 & 1 & 0 \\ 0 & -2 & 0 \\ 4 & -2 & 0 \end{array}\right] \sim \left[\begin{array}{cc|c} 1 & 1 & 0 \\ 0 & -2 & 0 \\ 0 & -6 & 0 \end{array}\right] \sim \left[\begin{array}{cc|c} 1 & 1 & 0 \\ 0 & 1 & 0 \\ 0 & -6 & 0 \end{array}\right] \sim \left[\begin{array}{cc|c} 1 & 1 & 0 \\ 0 & 1 & 0 \\ 0 & 0 & 0 \end{array}\right]$$

The second equation says that $s = 0$, plugging this into the first equation gives $t = 0$. Notice when $t = 0$ and $s = 0$ in the parametric equations of the lines, they both result in $x = 2$, $y = 3$, and $z = 1$. So the point of intersection is (2,3,1). To find the angle of intersection, you must find the angle between the two direction vectors $\mathbf{u} = \langle 4, 0, -1 \rangle$ and $\mathbf{v} = \langle 2, 2, 1 \rangle$. You get $\cos(\theta) = \frac{\mathbf{u} \cdot \mathbf{v}}{||\mathbf{u}|| \, ||\mathbf{v}||} = \frac{7}{\sqrt{17} \sqrt{9}} = \frac{7}{3\sqrt{17}}$. Therefore $\theta = \arccos\left(\frac{7}{3\sqrt{17}}\right) \approx 0.97$ radians or $55.5°$.

3a You need to determine if there are values for t and s where (x, y) are the same for both lines. So we need to solve these two equations for the two unknown values of s and t.

$$\begin{array}{rcl} 4t + 2 &=& s + 1 \\ 6t + 3 &=& 2s + 4 \end{array} \quad \sim \quad \begin{array}{rcl} 4t - s &=& -1 \\ 6t - 2s &=& 1 \end{array} \quad \sim \quad \left[\begin{array}{cc} 4 & -1 \\ 6 & -2 \end{array}\right]\left[\begin{array}{c} t \\ s \end{array}\right] = \left[\begin{array}{c} -1 \\ 1 \end{array}\right]$$

The determinant is -8 +6 = -2 so there is a unique solution for s and t. You can use Gaussian Elimination or the inverse of the matrix to get the solutions $t = -1.5$ and $s = -5$.

$$\left[\begin{array}{c} t \\ s \end{array}\right] = \left[\begin{array}{cc} 4 & -1 \\ 6 & -2 \end{array}\right]^{-1}\left[\begin{array}{c} -1 \\ 1 \end{array}\right] = \frac{1}{-2}\left[\begin{array}{cc} -2 & 1 \\ -6 & 4 \end{array}\right]\left[\begin{array}{c} -1 \\ 1 \end{array}\right] = \frac{-1}{2}\left[\begin{array}{c} 3 \\ 10 \end{array}\right] = \left[\begin{array}{c} -1.5 \\ -5 \end{array}\right]$$

So the point of intersection occurs when $t = -1.5$ or $s = -5$

$x = 4(-1.5) + 2$, $y = 6(-1.5) + 3 \quad \rightarrow \quad (x, y) = (-4, -6)$

$x = -5 + 1$, $y = 2(-5) + 4 \quad \rightarrow \quad (x, y) = (-4, -6)$

To find the angle of intersection, you must find the angle between the two direction vectors $\mathbf{u} = \langle 4, 6 \rangle$ and $\mathbf{v} = \langle 1, 2 \rangle$. You get $\cos(\theta) = \frac{\mathbf{u} \cdot \mathbf{v}}{||\mathbf{u}|| \, ||\mathbf{v}||} = \frac{16}{\sqrt{52} \sqrt{5}} = \frac{16}{2\sqrt{65}}$. Therefore $\theta = \arccos\left(\frac{8}{\sqrt{65}}\right) \approx 0.1244$ radians or $7.125°$.

3c You need to determine if there are values for t and s where (x, y) are the same for both lines. So we need to solve these two equations for the two unknown values of s and t.

$$\begin{array}{rcl} t - 2 &=& -3s + 1 \\ -t + 5 &=& 3s - 4 \end{array} \quad \sim \quad \begin{array}{rcl} t + 3s &=& 3 \\ -t - 3s &=& -9 \end{array} \quad \sim \quad \left[\begin{array}{cc} 1 & 3 \\ -1 & -3 \end{array}\right]\left[\begin{array}{c} t \\ s \end{array}\right] = \left[\begin{array}{c} 3 \\ -9 \end{array}\right]$$

The determinant is -3 + 3 = 0 and there is not a unique solution. You can perform Gaussian Elimination from here but you should notice that the two lines are parallel but do not go through the same point. Therefore there is no solution and no point of intersection.

4a $x(t) = 1 + t(-2 - 1) = 1 - 3t$

$y(t) = 2 + t(5 - 2) = 2 + 3t$

for $t \in [0, 1]$

5a You need to determine if there are values for t and s where (x, y) are the same for both lines. So we need to solve these two equations for the two unknown values of s and t.

$$\overrightarrow{PQ} = \overrightarrow{RS}$$

$$x: \quad 1 + t(10 - 1) = 3 + s(5 - 3) \quad \text{can be set up as a system of equations}$$
$$y: \quad 8 + t(2 - 8) = 1 + s(11 - 1)$$

$$\begin{matrix} 1 + 9t = 3 + 2s \\ 8 - 6t = 1 - 10s \end{matrix} \sim \begin{matrix} 9t - 2s = 2 \\ -6t + 10s = -7 \end{matrix} \sim \begin{bmatrix} 9 & -2 \\ -6 & 10 \end{bmatrix} \begin{bmatrix} t \\ s \end{bmatrix} = \begin{bmatrix} 2 \\ -7 \end{bmatrix}$$

Solving this for t and s you get $t = 1/3$ and $s = 1/2$. Since both of these are between 0 and 1, there is a hit. The point of collision occurs at
$P + t(\overrightarrow{PQ}) = (1, 8) + 1/3(9, -6) = (4, 6)$ or $R + s(\overrightarrow{RS}) = (3, 1) + 1/2(2, 10) = (4, 6)$.
So there is a hit at **(4,6)**.

6a We'll use the formula for the distance between a point Q and a line with direction vector $\mathbf{v}$;

$$D = \frac{||\overrightarrow{PQ} \times \mathbf{v}||}{||\mathbf{v}||},$$

where P is any point on the line. The direction vector for our line is $\mathbf{v} = \langle 4, 0, -1 \rangle$ and a good choice for P is found by letting $t = 0$ in the parametric equations for the line. Doing this give $P = (-2, 3, 1)$, and therefore $\overrightarrow{PQ} = \langle 3, 2, -3 \rangle$. So now in order to use the formula above we must first fine $\overrightarrow{PQ} \times \mathbf{v}$

$$\overrightarrow{PQ} \times \mathbf{v} = \begin{vmatrix} \mathbf{i} & \mathbf{j} & \mathbf{k} \\ 3 & 2 & -3 \\ 4 & 0 & -1 \end{vmatrix} = -2\mathbf{i} - 9\mathbf{j} - 8\mathbf{k} = \langle -2, -9, -8 \rangle. \text{ Now the distance from } Q \text{ to the line is}$$

$$D = \frac{||\overrightarrow{PQ} \times \mathbf{v}||}{||\mathbf{v}||} = \frac{\sqrt{149}}{\sqrt{17}} \approx 2.96$$

7a The x-radius is 2, and the y-radius is 1
$x(t) = 2 + 2\cos(t), \quad y(t) = 3 + \sin(t), \qquad t \in [-\pi, 0] \text{ or } t \in [\pi, 2\pi]$
There are other answers that trace out the exact same curve.

8a Blue Helix:
$$x(t) = \cos(t)$$
$$y(t) = \sin(t)$$
$$z(t) = 8t,$$
for $t \in [0, 6\pi]$

Red Helix:
$$x(t) = \cos(t + \pi)$$
$$y(t) = \sin(t + \pi)$$
$$z(t) = 8t,$$
for $t \in [0, 6\pi]$

Others are possible

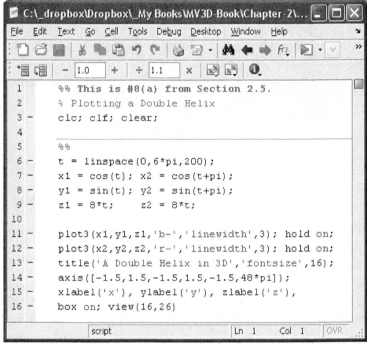

10a Trajectory: $\mathbf{r}(t) = \langle x(t),\ y(t) \rangle = \left\langle [v_o \cos(\theta)]t,\quad h + [v_o \sin(\theta)]t - \dfrac{1}{2}gt^2 \right\rangle.$

with $\theta = 0$, $h = 400$, $g = 32$, and $v_o = 60$ we get $\mathbf{r}(t) = \left\langle 60t,\quad 400 - 16t^2 \right\rangle = \langle x(t),\ y(t) \rangle.$

10b You get the height at $t = 2$ from $y(2) = 400 - 16 \cdot 2^2 =$ **336 feet.**

10c Solving $y(t) = 0$ you get the ball hits the ground at $t = 5$, and plugging $t = 5$ into $x(t)$ gives the total distance traveled as $x(5) = $ **300**.

You can also do this using the formulas

hits the ground at $t = \dfrac{v_o \sin(\theta) + \sqrt{v_o^2 \sin^2(\theta) + 2gh}}{g} = \dfrac{0 + \sqrt{0 + 2(32)(400)}}{32} = \dfrac{\sqrt{25600}}{32} = 5$ seconds.

total distance $= \dfrac{v_o^2 \cos(\theta)}{g}\left(\sin(\theta) + \sqrt{\sin^2(\theta) + \dfrac{2gh}{v_o^2}} \right) = 112.5\sqrt{\dfrac{25600}{3600}} = 300$ ft.

Chapter 2.6

1a We need a point on the plane (we have three) and a normal vector. To get the normal vector $\mathbf{n}$ we set $\mathbf{n} = \overrightarrow{PQ} \times \overrightarrow{PR}$ which will be orthogonal to both vectors that form the plane. In our case, $\overrightarrow{PQ} = \langle 1, -1, 1 \rangle$, $\overrightarrow{PR} = \langle -2, 2, 2 \rangle$, and

$$\mathbf{n} = \overrightarrow{PQ} \times \overrightarrow{PR} = \begin{vmatrix} \mathbf{i} & \mathbf{j} & \mathbf{k} \\ 1 & -1 & 1 \\ -2 & 2 & 2 \end{vmatrix} = -4\mathbf{i} - 4\mathbf{j} + 0\mathbf{k} = \langle -4, -4, 0 \rangle.$$

Using the point $P(0, 1, 2)$ as the point,

$$-4(x - 0) - 4(y - 1) + 0(z - 2) = 0 \quad \text{standard equation}$$
$$-4x - 4y + 4 = 0 \quad \text{intermediate step. now} \div \text{-4}$$
$$x + y - 1 = 0 \quad \text{general equation: simplest form}$$

Note: Any multiple of this last equation is also an equation for the plane.

1c We have a point, now we need a normal vector. Since the z-axis is normal to the xy-plane, so it must be normal to our desired plane. The easiest vector parallel to the z-axis is $\mathbf{n} = \langle 0, 0, 1 \rangle$.

$$0(x - 1) + 0(y - 2) + 1(z - 3) = 0 \quad \text{standard equation}$$
$$z - 3 = 0 \quad \text{intermediate step and general equation}$$

Note: This is just the xy-plane shifted up (along the z-axis) 3 units. You might have been able to come up with the answer without using the standard procedure described above.

2a

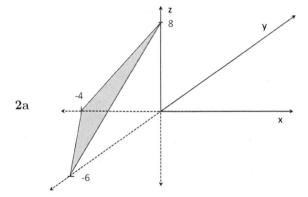

$$6x + 4y - 3z + 24 = 0$$

x-intercept: $6x + 24 = 0 \rightarrow x = -4$

y-intercept: $4y + 24 = 0 \rightarrow y = -6$

z-intercept: $-3z + 24 = 0 \rightarrow z = 8$

3a The normal to the first plane is $\mathbf{n}_1 = \langle 1, 2, -2 \rangle$, and the normal to the second plane is $\mathbf{n}_2 = \langle 3, 0, -3 \rangle$, the angle of intersection is given by

$$\theta = \arccos \left(\frac{|\mathbf{n}_1 \cdot \mathbf{n}_2|}{\|\mathbf{n}_1\| \, \|\mathbf{n}_2\|} \right) = \arccos \left(\frac{9}{\sqrt{9} \, \sqrt{18}} \right) = \arccos \left(\frac{9}{3 \, (3) \sqrt{2}} \right) =$$

$$\theta = \arccos \left(\frac{1}{\sqrt{2}} \right) = \arccos \left(\frac{\sqrt{2}}{2} \right) = \frac{\pi}{4} = 45^o$$

3b Here, we use Method 2.

Now we know that the direction vector is given by $\mathbf{v} = \mathbf{n}_1 \times \mathbf{n}_2$;

$$\mathbf{v} = \mathbf{n}_1 \times \mathbf{n}_2 = \begin{vmatrix} \mathbf{i} & \mathbf{j} & \mathbf{k} \\ 1 & 2 & -2 \\ 3 & 0 & -3 \end{vmatrix} = -6\mathbf{i} - 3\mathbf{j} - 6\mathbf{k} = \langle -6, -3, -6 \rangle . \text{ Since any vector parallel to this will work,}$$

you can divide this by -3 to get
$\mathbf{v} = \langle 2, 1, 2 \rangle$.

Now we must find a point on the intersection of both planes. This means we must find values of x, y and z that satisfy both plane equations or

$$\begin{array}{rcl} x + 2y - 2z & = & 4 \\ 3x + 0y - 3z & = & 6 \end{array} \quad \sim \quad \begin{bmatrix} 1 & 2 & -2 \\ 3 & 0 & -3 \end{bmatrix} \begin{bmatrix} x \\ y \\ z \end{bmatrix} = \begin{bmatrix} 4 \\ 6 \end{bmatrix}$$

Expressing these equations in augmented matrix form, you can use Gaussian Elimination to solve for the variables (or have software do it for you). You will get infinitely many solutions provided the planes actually intersect.

$$\left[\begin{array}{ccc|c} 1 & 2 & -2 & 4 \\ 3 & 0 & -3 & 6 \end{array}\right] \quad \sim \quad \left[\begin{array}{ccc|c} 1 & 2 & -2 & 4 \\ 0 & -6 & 3 & -6 \end{array}\right] \quad \sim \quad \left[\begin{array}{ccc|c} 1 & 2 & -2 & 4 \\ 0 & 2 & -1 & 2 \end{array}\right]$$

You can see we will get infinitely many solutions. Looking at the last equation you see that $2y - z = 2$. If we let $z = 0$, then $y = 1$. Looking at the first equation $x + 2y - 2z = 4$. If $z = 0$ and $y = 1$, the $x + 2 = 4$ or $x = 2$. So a point on both planes is $P(2, 1, 0)$.

Now we have a direction vector $\mathbf{v} = \langle 2, 1, 2 \rangle$ and a point $(2, 1, 0)$. So the parametric equations for the line of intersection are

$$x = 2 + 2t, \quad y = 1 + t, \quad z = 2t, \quad \text{for} \quad t \in (-\infty, \infty)$$

There are infinitely many ways to express this line but it must have a direction vector parallel to $\langle 2, 1, 2 \rangle$ and go through the point $(2,1,0)$.

5a The distance is given by $D = \|\text{proj}_{\mathbf{n}} \overrightarrow{PQ}\| = \dfrac{|\overrightarrow{PQ} \cdot \mathbf{n}|}{\|\mathbf{n}\|}$
where $\mathbf{n}$ is the normal to the plane, Q is the point of interest, and P is any point on the plane.

Here, $\mathbf{n} = \langle 6, -3, 2 \rangle$, $Q = (1, -1, 1)$, and we'll let $P = (0, 0, 4)$. Therefore $\overrightarrow{PQ} = \langle -1, 1, 3 \rangle$.
So, $D = \dfrac{|\langle -1, 1, 3 \rangle \cdot \langle 6, -3, 2 \rangle|}{\|\langle 6, -3, 2 \rangle\|} = \dfrac{|-3|}{\sqrt{49}} = \dfrac{3}{7} \approx 0.43$

6a The sphere has center at $Q(1, -2, 0)$ and radius $= 2$. So we check the distance from the center point to the plane. This distance is

$$D = \|\text{proj}_{\mathbf{n}} \overrightarrow{PQ}\| = \dfrac{|\overrightarrow{PQ} \cdot \mathbf{n}|}{\|\mathbf{n}\|}$$

where $\mathbf{n}$ is the normal to the plane, and P is any point on the plane. Here, $\mathbf{n} = \langle 2, -3, 1 \rangle$ and we'll let $P = (0, 0, 2)$. Therefore $\overrightarrow{PQ} = \langle -1, 2, 2 \rangle$.
So,

$$D = \dfrac{|\overrightarrow{PQ} \cdot \mathbf{n}|}{\|\mathbf{n}\|} = \dfrac{|-6|}{\sqrt{14}} = \dfrac{6}{\sqrt{14}} \approx 1.60$$

Since the radius of the sphere is 2 and the distance from the point to the plane ≈ 1.60 we conclude that the sphere and the plane do intersect.

7 We will use the formula for the distance between a point Q and the plane with normal vector $\mathbf{n}$ by

$$D = ||\text{proj}_{\mathbf{n}} \overrightarrow{PQ}|| = \frac{|\overrightarrow{PQ} \cdot \mathbf{n}|}{||\mathbf{n}||}$$

where P is a point in the plane. In our case, $\mathbf{n} = \langle 2, 1, 1 \rangle$, $Q = (2, 4, 8)$, and we'll let $P = (0, 0, 5)$. Therefore, $\overrightarrow{PQ} = \langle -2, -4, -3 \rangle$. And

$$D = \frac{|\overrightarrow{PQ} \cdot \mathbf{n}|}{||\mathbf{n}||} = \frac{|-11|}{\sqrt{6}} = \frac{11}{\sqrt{16}} \approx 4.49$$

Here is the code I used to get the distance, draw the point, the plane, and the directed line segment:

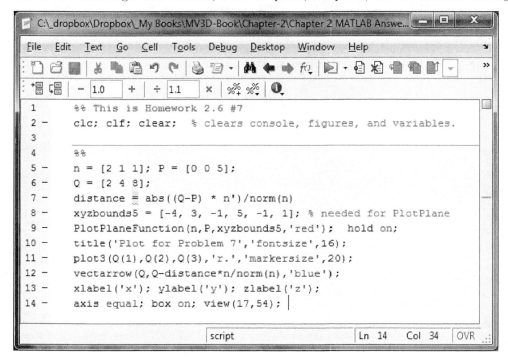

8 We'll use the formula for the distance between a point and a plane:

$$D = ||\text{proj}_{\mathbf{n}} \overrightarrow{PQ}|| = \frac{|\overrightarrow{PQ} \cdot \mathbf{n}|}{||\mathbf{n}||}.$$

There are many ways to set this up. I'll choose some point (Q) from the second plane and find the distance from that point to the first plane. The easiest selection for Q is $Q = (6, 0, 0)$. The normal to the first plane is $\mathbf{n} = \langle 1, -3, 4 \rangle$ and a nice point P from the first plane is $P = (10, 0, 0)$. Therefore, $\overrightarrow{PQ} = \langle 4, 0, 0 \rangle$. So,

$$D = \frac{|\overrightarrow{PQ} \cdot \mathbf{n}|}{||\mathbf{n}||} = \frac{|4|}{\sqrt{26}} \approx 0.78.$$

Here is the code I used to find the distance, sketch the planes and the directed line segment between them:

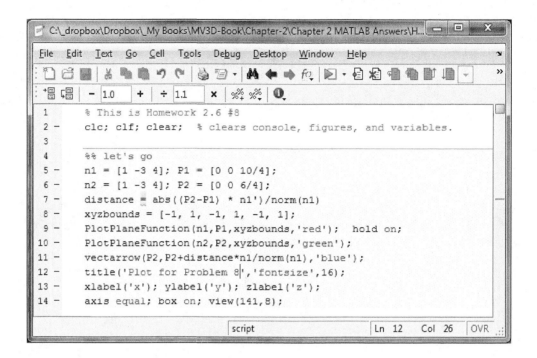

```
1    % This is Homework 2.6 #8
2 -  clc; clf; clear;  % clears console, figures, and variables.
3
4    %% let's go
5 -  n1 = [1 -3 4]; P1 = [0 0 10/4];
6 -  n2 = [1 -3 4]; P2 = [0 0 6/4];
7 -  distance = abs((P2-P1) * n1')/norm(n1)
8 -  xyzbounds = [-1, 1, -1, 1, -1, 1];
9 -  PlotPlaneFunction(n1,P1,xyzbounds,'red');  hold on;
10 - PlotPlaneFunction(n2,P2,xyzbounds,'green');
11 - vectarrow(P2,P2+distance*n1/norm(n1),'blue');
12 - title('Plot for Problem 8','fontsize',16);
13 - xlabel('x'); ylabel('y'); zlabel('z');
14 - axis equal; box on; view(141,8);
```

Chapter 2.7

1 The point of intersection is given by

$$P = P_L + t\,\mathbf{v}$$

where

$$t = \frac{\mathbf{n} \cdot \langle P_P - P_L \rangle}{\mathbf{n} \cdot \mathbf{v}},$$

$\mathbf{n}$ is a normal to the plane, P_p is a point on the plane, $\mathbf{v}$ is a direction vector for the line, and P_L is a point on the line. So,

$$
\begin{aligned}
\mathbf{n} &= \langle 2, 1, -1 \rangle \\
P_p &= (0, 0, 1) \\
\mathbf{v} &= \overrightarrow{MQ} = \langle 20, 20, 20 \rangle \\
P_L &= M = (-10, -10, -10)
\end{aligned}
$$

$$t = \frac{\mathbf{n} \cdot \langle P_P - P_L \rangle}{\mathbf{n} \cdot \mathbf{v}} = \frac{\langle 2, 1, -1 \rangle \cdot \langle 10, 10, 11 \rangle}{\langle 2, 1, -1 \rangle \cdot \langle 20, 20, 20 \rangle} = \frac{19}{40} = 0.475$$

and

$$P = P_L + t\,\mathbf{v} = (-10, -10, -10) + \frac{19}{40} \langle 20, 20, 20 \rangle = (-0.5, -0.5, -0.5)$$

2 To get things started we first need $\overrightarrow{MP} = \langle 9.5, 9.5, 9.5 \rangle$, then

$$
\begin{aligned}
\mathbf{v} &= \overrightarrow{MP} - \operatorname{Proj}_{\mathbf{n}}\overrightarrow{MP} \approx \langle 3.17, 6.33, 12.67 \rangle \\
R &= M + 2\mathbf{v} \approx (-3.67, 2.67, 15.33) \\
\overrightarrow{PB} &= \frac{\|\overrightarrow{PQ}\|}{\|\overrightarrow{PR}\|}\overrightarrow{PR} = \langle -3.5, 3.5, 17.5 \rangle \\
B &= P + \overrightarrow{PB} = (-.5, -.5, -.5) + (-3.5, 3.5, 17.5) = (-4,\ 3,\ 17)
\end{aligned}
$$

3 Below is the code for the calculations for the first two problems as well as the resulting graph.

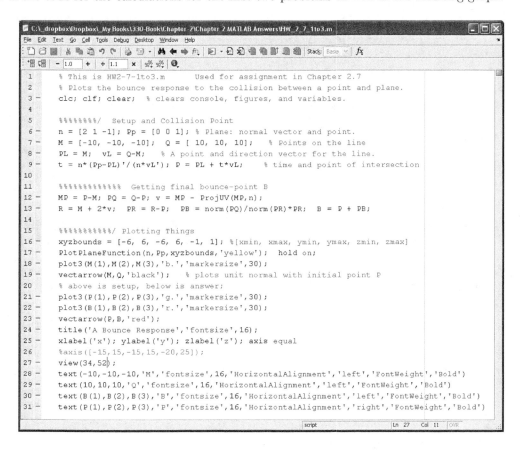

Chapter 3.1

1 (a) You want a circle in the xy-plane that increases in radius as t increases and z increases as t increases. There are about 10 rotations so $t \in [0, 20\pi]$.

$$
x(t) = t\,\cos(t), \quad y(t) = t\,\sin(t), \quad z = t, \quad t \in [0, 20\pi]
$$

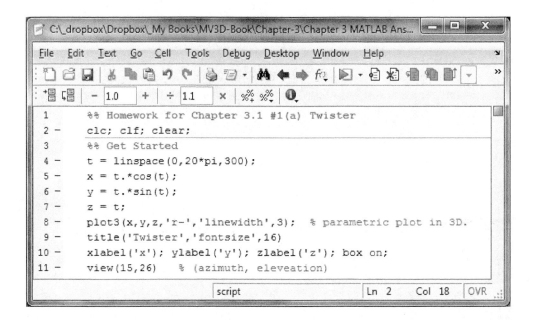

(b) You want x and y to create a circle in the xy-plane and let z oscillate more quickly.

$$x(t) = 2\cos(t), \quad y(t) = 2\sin(t) \quad z = \sin(kt), \quad t \in [0, 2\pi]$$

where k is an integer representing the number of complete sine waves.

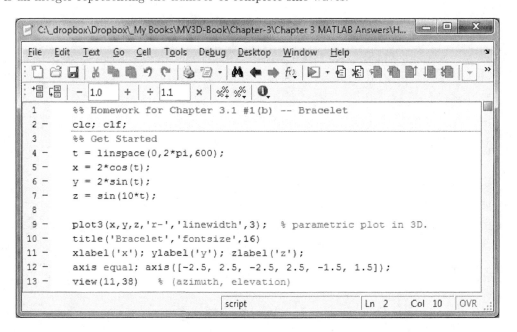

3a Here, $h = 60$, $\phi = 30^o = \pi/6$, $\theta = 45^o = \pi/4$, $v_o = 100$ ft/sec, and $g = 32$ feet/sec^2.

Note: $\sin(\pi/6) = \frac{1}{2}$, $\cos(\pi/6) = \frac{\sqrt{3}}{2}$, $\cos(\pi/4) = \sin(\pi/4) = \frac{\sqrt{2}}{2}$.

Plugging these values into equation (3.9) for when the ball hits the ground we get

$$t^* = \frac{v_o \sin(\phi) + \sqrt{v_o^2 \sin^2(\phi) + 2gh}}{g} \approx 4.05 \text{ seconds}$$

3b Now that we have the total time the ball is in the air, we use equation (3.8) for the actual trajectory:

$$
\begin{aligned}
\mathbf{r}(t) &= \langle\, x(t),\, y(t),\, z(t)\, \rangle \\
&= \left\langle v_o \cos(\theta)\cos(\phi)\, t,\quad v_o \sin(\theta)\cos(\phi)\, t,\quad h + v_o \sin(\phi)\, t - \frac{1}{2}g\, t^2 \right\rangle \\
&\approx \left\langle 61.2\, t,\, 61.2\, t,\, 60 + 50\, t - 16\, t^2 \right\rangle. \\
&\text{for}\quad t \in [0, t^*]
\end{aligned}
$$

3c To find where the ball lands in the xy-plane we just evaluate $x(t)$ and $y(t)$ at $t = t^*$.

It lands at $(x(t^*),\, y(t^*),\, 0)$ where

$$x(t^*) \approx 248.1, \quad \text{and} \quad y(t*) \approx 248.1$$

3d

$$\text{total distance in } xy\text{-plane} = \sqrt{[x(t^*)]^2 + [y(t^*)]^2} \approx 350.8 \text{ feet.}$$

3e The maximum height is achieved at $t = \tilde{t}$:

$$\tilde{t} = \frac{v_o \sin(\phi)}{g} \approx 1.56 \text{ seconds}$$

and the maximum height is $z(\tilde{t})$

$$z(\tilde{t}) \approx 99.1 \text{ feet.}$$

4 Below is the code I used to answer the questions above and plot the requested graph.

```
 ☰ C:\_dropbox\Dropbox\_My Books\330-Book\Chapter-3\Chapter 3 MATLAB Answers\HW_3_1_4.m      ☐☐☒
 File  Edit  Text  Go  Cell  Tools  Debug  Desktop  Window  Help
 ☐ ☐ ☐ | ☐ ☐ ☐ ☐ ☐ | ☐ ☐ · | ☐ ☐ ☐ | ☐ · | ☐ ☐ ☐ ☐ ☐ ☐ ☐ ☐ | Stack: Base ☐ | ☐☐
 ☐☐ ☐☐ | ─ |1.0 | + | ÷ |1.1 | × | ☐ ☐ | ☐.

  1        % Homework for Chapter 3.1 #4
  2 -      clc; clf; clear;
  3
  4        %%%% Initial Values
  5 -      h = 60; phidegrees=30; thetadegrees=45; vo=100; g = 32;
  6 -      theta = thetadegrees*pi/180; phi = phidegrees*pi/180
  7        |
  8        %%%%%%%/   critical values
  9 -      tstar = (vo*sin(phi) + sqrt(vo^2 * (sin(phi))^2 + 2*g*h))/g;
 10 -      ttilde = vo*sin(phi)/g;  % time of max heght
 11 -      xmax = vo * cos(theta) * cos(phi) * tstar;
 12 -      ymax = vo * sin(theta) * cos(phi) * tstar;
 13 -      fprintf('It lands at (%1.1f, %1.1f, 0) \n', xmax, ymax);
 14 -      distance = sqrt(xmax^2 + ymax^2);
 15 -      fprintf('The total distance is %1.1f feet \n', distance);
 16 -      zmax = h + vo*sin(phi)*ttilde - 1/2*g*ttilde^2;
 17 -      fprintf('The max height is %1.1f feet \n', zmax);
 18
 19        %%%%%%%%%%%%/  Create Trajectory points
 20 -      t = linspace(0,tstar,100);
 21 -      x = vo * cos(theta) * cos(phi) * t;
 22 -      y = vo * sin(theta) * cos(phi) * t;
 23 -      z = h + vo*sin(phi)*t - 1/2*g*t.^2;
 24
 25        %%% Plotting directives
 26 -      xyzbounds = [-1.5, 1.1*xmax, -1.5, 1.1*ymax, -5, 1.1*zmax];
 27
 28        %%%%%%%%%%%%%%%%  initial plot
 29 -      plot3(x,y,z,'r-','linewidth',3);  % parametric plot in 3D.
 30 -      axis(xyzbounds); view(13,32); grid on;
 31 -      xlabel('x'); ylabel('y'); zlabel('z');
 32 -      title('Projectile in 3D','fontsize',16)

                                            script          Ln 7    Col 1    OVR
```

Chapter 3.2

1a In order to find the velocity function we differentiate the position vector with respect to t.

$$\mathbf{r}(t) = \langle\, 2\cos(t), \quad 8\sin(t)\,\rangle \quad \rightarrow \quad \mathbf{v}(t) = \mathbf{r}'(t) = \langle\, -2\sin(t), \quad 8\cos(t)\,\rangle.$$

1b In this case it is pretty obvious that $t = 0$. However, if you want to direct a machine to confirm this, we know that

$$
\begin{aligned}
2\cos(t) &= 2 &\rightarrow& \quad \cos(t) = 1 \\
8\sin(t) &= 0 &\rightarrow& \quad \sin(t) = 0 \\
t &= \texttt{atan2}(0,1) = 0
\end{aligned}
$$

So, $t = 0$ and the velocity vector is

$$
v(0) = \langle\, -2\sin(0), \quad 8\cos(0)\,\rangle = \langle\, \mathbf{0,8}\,\rangle
$$

1c In this case it is pretty obvious that t is 270° or -180° which is $3\pi/2$ or $-\pi/2$ respectively. However, if we were to solve for t using a machine, we know that

$$
\begin{aligned}
2\cos(t) &= 0 &\rightarrow& \quad \cos(t) = 0 \\
8\sin(t) &= -8 &\rightarrow& \quad \sin(t) = -1 \\
t &= \texttt{atan2}(-1,0) = -1.570796 = -\pi/2
\end{aligned}
$$

So, $t = -\pi/2$ and the velocity vector is

$$
v(-\pi/2) = \langle\, -2\sin(-\pi/2), \quad 8\cos(-\pi/2)\,\rangle = \langle\, \mathbf{2,0}\,\rangle
$$

1d It is a little trickier determining t in this situation. The reason this is tricky is because the value of t is not the same as the angle made by the vector through this point. If we were to solve for t using a machine, we know that

$$
\begin{aligned}
2\cos(t) &= -\sqrt{2} &\rightarrow& \quad \cos(t) = -\frac{\sqrt{2}}{2} \\
8\sin(t) &= 4\sqrt{2} &\rightarrow& \quad \sin(t) = \frac{\sqrt{2}}{2} \\
t &= \texttt{atan2}\left(\frac{\sqrt{2}}{2}, -\frac{\sqrt{2}}{2}\right) = 2.3562 = \frac{3\pi}{4}
\end{aligned}
$$

So, $t = 3\pi/4$ and the velocity vector is

$$
\begin{aligned}
v(3\pi/4) &= \langle\, -2\sin(3\pi/4), \quad 8\cos(3\pi/4)\,\rangle \\
&= \left\langle\, -2\,\frac{\sqrt{2}}{2}, \ 8\,\frac{-\sqrt{2}}{2}\,\right\rangle \\
&= \langle\, -\sqrt{2}, -4\sqrt{2}\,\rangle \approx \langle\, \mathbf{-1.41}, \mathbf{-5.66}\,\rangle.
\end{aligned}
$$

1e Here is the code and the graph.

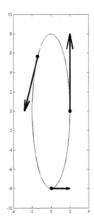

3a

$$\mathbf{v}(t) = \langle -\sin(t), \cos(t), 1 \rangle$$

$$\mathbf{a}(t) = \langle -\cos(t), -\sin(t), 0 \rangle$$

3b There is no acceleration in the z-direction, the velocity is constant in that direction.

3c Here is the code and graph

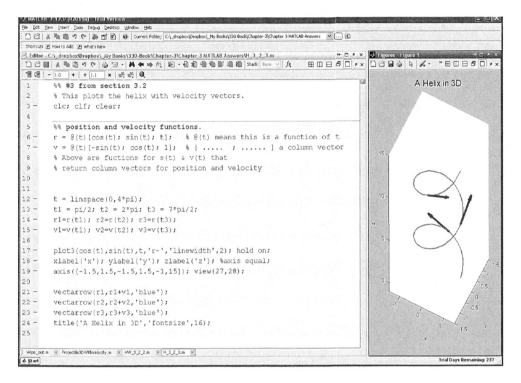

5a Differentiating term-by-term, (using the product rule on $x(t)$),

$$\mathbf{v}(t) = \langle -t\sin(t) + \cos(t),\ 4\cos(4t),\ 6t \rangle$$

5b

$$\mathbf{v}(0) = \langle\, 1,\ 4, 0\,\rangle\,.$$
$$\text{speed} = \sqrt{1 + 16 + 0} = \sqrt{17}.$$

5c This is a little refresher in differentiation with respect to $x'(t)$ so let's start with that one

$$
\begin{aligned}
x'(t) &= -t\sin(t) + \cos(t) \\
x''(t) &= -t(\cos(t)) + \sin(t)(-1) - \sin(t) \\
&= -t\cos(t) - 2\sin(t),
\end{aligned}
$$

$$y'(t) = 4\cos(4t) \quad \rightarrow \quad y''(t) = -16\sin(4t),$$

and

$$z'(t) = 6t \quad \rightarrow \quad z''(t) = 6$$

Finally,

$$\mathbf{a}(t) = \mathbf{v}'(t) = \langle\, -t\cos(t) - 2\sin(t),\ -16\sin(4t),\ 6\,\rangle$$

6 $\mathbf{v}(t) = \left\langle 2,\ 2t,\ \frac{3}{2}t^2 \right\rangle$ but you need t. If the point is (4,5,4) this means that $2t = 4$ or $t = 2$. So, $\mathbf{v}(2) = \langle \mathbf{2},\ \mathbf{4},\ \mathbf{6} \rangle$

8 Here, $h = 60$, $\phi = 30^o = \pi/6$, $\theta = 45^o = \pi/4$, $v_o = 100$ ft/sec, and $g = 32$ feet/sec^2.

Note: $\sin(\pi/6) = \frac{1}{2}$, $\cos(\pi/4) = \frac{\sqrt{2}}{2}$, $\sin(\pi/2) = \frac{\sqrt{2}}{2}$

First we must determine when the ball hits the ground. You did this in the last section (using equation (3.9)) and found:

$$t^* = \frac{v_o \sin(\phi) + \sqrt{v_o^2 \sin^2(\phi) + 2gh}}{g} \approx 4.05 \text{ seconds}$$

8a The velocity vector is found by differentiating the position vector:

$$
\begin{aligned}
\mathbf{r}(t) &= \left\langle v_o \cos(\theta)\cos(\phi)\, t, \quad v_o \sin(\theta)\cos(\phi)\, t, \quad h + v_o \sin(\phi)\, t - \frac{1}{2}g\, t^2 \right\rangle \\
\mathbf{v}(t) &= \left\langle v_o \cos(\theta)\cos(\phi), \quad v_o \sin(\theta)\cos(\phi), \quad v_o \sin(\phi) - g\, t \right\rangle \\
&\approx \langle 61.2, \quad 61.2, \quad 50 - 32\, t \rangle.
\end{aligned}
$$

So the velocity vector when it hits the ground is just $\mathbf{v}(t^*)$

$$
\begin{aligned}
\mathbf{v}(t^*) &= \langle 61.2, \quad 61.2, \quad 50 - 32\, t^* \rangle \\
&\approx \langle 61.2, 61.2, -79.6 \rangle
\end{aligned}
$$

8b The speed when it hits the ground is given by $\|\mathbf{v}(t^*)\|$.

$$\|\mathbf{v}(t^*)\| = \| \langle 61.2, 61.2, -79.6 \rangle \| \approx 117.64 \text{ feet/sec}$$

8c A perfect bounce is given by the formula in equation (3.22)

$$\mathbf{v}_1 = \mathbf{v}_0 - 2\, \text{Proj}_\mathbf{n}\mathbf{v}_0 = \langle 61.2, 61.2, 79.6 \rangle$$

where $\mathbf{v}_0$ is the incoming velocity (found in part (a) = $\mathbf{v}(t^*)$), n is the normal to the ground = $\langle 0, 0, 1 \rangle$, and $\mathbf{v}_1$ is the bounce vector. Notice, for now, all the perfect bounce does is change the sign of the z component of the incoming velocity vector.

Chapter 3.3

1a Using equation (2.17) (page 92) from Chapter 2.5.2 for the distance traveled,

total distance $= \dfrac{v_o^2 \cos(\theta)}{g} \left(\sin(\theta) + \sqrt{\sin^2(\theta) + \dfrac{2gh}{v_o^2}} \right)$

with $\theta = \pi/6$, $v_o = 80$, $g = 32$, and $h = 10$, you should get **189.07** feet.

1b With $\Delta t = 0.10$, the ball hits the ground at $x \approx 200.9$ feet.

1e If you use $\Delta t = 0.001$ you should get a landing point of $x \approx 189.14$ which is within 0.1 of the actual landing position. It takes a long time for the program to run with such a small step size.

Chapter 3.4

3 The code remains essentially the same with the prescribed differences in v_o, θ, D, and Δt. The trick is in the triangle collision detection and bounce response. Here, $W = (100, 0)$ and $W_1 = (160, 40)$ producing $\mathbf{w} = \langle 60, 40 \rangle$, which are easily obtained from the graph. It's all algebra from here to get the collision detection. We want to check if R_1 is in the triangle. So, the x-value has to be between 100 and 160 but the y-value must be below the line connecting W and W_1. That line is defined by $(y - 0) = m(x - 100)$ where $m = \frac{40}{60}$. So, you need to check if $R(2) < m(x - 100)$. If it is (while $R(1)$ is between 100 and 160), you've got a hit. Below is the code

```
C:\_dropbox\Dropbox\_My Books\MV3D-Book\Chapter-3\Chapter 3 MATLAB Answers\HW_3_4_3.m
File Edit Text Go Cell Tools Debug Desktop Window Help

1    %% This is HW_3_4_3.m
2    % Performs a bouncing ball simulation with a non-horizontal wall
3 -  clf; clc; clear;
4    %% Initial Values
5 -  vo = 80; thetadegrees = 20; h=0; g = 32;
6 -  t_end = 9; delta_t = .05; t_steps = t_end/delta_t;
7 -  R=[0,h];      %/ initial position.
8 -  theta = thetadegrees*pi/180;
9 -  accel = [0,-g];    %/ the constant acceleration vector.
10 - D = .8;      %/ D = damping on the bounce (between 0 and 1)
11   %% Wall
12 - W_x_values = [100,160,160,100]; W_y_values = [0,40,0,0];
13 - W=[100,0]; W1=[160,40]; w=(W1-W); slopeW = w(2)/w(1);
14   %% Plot first Point and  Wall
15 - plot(R(1),R(2),'r.'); hold on;
16 - plot(W_x_values,W_y_values,'k-','linewidth',4);
17 - hold on; axis equal; axis([0,200,0,100]); grid on;
18 - title('click to start','fontsize',16);
19 - waitforbuttonpress % waits for a click on the graph.
20 - title('Euler Bounce with Wall','fontsize',16);
21   %% Animation Loop
22 - v = vo*[cos(theta), sin(theta)];    % initial velocity vector
23 - for i = 1:1:t_steps
24 -     V = delta_t*v;
25 -     R1 = R + V;        % Next Position
26 -     v1 = v + delta_t*accel;   % Next Velocity Vector
27 -     if R1(2)<0                  % Detect ground hit
28 -         disp('hit ground');
29 -         V1 = D*(2*ProjUV(V,[1,0]) - V);    % New V1
30 -         R1 = [R(1) - R(2)* V(1)/V(2), 0];  % New R1
31 -         v1 = V1/delta_t;
32 -     end
33 -     if R1(1) >= W(1) & R1(1) <= W1(1) & R1(2) <= W(2)+slopeW*(R1(1)-W(1))
34 -         disp('hit wall')                   % detect wall hit
35 -         V1 = D*(2*ProjUV(V,w) - V);        % New V1
36 -         rs=[-w(1),V(1);-w(2),V(2)]\[W(1)- R(1); W(2) - R(2)];
37 -         R1 = R + rs(2)*V;                  % New R1
38 -         v1 = V1/delta_t;                   % New v1
39 -     end
40 -     pause(.005);
41 -     plot(R1(1),R1(2), 'r.','markersize',20);   %% plot the new point.
42 -     R = R1; v = v1;   % Reset R and v.
43 - end
```

Chapter 4.1

1a In the xz plane, $y = 0$, and z is given by $z = \cos\left(\sqrt{x^2}\right) = \cos|x| = \cos(x)$

1b In the yz plane, $x = 0$, and z is given by $z = \cos\left(\sqrt{y^2}\right) = \cos|y| = \cos(y)$

Below are the graphs of the traces and the code I used to make this graph.

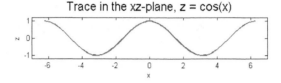

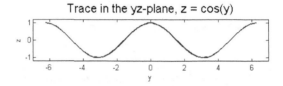

```
 1    %% This is HW4-1-1-ab.m      It does #1 (a) and (b) in Chapter 4.1
 2    % It plots some traces of z = cos(\sqrt(x^2 + y^2))
 3 —  clc; clf; clear; % clears console, figures, variables
 4
 5    %% The surface function
 6 —  surface = @(x,y)[cos(sqrt(x.^2 + y.^2))];
 7
 8    %% The x and y values
 9 —  xvec = linspace(-2*pi,2*pi,40);    % create the vector of x-values
10 —  yvec = linspace(-2*pi,2*pi,40);    % create the vector of y-value
11
12    %% Plotting Traces
13    %  In the xz plane, y = 0.
14 —  subplot(2,1,1)
15 —  plot(xvec,surface(xvec,0*yvec),'r-', 'linewidth',2)
16 —  axis equal; axis([-7,7,-1.2,1.2]);
17 —  title('Trace in the xz-plane, z = cos(x)','fontsize',16), xlabel('x'), ylabel('z')
18    %   In the yz plane, x = 0.
19 —  subplot(2,1,2)
20 —  plot(yvec,surface(0*xvec,yvec),'b-','linewidth',2)
21 —  axis equal; axis([-7,7,-1.2,1.2]);
22 —  title('Trace in the yz-plane, z = cos(y)','fontsize',16), xlabel('y'), ylabel('z')
```

1c Below is the graph and below that the code.

red = xz-trace, blue = yz-trace

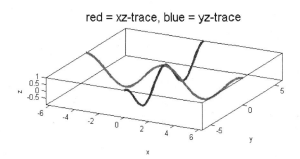

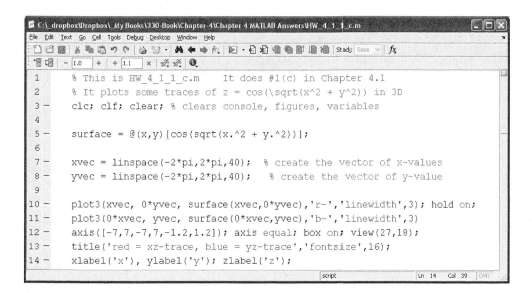

```
1        % This is HW_4_1_1_c.m    It does #1(c) in Chapter 4.1
2        % It plots some traces of z = cos(\sqrt(x^2 + y^2)) in 3D
3 -      clc; clf; clear; % clears console, figures, variables
4
5 -      surface = @(x,y)[cos(sqrt(x.^2 + y.^2))];
6
7 -      xvec = linspace(-2*pi,2*pi,40);   % create the vector of x-values
8 -      yvec = linspace(-2*pi,2*pi,40);   % create the vector of y-value
9
10 -     plot3(xvec, 0*yvec, surface(xvec,0*yvec),'r-','linewidth',3); hold on;
11 -     plot3(0*xvec, yvec, surface(0*xvec,yvec),'b-','linewidth',3)
12 -     axis([-7,7,-7,7,-1.2,1.2]); axis equal; box on; view(27,18);
13 -     title('red = xz-trace, blue = yz-trace','fontsize',16);
14 -     xlabel('x'), ylabel('y'); zlabel('z');
```

1(d)i If $z = \cos\left(\sqrt{x^2 + y^2}\right)$ and $z = 0$ then $\cos\left(\sqrt{x^2 + y^2}\right) = 0$ or

$$\sqrt{x^2 + y^2} = \frac{\text{any odd integer}}{2} \cdot \pi = \frac{2k+1}{2}\,\pi \quad \text{for any integer } k$$

This results in concentric circles

$$x^2 + y^2 = \left(\frac{2k+1}{2}\pi\right)^2$$

which are circles with radius $= \left|\dfrac{2k+1}{2}\pi\right|$.

1(d)ii If $z = \cos\left(\sqrt{x^2 + y^2}\right)$ and $z = -1$ then $\cos\left(\sqrt{x^2 + y^2}\right) = -1$ or

$$\sqrt{x^2 + y^2} = (\text{any odd integer}) \cdot \pi = (2\,k+1)\,\pi \quad \text{for any integer } k$$

This results in concentric circles

$$x^2 + y^2 = [(2k+1)\pi]^2$$

which are circles with radius $= |(2k+1)\pi|$.

1(d)iii If $z = \cos\left(\sqrt{x^2 + y^2}\right)$ and $z = 1$ then $\cos\left(\sqrt{x^2 + y^2}\right) = 1$ or

$$\sqrt{x^2 + y^2} = (\text{any even integer}) \cdot \pi = (2\,k)\,\pi \quad \text{for any integer } k$$

This results in concentric circles

$$x^2 + y^2 = [2k\,\pi]^2$$

which are circles with radius $= |2k\,\pi|$.

Below are the level-curves in 3-space with the traces from parts (a) and (b).

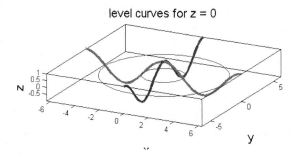

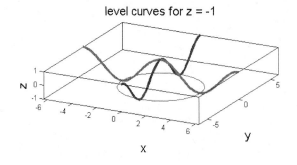

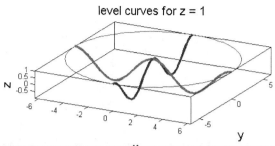

level curves for z = 1

```
 1 │     %% This is HW4_1_1_d.m      It does #1(d) in Chapter 4.1
 2 │     % It plots some traces of z = cos(\sqrt(x^2 + y^2)) in 3D
 3 │ –   clc; clf; clear; % clearrs console, figures, variables
 4 │
 5 │     surface = @(x,y)[cos(sqrt(x.^2 + y.^2))]
 6 │     xvec = linspace(-2*pi,2*pi,40);  % create the vector of x-values
 7 │ –   yvec = linspace(-2*pi,2*pi,40);   % create the vector of y-value
 8 │
 9 │     %%     Traces in the xz and yz planes
10 │ –   plot3(xvec, 0*yvec, surface(xvec,0*yvec),'r-','linewidth',3); hold on;
11 │     plot3(0*xvec, yvec, surface(0*xvec,yvec),'b-','linewidth',3)
12 │
13 │     %%%%%%%/   Level curves.  uncomment the ones you want.
14 │ –   tvec = linspace(0,2*pi, 100);  % parameter for level curves.
15 │     % z = 0; plot3(pi/2*cos(tvec), pi/2*sin(tvec), 0*tvec+z);
16 │     % z = 0; plot3(3*pi/2*cos(tvec), 3*pi/2*sin(tvec), 0*tvec+z)
17 │     % z = -1; plot3(pi*cos(tvec), pi*sin(tvec), 0*tvec+z)
18 │ –     z = 1; plot3(2*pi*cos(tvec), 2*pi*sin(tvec), 0*tvec+z).
19 │
20 │ –   axis([-7,7,-7,7,-1.2,1.2]); axis equal; box on; view(27,18);
21 │ –   text1 = sprintf('level curves for z = %1.0f',z)
22 │ –   title(text1,'fontsize',16)
23 │ –   xlabel('x','fontsize',16), ylabel('y','fontsize',16); zlabel('z','fontsize',16);
24 │
25 │
26 │
```

1e Below is the graph of the surface. Below that is the code.

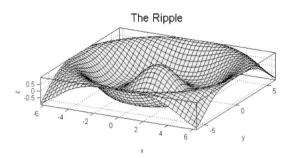

```
 1     % This is HW_4_1_1_e.m     It does #1(e) in Chapter 4.1
 2     % It plots some traces of z = cos(\sqrt(x^2 + y^2)) in 3D
 3 -   clc; clf; clear; % clearrs console, figures, variables
 4
 5 -   surface = @(x,y)[cos(sqrt(x.^2 + y.^2))]
 6 -   xvec = linspace(-2*pi,2*pi,40);   % vector of x-values
 7 -   yvec = linspace(-2*pi,2*pi,40);    % vector of y-value
 8
 9     % Plot z = x^2 + y^2 + 2
10 -   [x y] = meshgrid(xvec,yvec);   % create a full array of x & y
11 -   z = surface(x,y);   % define z
12 -   surf(x, y, z,'facecol', 'yellow');
13 -   title('The Ripple','fontsize',16)
14 -   axis([-7,7,-7,7,-1.2,1.2]); axis equal; box on; view(27,18);
15 -   xlabel('x'); ylabel('y');   zlabel('z');
```

3a In the xz-plane, $y = 0$, and z is given by $z = \dfrac{3}{1 + x^2}$

In the yz-plane, $x = 0$, and z is given by $z = \dfrac{3}{1 + y^2}$

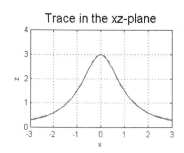

Trace in the xz-plane

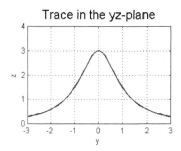

Trace in the yz-plane

3b The surface:

$$f(x, y) = \frac{3}{1 + x^2 + y^2}$$

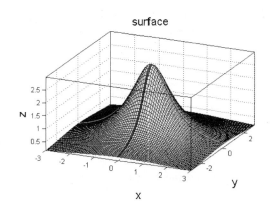

surface

5a Solving the equation for z we get,

$$z = f(x, y) = \frac{3}{4}x + \frac{1}{2}y - \frac{3}{2}$$

5b This can be done in two ways:

$$F(x, y, z) = 3x + 2y - 4z - 6 \qquad \text{or} \qquad F(x, y, z) = -3x - 2y + 4z + 6$$

Either way, the equation $F(x, y, z) = 0$ represents the equation for the same plane.

Chapter 4.2

1 We have already calculated the partial derivatives needed for this problem. The function which defines the surface has gradient given by

$$\nabla f = \langle\, f_x,\ f_y \,\rangle = \left\langle\ \frac{-x \sin(\sqrt{x^2 + y^2})}{\sqrt{x^2 + y^2}},\ \frac{-y \sin(\sqrt{x^2 + y^2})}{\sqrt{x^2 + y^2}}\ \right\rangle$$

So our normal vector to the curve is either

$$\mathbf{n} = \langle f_x, f_y, -1 \rangle \quad \text{or} \quad \langle -f_x, -f_y, 1 \rangle$$

If we want the normal vector that points up, we choose the second form with positive z-component so

$$\mathbf{n} = \langle -f_x, -f_y, 1 \rangle = \left\langle \frac{x \sin(\sqrt{x^2 + y^2})}{\sqrt{x^2 + y^2}}, \frac{y \sin(\sqrt{x^2 + y^2})}{\sqrt{x^2 + y^2}}, 1 \right\rangle$$

Now we just evaluate this at the point $(x, y) = (1, 0)$. or

$$\mathbf{n} = \langle \sin(1), 0, 1 \rangle \approx \langle 0.84, 0, 1 \rangle$$

Below is the code used to generate the graph. In order to make the normal vector appear normal, you must set axis to equal.

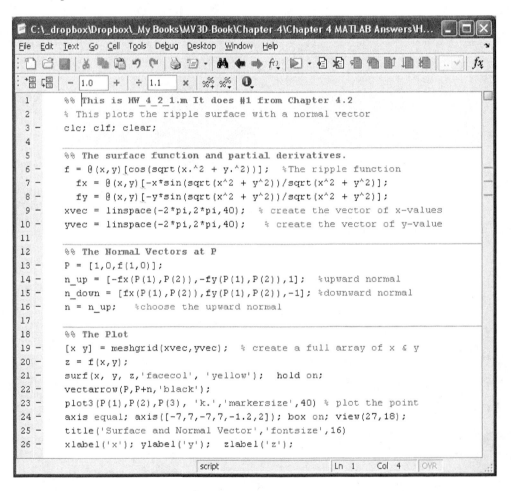

3a $f_x = -3 \left(1 + x^2 + y^2\right)^{-2} 2x = \dfrac{-6x}{\left(1 + x^2 + y^2\right)^2}$

3b $f_y = -3 \left(1 + x^2 + y^2\right)^{-2} 2y = \dfrac{-6y}{\left(1 + x^2 + y^2\right)^2}$

3c $\mathbf{n} = \langle f_x, f_y, -1 \rangle$ or $\mathbf{n} = \langle -f_x, -f_y, 1 \rangle$. We choose the second one because it points up and out.

$f_x(-1,1) = \dfrac{6}{(1+1+1)^2} = \dfrac{6}{9} = \dfrac{2}{3}$ so $-f_x(-1,1) = -\dfrac{2}{3}$

$f_x(-1,1) = \dfrac{-6}{(1+1+1)^2} = \dfrac{-6}{9} = \dfrac{-2}{3}$ so $-f_x(-1,1) = \dfrac{2}{3}$

$\mathbf{n} = \langle -\frac{2}{3}, \frac{2}{3}, 1 \rangle \approx \langle -0.67, 0.67, 1 \rangle$

So, the proper **unit** normal vector is then

$$\mathbf{u} = \frac{n}{||n||} \approx \langle -0.4851,\ 0.4851,\ 0.7276 \rangle$$

6a When you solve for z you get

$z = f(x,y) = -2 \pm \sqrt{25 - (x-2)^2 - (y-1)^2}$. Since our point $(2,4,-6)$ is on the bottom half of the sphere, we choose the minus sign and

$$
\begin{aligned}
z = f(x,y) &= -2 - \sqrt{25 - (x-2)^2 - (y-1)^2} \\
&= -2 - \left(25 - (x-2)^2 - (y-1)^2 \right)^{1/2}
\end{aligned}
$$

Now, using the chain rule with the power rule, the partial derivatives f_x and f_y are given by

$$
\begin{aligned}
f_x &= -\frac{1}{2}(25 - (x-2)^2 - (y-1)^2)^{-1/2}(-2(x-2)) = \frac{x-2}{\sqrt{25 - (x-2)^2 - (y-1)^2}} \\
f_y &= -\frac{1}{2}(25 - (x-2)^2 - (y-1)^2)^{-1/2}(-2(y-1)) = \frac{y-1}{\sqrt{25 - (x-2)^2 - (y-1)^2}}.
\end{aligned}
$$

Now, evaluating these at $x = 2$, and $y = 4$,

$$
\begin{aligned}
f_x(2,4) &= \frac{2-2}{\sqrt{25 - (2-2)^2 - (4-1)^2}} = 0 \\
f_y(2,4) &= \frac{4-1}{\sqrt{25 - (2-2)^2 - (4-1)^2}} = \frac{3}{4}.
\end{aligned}
$$

and

$$\mathbf{n} = \pm \langle f_x, f_y, -1 \rangle = \pm \left\langle 0, \frac{3}{4}, -1 \right\rangle \quad \text{choose } (+) \rightarrow \quad \mathbf{n} = \left\langle 0, \frac{3}{4}, -1 \right\rangle$$

Since our point is on the bottom half of the sphere, the outward-pointing normal will have a negative z-component so you choose the positive $(+)$ version of these normal vectors.

6b Taking the equation for the sphere and getting a zero on the right hand side:

$$F(x,y,z) = (x-2)^2 + (y-1)^2 + (z+2)^2 - 25$$

then

$$F_x = 2(x-2) \qquad F_y = 2(y-1) \qquad F_z = 2(z+2)$$

and plugging in $x = 2$, $y = 4$, and $z = -6$ yields

$$F_x = 2(2-2) = 0 \qquad F_y = 2(4-1) = 6 \qquad F_z = 2(-6+2) = -8$$

and

$$\mathbf{n} = \pm \nabla F = \pm \left\langle 0, 6, -8 \right\rangle.$$

Again, since our point (2,4,-6) is on the bottom of the sphere we choose the $(+)$ version and $\mathbf{n} = \left\langle 0, 6, -8 \right\rangle$. Notice this is parallel to the normal found in part (a) and was a lot easier to obtain.

7a $f_x = y + 2x$ and $f_y = x + 2y$

7c f_x requires the product rule treating y as a constant.
$f_x = y \left[x(-\sin(2x)\, 2) + \cos(2x) \right] = y \left[-2x \sin(2x) + cos(2x) \right]$
$f_y = x \cos(2x)$

8a $\nabla F = \left\langle F_x,\ F_y,\ F_z \right\rangle = \left\langle\ 6x,\ -2,\ -3\cos(z)\ \right\rangle$

9 Subtracting $4x^2 - y^2$ from both sides gives $F(x, y, z) = 2z^2 - 4x^2 + y^2$.
Subtracting $2z^2$ from both sides gives $F(x, y, z) = 4x^2 - y^2 - 2z^2$
Either one works.

Chapter 4.3

1 In the previous chapter, we found the normal vector to the surface at $(1, 0, \cos(1))$.
$\mathbf{n} = \left\langle\ \sin(1),\ 0,\ 1\ \right\rangle \approx \left\langle\ 0.84,\ 0,\ 1\ \right\rangle$
Now we use the equation: $\mathbf{v}_1 = \mathbf{v}_o - 2\text{Proj}_{\mathbf{n}}\mathbf{v}_o$, where

$$\text{Proj}_{\mathbf{n}}\mathbf{v}_o = \frac{\mathbf{n}\cdot\mathbf{v}_o}{||\mathbf{n}||^2}\mathbf{n} = \frac{\langle \sin(1),0,1\rangle\cdot\langle 0,0,-3\rangle}{\sin^2(1)+1} \langle \sin(1),0,1 \rangle = \frac{-3}{\sin^2(1)+1} \langle \sin(1),0,1 \rangle$$

Now, $\mathbf{v}_1 = \mathbf{v}_o - 2\text{Proj}_{\mathbf{n}}\mathbf{v}_o = \langle 0,0,-3 \rangle + \frac{6}{\sin^2(1)+1} \langle \sin(1),0,1 \rangle \approx \langle \mathbf{2.9559},\ \mathbf{0.000},\ \mathbf{0.5127} \rangle$

3 In the previous chapter, we found the normal vector to the surface at $(-1, 1, 1)$.
$\mathbf{n} = \left\langle -\dfrac{2}{3}, \dfrac{2}{3}, 1 \right\rangle \approx \langle -0.67, 0.67, 1 \rangle$.
Now we use the equation: $\mathbf{v}_1 = \mathbf{v}_o - 2\text{Proj}_{\mathbf{n}}\mathbf{v}_o$, where

$$\text{Proj}_{\mathbf{n}}\mathbf{v}_o = \frac{\mathbf{n}\cdot\mathbf{v}_o}{||\mathbf{n}||^2}\mathbf{n} = \frac{\langle -\frac{2}{3},\frac{2}{3},1\rangle\cdot\langle 0,-1,-1\rangle}{17/9} \left\langle -\tfrac{2}{3},\tfrac{2}{3},1 \right\rangle = \frac{-5/3}{17/9}\left\langle -\tfrac{2}{3},\tfrac{2}{3},1 \right\rangle = \frac{-15}{17}\left\langle -\tfrac{2}{3},\tfrac{2}{3},1 \right\rangle = \frac{-5}{17}\langle -2,2,3 \rangle$$

Now, $\mathbf{v}_1 = \mathbf{v}_o - 2\text{Proj}_{\mathbf{n}}\mathbf{v}_o = \langle 0,-1,-1 \rangle + \frac{10}{17}\langle -2,2,3 \rangle = \left\langle \frac{-20}{17}, \frac{3}{17}, \frac{13}{17} \right\rangle \approx \langle \mathbf{-1.1765},\ \mathbf{0.1765},\ \mathbf{0.7647} \rangle$

5 $\mathbf{v}_1 = \mathbf{v}_0 - 2\text{Proj}_n\mathbf{v}_0$, where $\mathbf{n}$ is a normal to the plane. $\mathbf{n} = \langle 2,2,-1 \rangle$.
$\mathbf{v}_1 = \mathbf{v}_0 - 2 * \frac{\mathbf{n}\cdot\mathbf{v}_0}{||\mathbf{n}||^2}\mathbf{n} = \langle 2,3,6 \rangle - 2\frac{\mathbf{n}\cdot\mathbf{v}_0}{||\mathbf{n}||^2}\langle 2,2,-1 \rangle = \langle 2,3,6 \rangle - 2\frac{\langle 2,2,-1\rangle\cdot\langle 2,3,6\rangle}{9}\langle 2,2,-1 \rangle$
$\mathbf{v}_1 = \langle 2,3,6 \rangle - 2\frac{4}{9}\langle 2,2,-1 \rangle = \langle 2,3,6 \rangle - \frac{8}{9}\langle 2,2,-1 \rangle = \left\langle \frac{18}{9}, \frac{27}{9}, \frac{54}{9} \right\rangle - \left\langle \frac{16}{9}, \frac{16}{9}, \frac{-8}{9} \right\rangle$
$\mathbf{v}_1 = \left\langle \frac{2}{9}, \frac{11}{9}, \frac{62}{9} \right\rangle \approx \langle \mathbf{0.22},\ \mathbf{1.22},\ \mathbf{6.89} \rangle$

Index